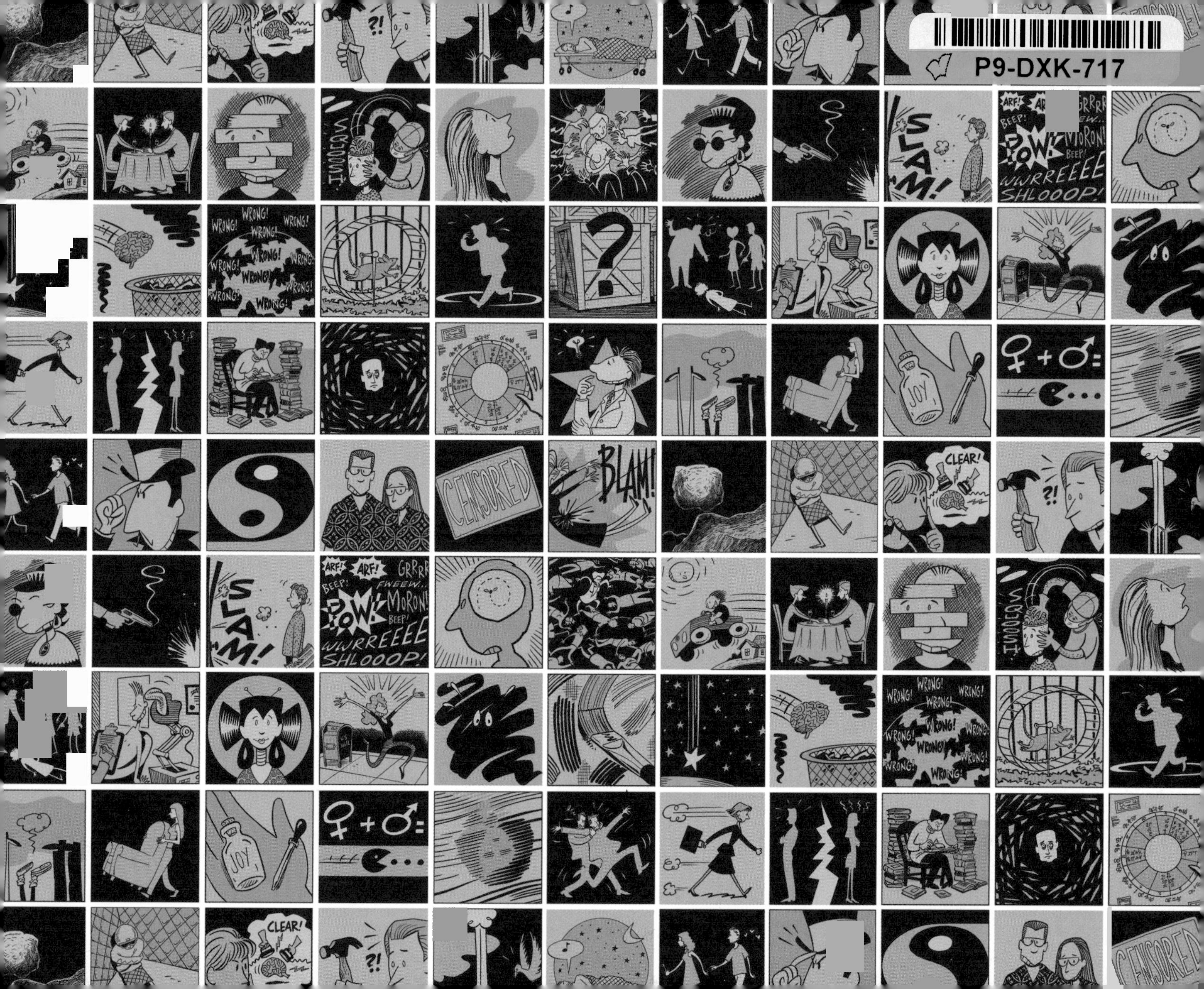
?!
CENSORED
SQUOOSH!
SLAM!
ARF! ARF! GRRRR BEEP! FWEEW... POW! MORON! BEEP! WWRREEEE SHLOOOP!
WRONG! WRONG! WRONG! WRONG! WRONG! WRONG! WRONG! WRONG! WRONG! WRONG!
?
JOY
♀ + ♂ =
CENSORED
BLAM!
CLEAR!
?!
SLAM!
ARF! ARF! GRRRR BEEP! FWEEW... POW! MORON! BEEP! WWRREEEE SHLOOOP!
SQUOOSH!
U.S. MAIL
WRONG! WRONG! WRONG! WRONG! WRONG! WRONG! WRONG! WRONG! WRONG! WRONG!
JOY
♀ + ♂ =
CLEAR!
?!
CENSORED

Carol Lay's Illiterature

ROSS RICHIE Chief Executive Officer • **MATT GAGNON** Editor-in-Chief • **FILIP SABLIK** VP-Publishing & Marketing • **LANCE KREITER** VP-Licensing & Merchandising • **PHIL BARBARO** Director of Finance
BRYCE CARLSON Managing Editor • **DAFNA PLEBAN** Editor • **SHANNON WATTERS** Editor • **ERIC HARBURN** Assistant Editor • **ADAM STAFFARONI** Assistant Editor • **CHRIS ROSA** Assistant Editor
STEPHANIE GONZAGA Graphic Designer • **CAROL THOMPSON** Production Designer • **JASMINE AMIRI** Operations Coordinator • **DEVIN FUNCHES** Marketing & Sales Assistant

CAROL LAY'S ILLITERATURE: STORY MINUTES Volume One — October 2012. Published by BOOM! Town, a division of Boom Entertainment, Inc. All contents, unless otherwise specified, Copyright © 2012 Carol Lay. All rights reserved. BOOM! Town™ and the BOOM! Town logo are trademarks of Boom Entertainment, Inc., registered in various countries and categories. All characters, events, and institutions depicted herein are fictional. Any similarity between any of the names, characters, persons, events, and/or institutions in this publication to actual names, characters, and persons, whether living or dead, events, and/or institutions is unintended and purely coincidental. BOOM! Town does not read or accept unsolicited submissions of ideas, stories, or artwork.

A catalog record of this book is available from OCLC and from the BOOM! Studios website, www.boom-studios.com, on the Librarians Page.

BOOM! Studios, 5670 Wilshire Boulevard, Suite 450, Los Angeles, CA 90036-5679. Printed in China. First Printing. ISBN: 978-1-60886-282-5

Carol Lay's Illiterature

Story Minutes
Vol. I

For my old friend Bill Glass, who once asked me if I might want to try drawing comics.

Cover and Contents by Carol Lay

Collected from Story Minute and Way Lay strips, originally published from 1997-1999

Assistant Editor
Adam Staffaroni

Design
Carol Thompson

Production Assistants
Cole Closser
Sophie Goldstein

INTRODUCTION
By Kim Deitch

I first met Carol Lay thirty years ago. Little did I know that in a matter of a few weeks we'd be working on a project together. It was a rush job. We had to get a comic book version of Paul Bartel's now famous film comedy, *Eating Raoul*, out and ready for the printer in a very short time.

We did it, but only because of Carol's solid efficiency, know-how and can-do spirit. I learned new things about how to make comics on that job that I'm still using and we've been friends ever since.

Carol doesn't brag about herself although, God knows, she easily could. Comic artist, painter, novelist, storyboard artist — I've seen her succeed at all of the above and always with all the confident professionalism that she is known for.

Of course there is a downside. At any given moment there always seems to be someone who wants to lure her away from her own artistic projects so she can put theirs over. Hell, I was guilty of it myself when I hired her to save my bacon on that *Eating Raoul* project!

She could easily be nothing more than a highly paid cog in somebody else's big, well-oiled machine. There are plenty of talented people who spend their whole lives doing just that. But Carol's better than that. She's always got a lot of irons in the fire. But she's taken care to also nurture and keep her own artistic vision up and running.

This book, a collection of her legendary, long running strip, "Story Minute," is stunning evidence of that. These strips absolutely overflow with ideas. There is more solid originality in them per square panel than any comic strip I have ever seen before or since. Of course a thing like that could be just too overpowering. Ah, but that's the beauty of it. It only takes a minute to read one and that brings up an interesting point. This book is not meant to be a page turner. In fact, to really enjoy and appreciate these strips, it's best if you can read them one at a time. I say if you can because, if not taken in small doses, I warn you; these Story Minutes can be addictive.

They are in turn, funny, intriguing, tragic, touching, and always entertaining. For the most part they are fictional and usually improbable; but like all good fiction, there is plenty of Carol's own life experience on display here. Reading them, you will immediately get a sense of this. It's part of why they are so good. Mostly, that experience is artfully woven into the book's many story lines.

I say mostly because in one instance, she departs from her usual approach and tells a completely true story. You'll know it immediately when you see it because it is the one page in this book where she abandons her usual, deft, cartoony style for a more realistic one. This is the page where she tells the story of her pet cat of fifteen years, Güsto. It is wonderful and my particular favorite in this collection.

To me, the key thing about these strips is this: while it may take a mere minute to read one, there's a lot to mentally chaw on in these pages that will stay with you for a long, long, time.

-Kim Deitch
June 2012

STORY MINUTE © CAROL LAY
"ROAD SIGNS"

SHE WASN'T SURE WHEN SHE SAW THE FIRST SIGN.

SHE WAS ON A LONELY DESERT ROAD WHEN SHE SAW WHAT APPEARED TO BE AN ADVERTISEMENT.

BUT IT DIDN'T PROMOTE ANY PRODUCT—IT JUST CAUGHT HER EYE WITH A CLEVER PHRASE.

DOWN THE ROAD, SHE CAME UPON ANOTHER SIGN THAT ADVANCED THE THEME OF THE FIRST.

THERE WERE MORE SIGNS AFTER THAT. THEY SEEMED TO BE TELLING A STORY.

THE STORY ECHOED HER ALONE-NESS AND APPEALED TO HER SENSE OF ADVENTURE.

SHE GOT SO INVOLVED THAT SHE MISSED HER TURN-OFF.

BUT HER APPOINTMENT COULD WAIT. SHE HAD TO SEE HOW THE STORY TURNED OUT.

THE SIGNS LED HER FURTHER AND FURTHER AWAY FROM HER FORMER DESTINATION.

THEY LED HER UP INTO THE MOUNTAINS, TO AN ISOLATED CABIN IN THE WOODS.

SHE KNOCKED ON THE CABIN'S DOOR SO SHE COULD FIND OUT HOW THE STORY ENDED.

AS IT TURNED OUT, IT WAS A MURDER MYSTERY.

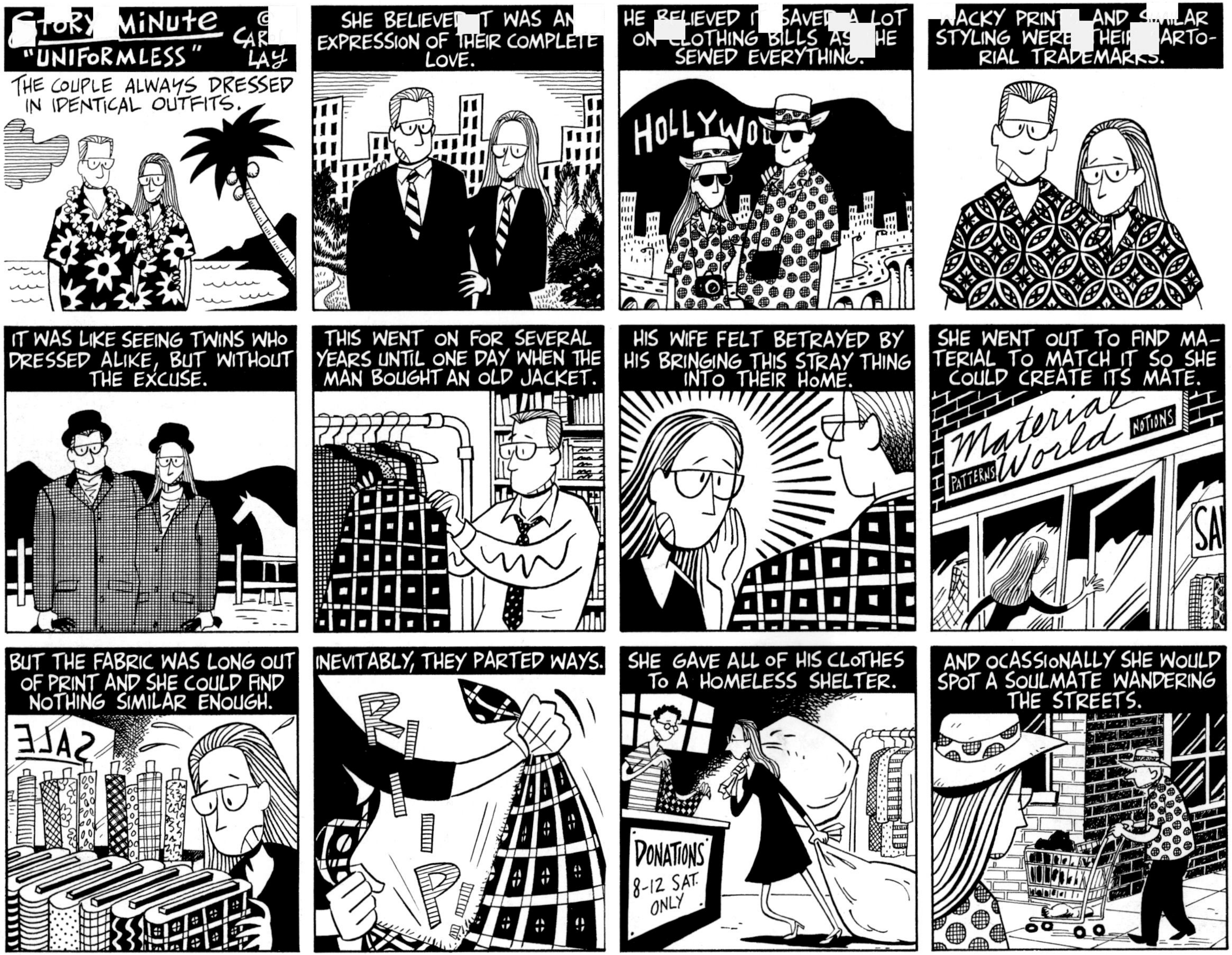

STORY MINUTE
"UNIFORMLESS"
© CAROL LAY
THE COUPLE ALWAYS DRESSED IN IDENTICAL OUTFITS.
SHE BELIEVED IT WAS AN EXPRESSION OF THEIR COMPLETE LOVE.
HE BELIEVED IT SAVED A LOT ON CLOTHING BILLS AS SHE SEWED EVERYTHING.
HOLLYWOO
WACKY PRINTS AND SIMILAR STYLING WERE THEIR SARTORIAL TRADEMARKS.
IT WAS LIKE SEEING TWINS WHO DRESSED ALIKE, BUT WITHOUT THE EXCUSE.
THIS WENT ON FOR SEVERAL YEARS UNTIL ONE DAY WHEN THE MAN BOUGHT AN OLD JACKET.
HIS WIFE FELT BETRAYED BY HIS BRINGING THIS STRAY THING INTO THEIR HOME.
SHE WENT OUT TO FIND MATERIAL TO MATCH IT SO SHE COULD CREATE ITS MATE.
Material World
PATTERNS
NOTIONS
BUT THE FABRIC WAS LONG OUT OF PRINT AND SHE COULD FIND NOTHING SIMILAR ENOUGH.
SALE
INEVITABLY, THEY PARTED WAYS.
RIIIP!
SHE GAVE ALL OF HIS CLOTHES TO A HOMELESS SHELTER.
DONATIONS 8-12 SAT. ONLY
AND OCASSIONALLY SHE WOULD SPOT A SOULMATE WANDERING THE STREETS.

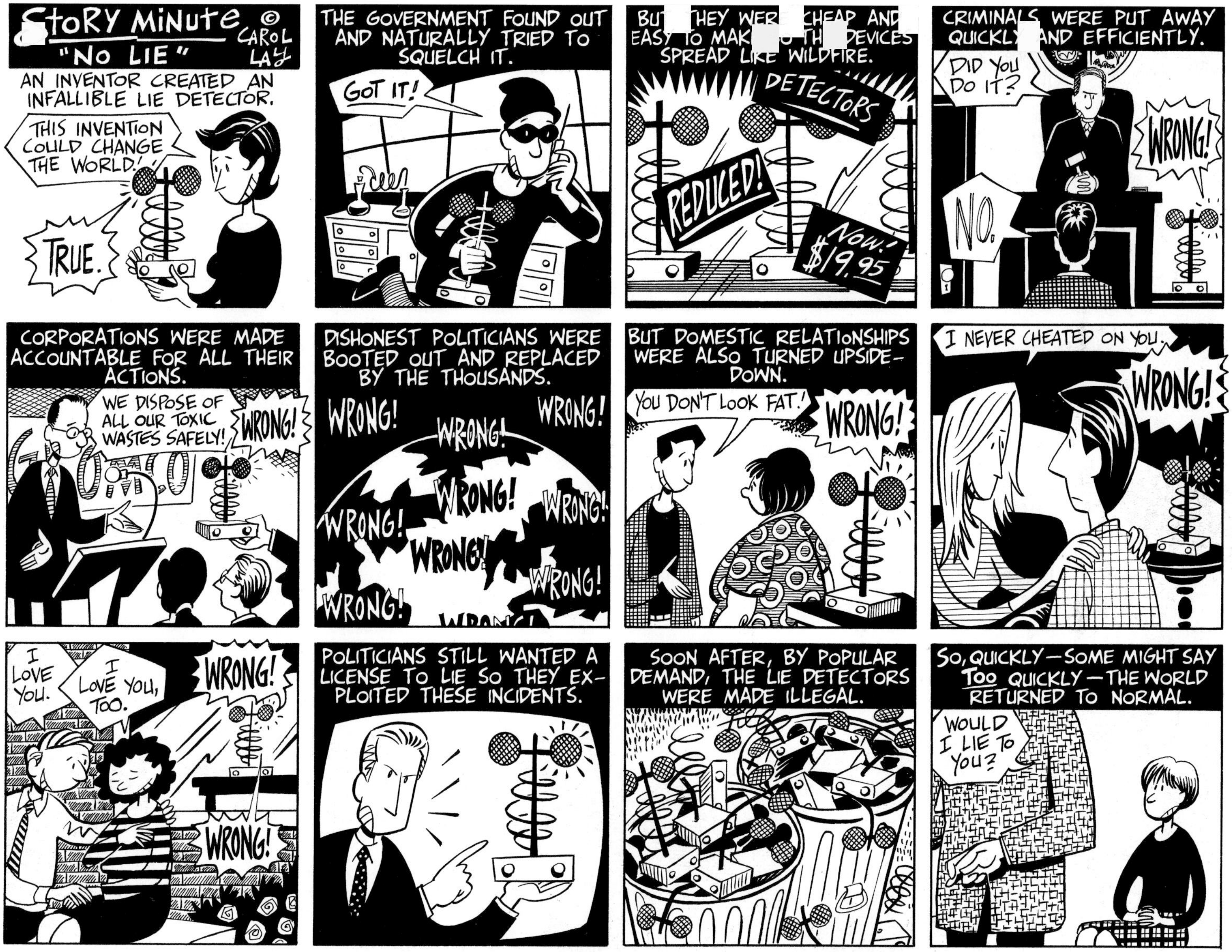
STORY MINUTE "NO LIE" © CAROL LAY
AN INVENTOR CREATED AN INFALLIBLE LIE DETECTOR.
THIS INVENTION COULD CHANGE THE WORLD!
TRUE.
THE GOVERNMENT FOUND OUT AND NATURALLY TRIED TO SQUELCH IT.
GOT IT!
BU THEY WER CHEAP AND EASY TO MAK TH DEVICES SPREAD LIKE WILDFIRE.
DETECTORS
REDUCED!
NOW! $19.95
CRIMINALS WERE PUT AWAY QUICKLY AND EFFICIENTLY.
DID YOU DO IT?
NO.
WRONG!
CORPORATIONS WERE MADE ACCOUNTABLE FOR ALL THEIR ACTIONS.
WE DISPOSE OF ALL OUR TOXIC WASTES SAFELY!
WRONG!
DISHONEST POLITICIANS WERE BOOTED OUT AND REPLACED BY THE THOUSANDS.
WRONG! WRONG! WRONG! WRONG! WRONG! WRONG! WRONG! WRONG! WRONG!
BUT DOMESTIC RELATIONSHIPS WERE ALSO TURNED UPSIDE-DOWN.
YOU DON'T LOOK FAT.
WRONG!
I NEVER CHEATED ON YOU.
WRONG!
I LOVE YOU.
I LOVE YOU, TOO.
WRONG!
WRONG!
POLITICIANS STILL WANTED A LICENSE TO LIE SO THEY EXPLOITED THESE INCIDENTS.
SOON AFTER, BY POPULAR DEMAND, THE LIE DETECTORS WERE MADE ILLEGAL.
SO, QUICKLY—SOME MIGHT SAY TOO QUICKLY—THE WORLD RETURNED TO NORMAL.
WOULD I LIE TO YOU?

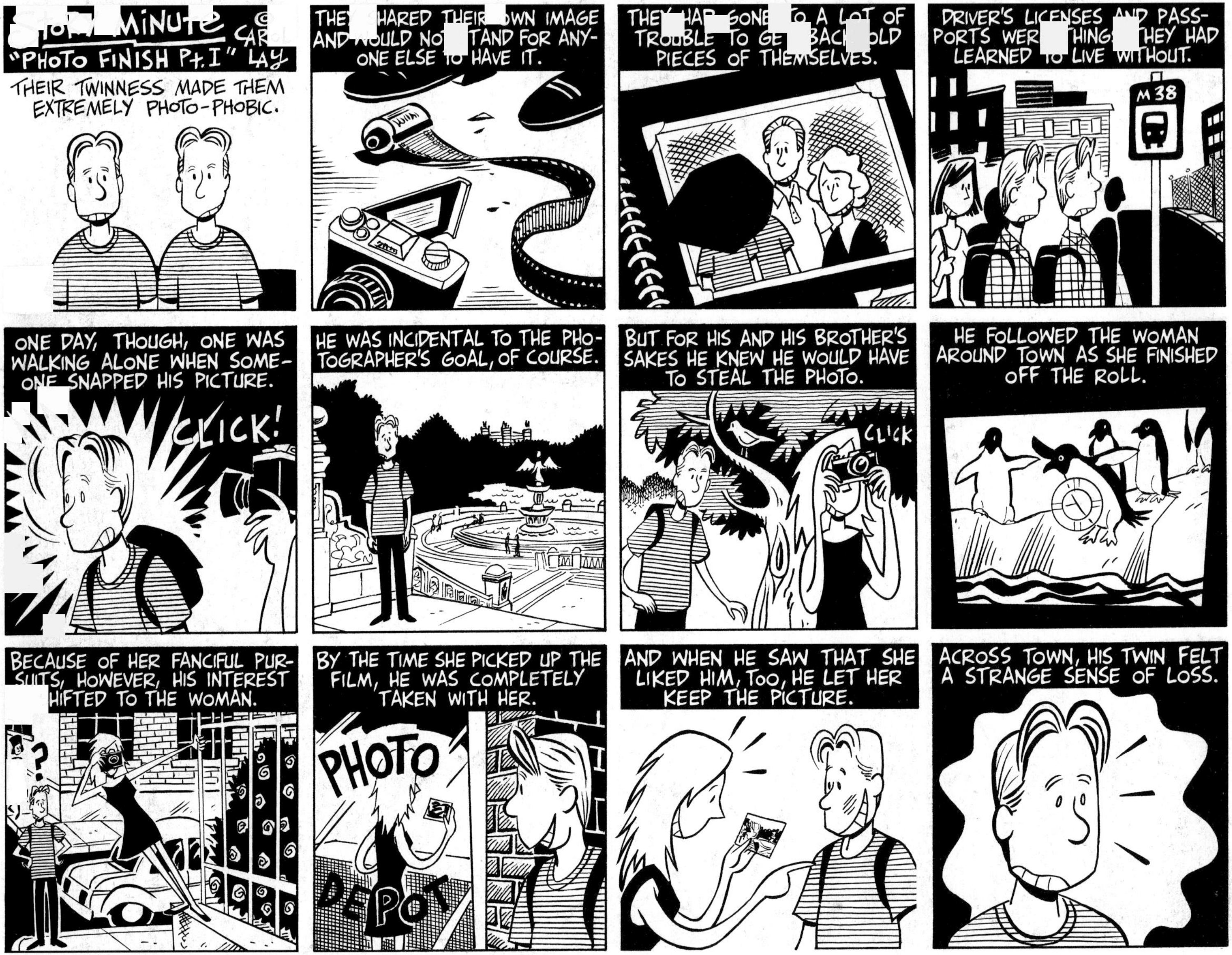

MINUTE © CAR LAY
"PHOTO FINISH Pt. I"
THEIR TWINNESS MADE THEM EXTREMELY PHOTO-PHOBIC.
THEY HARED THEIR WN IMAGE AND WOULD NO TAND FOR ANY- ONE ELSE HAVE IT.
THE HA GONE O A LOT OF TROUBLE TO GE BACK OLD PIECES OF THEMSELVES.
DRIVER'S LICENSES AND PASS- PORTS WER THING HEY HAD LEARNED TO LIVE WITHOUT.
M38
ONE DAY, THOUGH, ONE WAS WALKING ALONE WHEN SOME- ONE SNAPPED HIS PICTURE.
CLICK!
HE WAS INCIDENTAL TO THE PHO- TOGRAPHER'S GOAL, OF COURSE.
BUT FOR HIS AND HIS BROTHER'S SAKES HE KNEW HE WOULD HAVE TO STEAL THE PHOTO.
CLICK
HE FOLLOWED THE WOMAN AROUND TOWN AS SHE FINISHED OFF THE ROLL.
BECAUSE OF HER FANCIFUL PUR- SUITS, HOWEVER, HIS INTEREST HIFTED TO THE WOMAN.
?
BY THE TIME SHE PICKED UP THE FILM, HE WAS COMPLETELY TAKEN WITH HER.
PHOTO
DEPOT
AND WHEN HE SAW THAT SHE LIKED HIM, TOO, HE LET HER KEEP THE PICTURE.
ACROSS TOWN, HIS TWIN FELT A STRANGE SENSE OF LOSS.

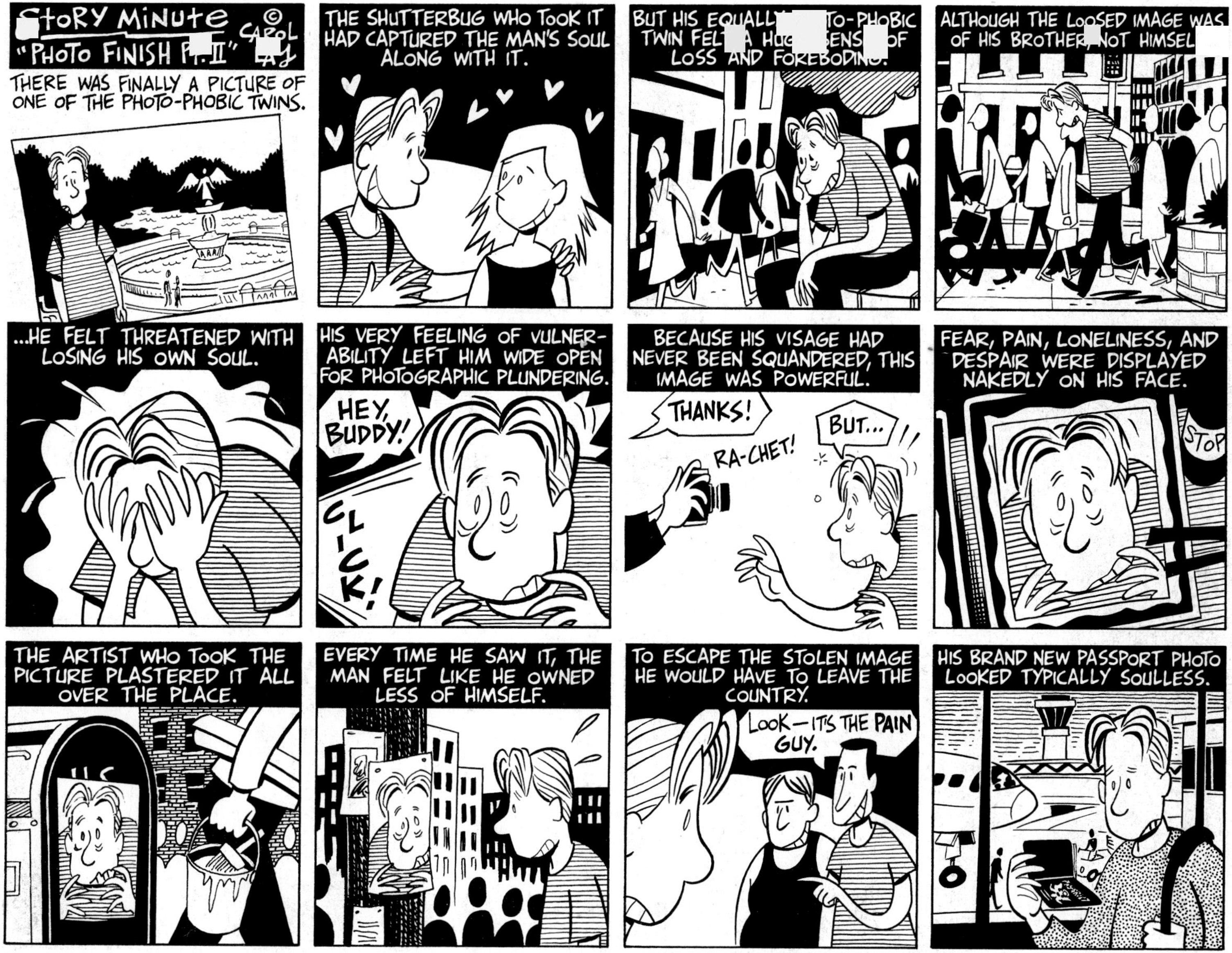

STORY MINUTE
"PHOTO FINISH PT. II"
© CAROL LAY
THERE WAS FINALLY A PICTURE OF ONE OF THE PHOTO-PHOBIC TWINS.
THE SHUTTERBUG WHO TOOK IT HAD CAPTURED THE MAN'S SOUL ALONG WITH IT.
BUT HIS EQUALLY TO-PHOBIC TWIN FEL A HU SENS OF LOSS AND FOREBODIN
ALTHOUGH THE LOOSED IMAGE WAS OF HIS BROTHER, NOT HIMSEL
...HE FELT THREATENED WITH LOSING HIS OWN SOUL.
HIS VERY FEELING OF VULNERABILITY LEFT HIM WIDE OPEN FOR PHOTOGRAPHIC PLUNDERING.
HEY, BUDDY!
CLICK!
BECAUSE HIS VISAGE HAD NEVER BEEN SQUANDERED, THIS IMAGE WAS POWERFUL.
THANKS!
RA-CHET!
BUT...
FEAR, PAIN, LONELINESS, AND DESPAIR WERE DISPLAYED NAKEDLY ON HIS FACE.
STOP
THE ARTIST WHO TOOK THE PICTURE PLASTERED IT ALL OVER THE PLACE.
EVERY TIME HE SAW IT, THE MAN FELT LIKE HE OWNED LESS OF HIMSELF.
TO ESCAPE THE STOLEN IMAGE HE WOULD HAVE TO LEAVE THE COUNTRY.
LOOK—IT'S THE PAIN GUY.
HIS BRAND NEW PASSPORT PHOTO LOOKED TYPICALLY SOULLESS.

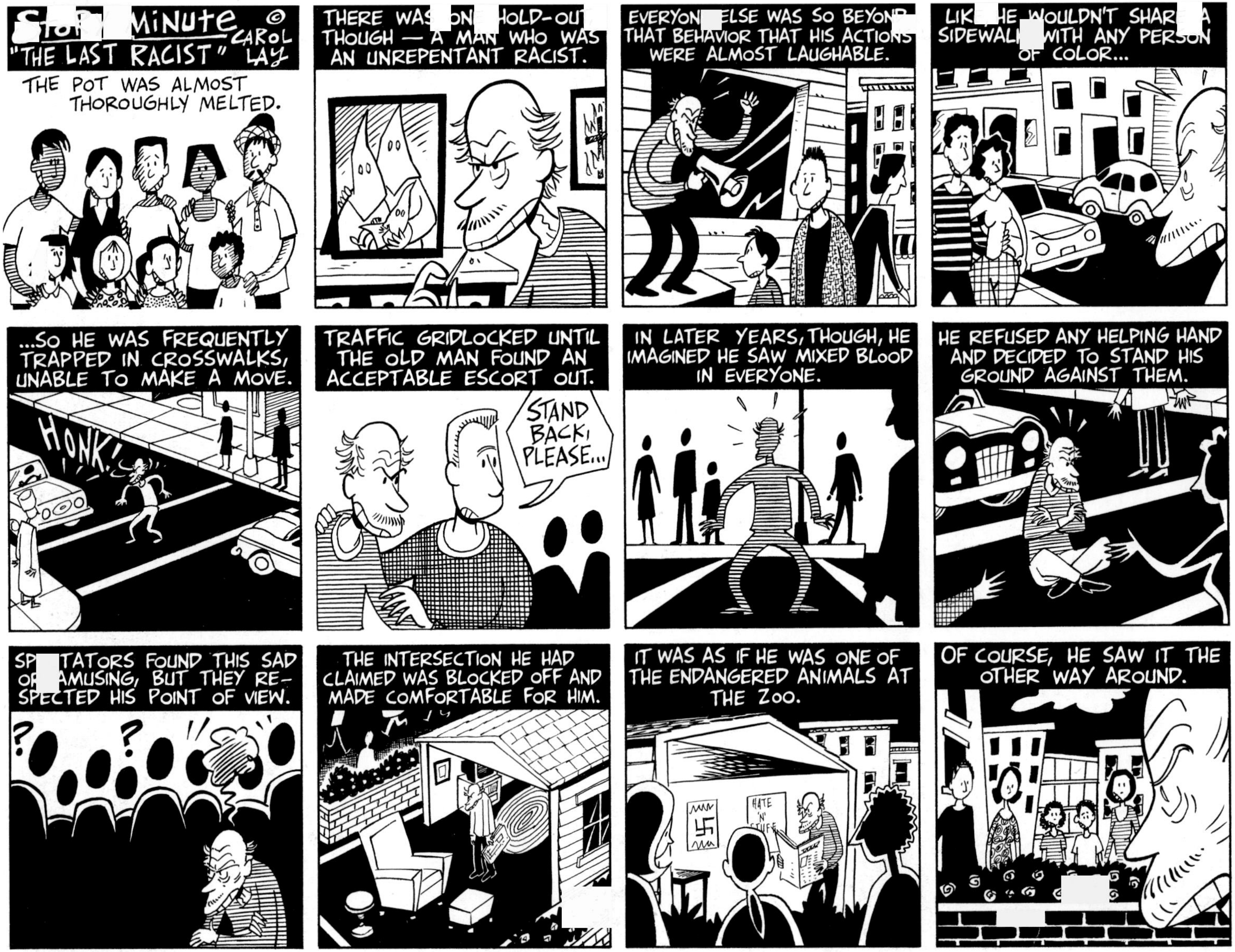

Minute ©
CAROL LAY
"THE LAST RACIST"
THE POT WAS ALMOST THOROUGHLY MELTED.
THERE WAS ONE HOLD-OUT THOUGH — A MAN WHO WAS AN UNREPENTANT RACIST.
EVERYON ELSE WAS SO BEYOND THAT BEHAVIOR THAT HIS ACTIONS WERE ALMOST LAUGHABLE.
LIK HE WOULDN'T SHAR A SIDEWAL WITH ANY PERSON OF COLOR...
...SO HE WAS FREQUENTLY TRAPPED IN CROSSWALKS, UNABLE TO MAKE A MOVE.
HONK!
TRAFFIC GRIDLOCKED UNTIL THE OLD MAN FOUND AN ACCEPTABLE ESCORT OUT.
STAND BACK, PLEASE...
IN LATER YEARS, THOUGH, HE IMAGINED HE SAW MIXED BLOOD IN EVERYONE.
HE REFUSED ANY HELPING HAND AND DECIDED TO STAND HIS GROUND AGAINST THEM.
SP TATORS FOUND THIS SAD O AMUSING, BUT THEY RE-SPECTED HIS POINT OF VIEW.
?
?
THE INTERSECTION HE HAD CLAIMED WAS BLOCKED OFF AND MADE COMFORTABLE FOR HIM.
IT WAS AS IF HE WAS ONE OF THE ENDANGERED ANIMALS AT THE ZOO.
HATE 'N' STUFF
OF COURSE, HE SAW IT THE OTHER WAY AROUND.

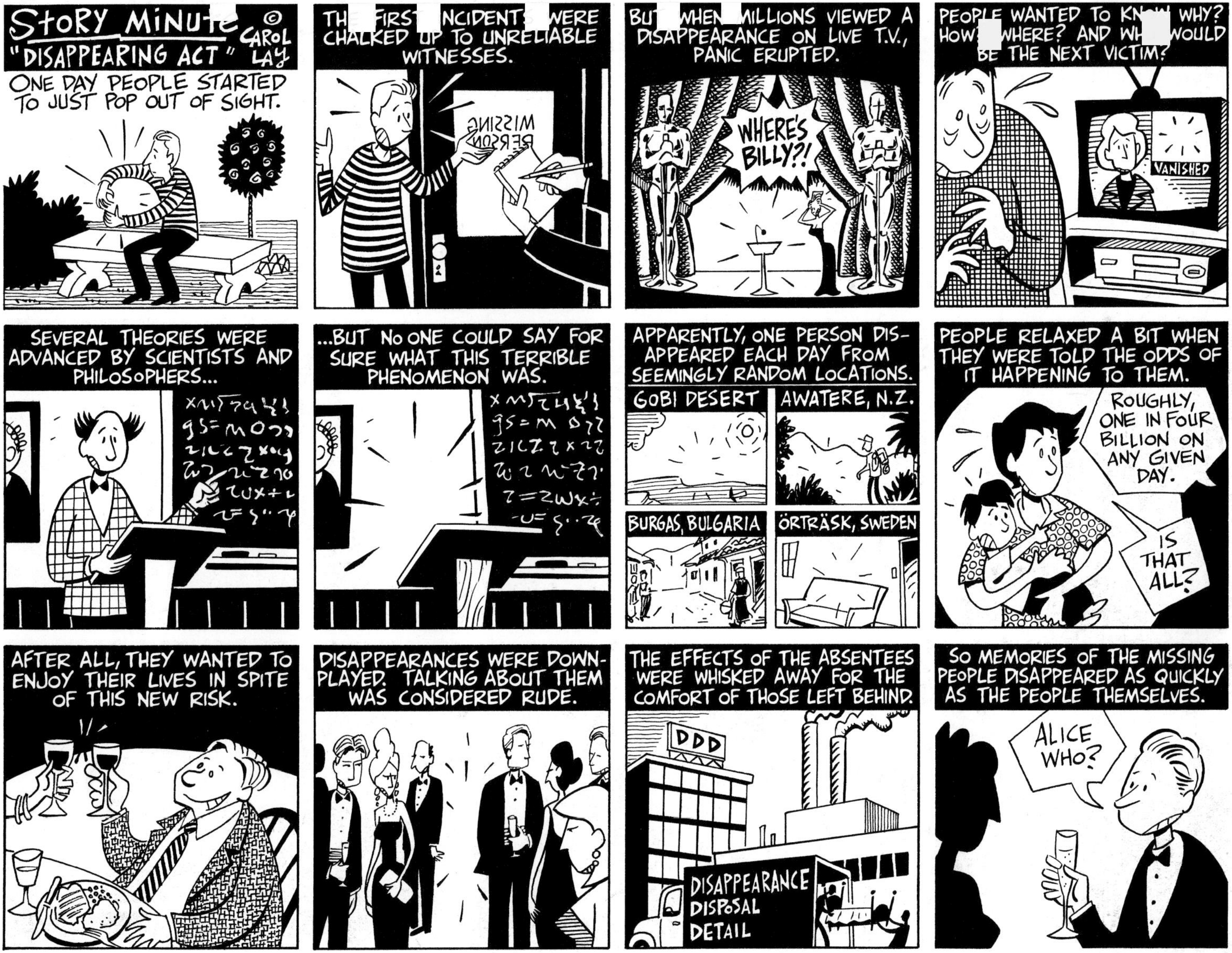

STORY MINUTE © CAROL LAY
"DISAPPEARING ACT"
ONE DAY PEOPLE STARTED TO JUST POP OUT OF SIGHT.
TH FIRST NCIDENTS WERE CHALKED UP TO UNRELIABLE WITNESSES.
MISSING PERSON
BU WHEN MILLIONS VIEWED A DISAPPEARANCE ON LIVE T.V., PANIC ERUPTED.
WHERE'S BILLY?!
PEOPL WANTED TO KN W WHY? HOW WHERE? AND WH WOULD BE THE NEXT VICTIM?
VANISHED
SEVERAL THEORIES WERE ADVANCED BY SCIENTISTS AND PHILOSOPHERS...
...BUT NO ONE COULD SAY FOR SURE WHAT THIS TERRIBLE PHENOMENON WAS.
APPARENTLY, ONE PERSON DISAPPEARED EACH DAY FROM SEEMINGLY RANDOM LOCATIONS.
GOBI DESERT
AWATERE, N.Z.
BURGAS, BULGARIA
ÖRTRÄSK, SWEDEN
PEOPLE RELAXED A BIT WHEN THEY WERE TOLD THE ODDS OF IT HAPPENING TO THEM.
ROUGHLY, ONE IN FOUR BILLION ON ANY GIVEN DAY.
IS THAT ALL?
AFTER ALL, THEY WANTED TO ENJOY THEIR LIVES IN SPITE OF THIS NEW RISK.
DISAPPEARANCES WERE DOWNPLAYED. TALKING ABOUT THEM WAS CONSIDERED RUDE.
THE EFFECTS OF THE ABSENTEES WERE WHISKED AWAY FOR THE COMFORT OF THOSE LEFT BEHIND.
DDD
DISAPPEARANCE DISPOSAL DETAIL
SO MEMORIES OF THE MISSING PEOPLE DISAPPEARED AS QUICKLY AS THE PEOPLE THEMSELVES.
ALICE WHO?

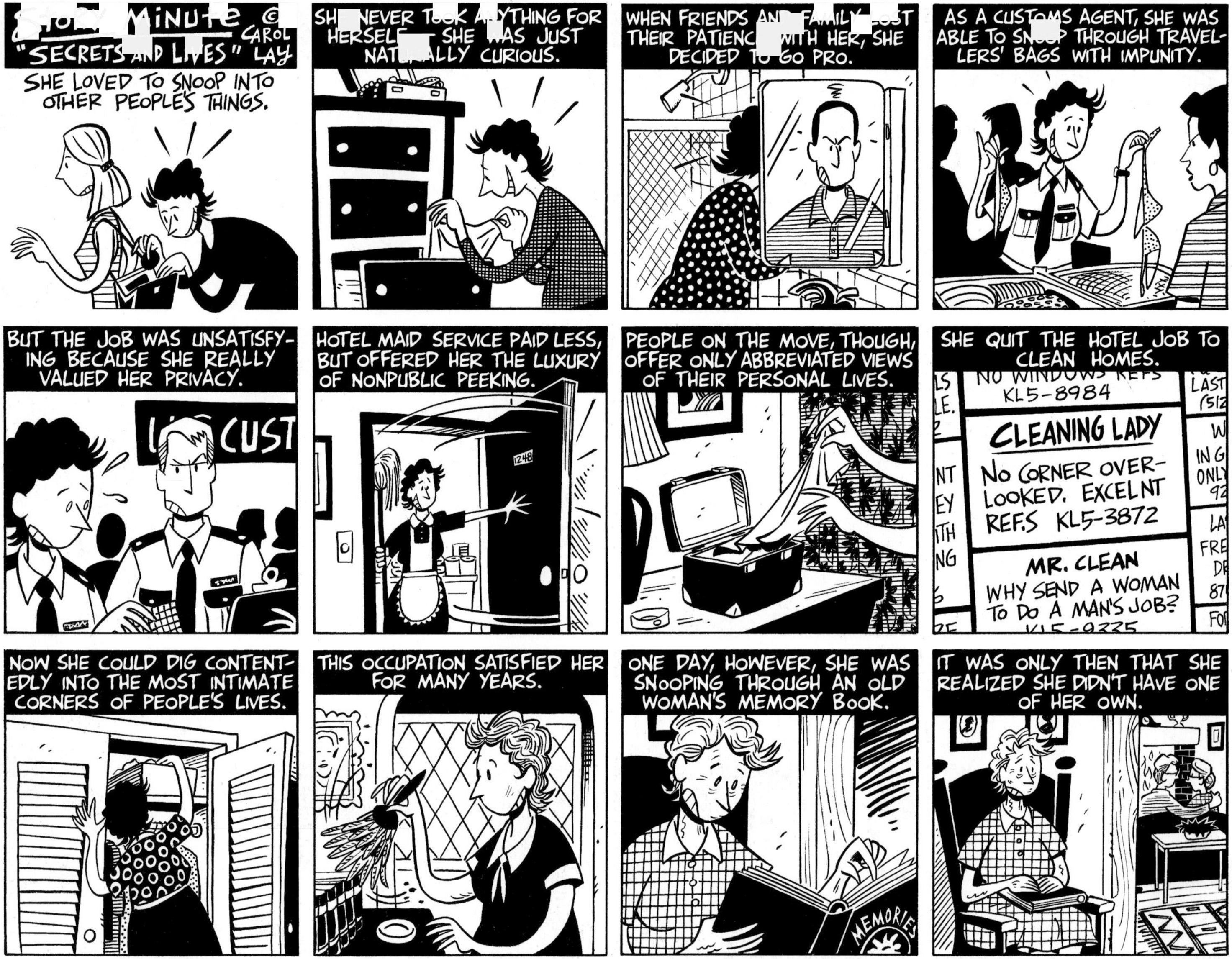

Minute © Carol Lay
"SECRETS AND LIVES"
SHE LOVED TO SNOOP INTO OTHER PEOPLE'S THINGS.
SHE NEVER TOOK ANYTHING FOR HERSELF — SHE WAS JUST NATURALLY CURIOUS.
WHEN FRIENDS AND FAMILY LOST THEIR PATIENCE WITH HER, SHE DECIDED TO GO PRO.
AS A CUSTOMS AGENT, SHE WAS ABLE TO SNOOP THROUGH TRAVELLERS' BAGS WITH IMPUNITY.
BUT THE JOB WAS UNSATISFYING BECAUSE SHE REALLY VALUED HER PRIVACY.
CUST
HOTEL MAID SERVICE PAID LESS, BUT OFFERED HER THE LUXURY OF NONPUBLIC PEEKING.
1248
PEOPLE ON THE MOVE, THOUGH, OFFER ONLY ABBREVIATED VIEWS OF THEIR PERSONAL LIVES.
SHE QUIT THE HOTEL JOB TO CLEAN HOMES.
KL5-8984
CLEANING LADY
NO CORNER OVERLOOKED. EXCELNT REF.S KL5-3872
MR. CLEAN
WHY SEND A WOMAN TO DO A MAN'S JOB?
NOW SHE COULD DIG CONTENTEDLY INTO THE MOST INTIMATE CORNERS OF PEOPLE'S LIVES.
THIS OCCUPATION SATISFIED HER FOR MANY YEARS.
ONE DAY, HOWEVER, SHE WAS SNOOPING THROUGH AN OLD WOMAN'S MEMORY BOOK.
MEMORIES
IT WAS ONLY THEN THAT SHE REALIZED SHE DIDN'T HAVE ONE OF HER OWN.

Story Minute © "STAR STUCK" CARLAY

THE WOMAN BELIEVED THAT THE STARS DETERMINED ALL.

SHE CHECKED HER CHARTS BEFORE EVERY MAJOR DECISION.

So FAR, EVERY CALCULATION HAD PROVED TO BE EXACTLY RIGHT.

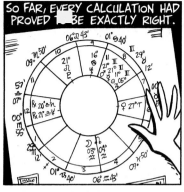

THE STARS EVEN TOLD HER ON WHAT DAY SHE WOULD MEET HER FUTURE HUSBAND.

WHEN THEY WERE LOOKING FOR A HOUSE TO BUY, SHE CONSULTED THE SKY.

AND SHE PLOTTED THE EXACT TIME THAT WOULD BE RIGHT FOR HER TO CONCEIVE A BABY.

NATURE HAD OTHER IDEAS, THOUGH, AND SHE BECAME PREGNANT A MONTH TOO SOON.

THE FETUS HAD BEEN CONCEIVED WITH LOVE, SO SHE KNEW SHE COULD NOT ABORT IT.

FOR ALTHOUGH ALL SIGNS POINTED TO IT GROWING UP TO BE A POSSIBLE SERIAL KILLER...

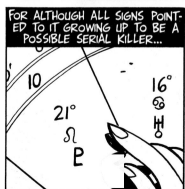

...SHE HOPED THAT A MOTHER'S LOVE COULD CANCEL OUT THOSE PREDISPOSED NEGATIVE PATHS.

BUT, SADLY, THE WOMAN DIED DURING CHILDBIRTH...

AND THUS BECAME THE SERIAL KILLER'S FIRST VICTIM.

STORY MINUTE © [...]ARO[...]
"LIKE FATHER" [...] LAY

HIS FATHER LEFT THEM WHEN HE WAS THREE.

SLAM!

HIS MOTHER TAUGHT HIM TO HATE THE MAN BY EXAMPLE.

THE RESENTMENT WOULD NOT HAVE BEEN [...] TOTAL HAD THE MAN PA[...] [CH]ILD SUPPORT.

BUT THE FATHER NEVER GAVE THEM A PENNY, EVEN THOUGH HE WAS STINKING RICH.

INDUSTRIALIST MAKES BILLIONS BY EXPLOITING FORESTS AND WETLANDS.

WORLD NEWS

THE SON WORKED HIS WAY THROUGH COLLEGE WITH GENUINE PURPOSE.

ENVIRONMENTAL LAW BECAME A WAY FOR HIM TO DO GOOD AND FEEL AVENGED.

HE WOULD MAKE A CAREER OF TRYING TO BRING DOWN FAT CATS LIKE HIS FATHER.

HE MARRIED AND HAD A SON OF HIS OWN IN BETWEEN HIS VARIOUS CRUSADES.

SOME YEARS LATER HIS FATHER DIED AND LEFT HIM $4 BILLION.

YOU'RE KIDDING ME.

CONFUSION. WHAT SHOULD HE DO WITH THIS MONEY FROM THE FATHER HE HATED?

WE'RE RICH!!

TO SPITE HIS DEAD FATHER, HE GAVE ALL THE MONEY TO HIS MANY CAUSES.

$

HIS WIFE AND SON NEVER FORGAVE HIM.

SLAM

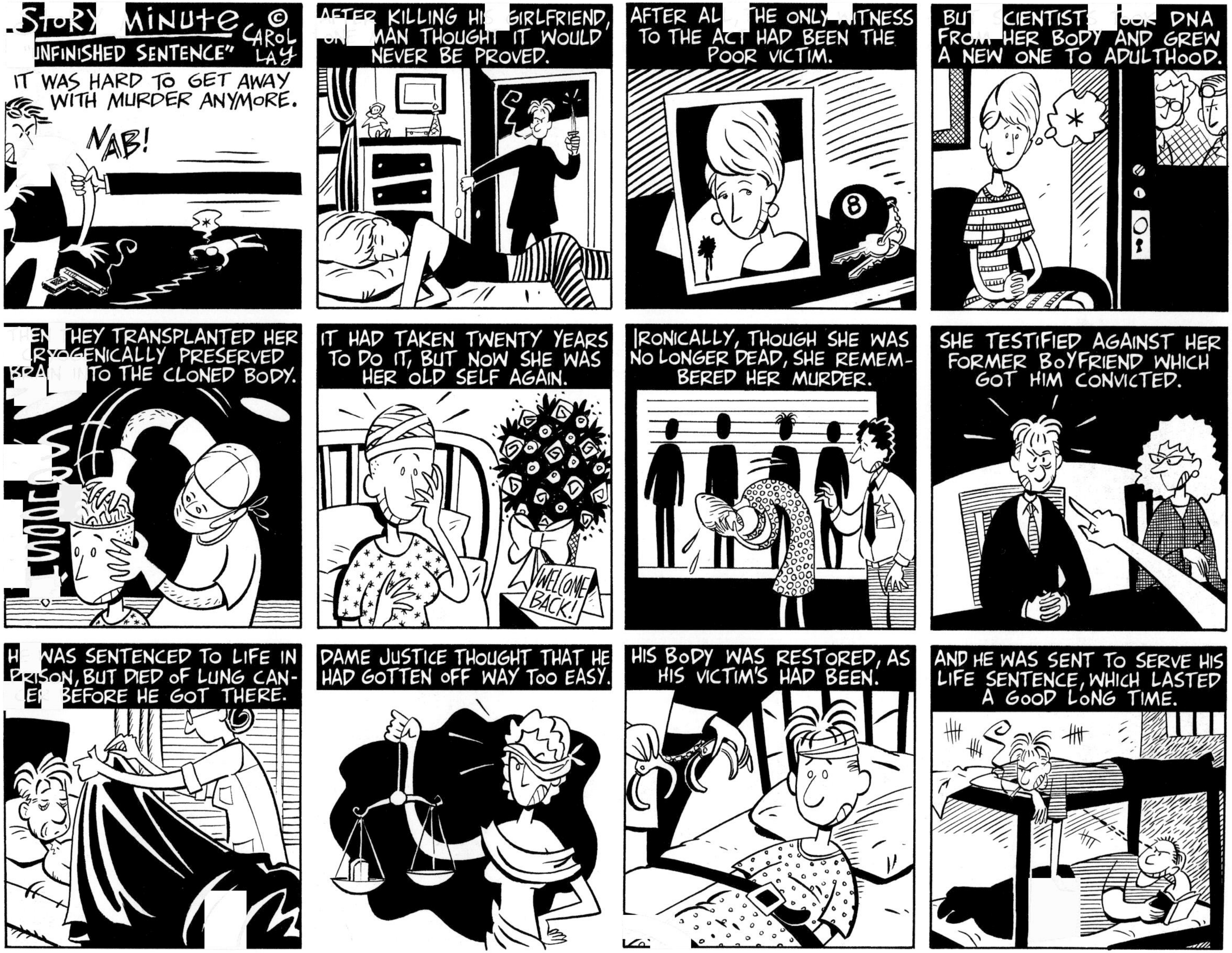
TORY MINUTE ©
UNFINISHED SENTENCE"
CAROL LAY
IT WAS HARD TO GET AWAY WITH MURDER ANYMORE.
NAB!
AFTER KILLING HI GIRLFRIEND, MAN THOUGHT IT WOULD NEVER BE PROVED.
AFTER AL THE ONLY ITNESS TO THE ACT HAD BEEN THE POOR VICTIM.
BU CIENTIST DNA FROM HER BODY AND GREW A NEW ONE TO ADULTHOOD.
THE THEY TRANSPLANTED HER RYOGENICALLY PRESERVED TO THE CLONED BODY.
IT HAD TAKEN TWENTY YEARS TO DO IT, BUT NOW SHE WAS HER OLD SELF AGAIN.
WELCOME BACK!
IRONICALLY, THOUGH SHE WAS NO LONGER DEAD, SHE REMEMBERED HER MURDER.
SHE TESTIFIED AGAINST HER FORMER BOYFRIEND WHICH GOT HIM CONVICTED.
H WAS SENTENCED TO LIFE IN RISON, BUT DIED OF LUNG CAN- BEFORE HE GOT THERE.
DAME JUSTICE THOUGHT THAT HE HAD GOTTEN OFF WAY TOO EASY.
HIS BODY WAS RESTORED, AS HIS VICTIM'S HAD BEEN.
AND HE WAS SENT TO SERVE HIS LIFE SENTENCE, WHICH LASTED A GOOD LONG TIME.

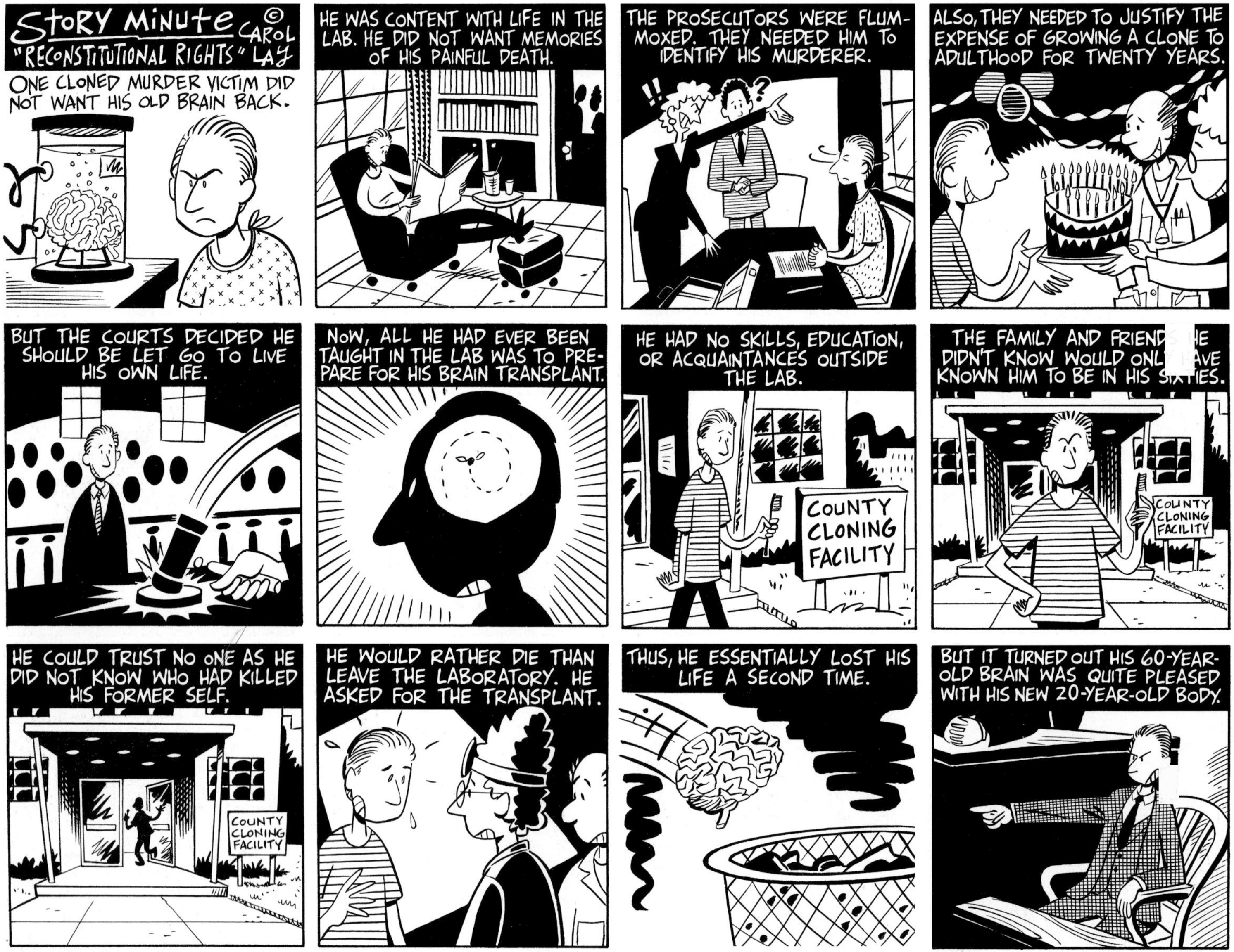
STORY MINUTE
"RECONSTITUTIONAL RIGHTS"
© CAROL LAY
ONE CLONED MURDER VICTIM DID NOT WANT HIS OLD BRAIN BACK.
HE WAS CONTENT WITH LIFE IN THE LAB. HE DID NOT WANT MEMORIES OF HIS PAINFUL DEATH.
THE PROSECUTORS WERE FLUMMOXED. THEY NEEDED HIM TO IDENTIFY HIS MURDERER.
!!
?
ALSO, THEY NEEDED TO JUSTIFY THE EXPENSE OF GROWING A CLONE TO ADULTHOOD FOR TWENTY YEARS.
BUT THE COURTS DECIDED HE SHOULD BE LET GO TO LIVE HIS OWN LIFE.
NOW, ALL HE HAD EVER BEEN TAUGHT IN THE LAB WAS TO PREPARE FOR HIS BRAIN TRANSPLANT.
HE HAD NO SKILLS, EDUCATION, OR ACQUAINTANCES OUTSIDE THE LAB.
COUNTY CLONING FACILITY
THE FAMILY AND FRIENDS HE DIDN'T KNOW WOULD ONLY HAVE KNOWN HIM TO BE IN HIS SIXTIES.
COUNTY CLONING FACILITY
HE COULD TRUST NO ONE AS HE DID NOT KNOW WHO HAD KILLED HIS FORMER SELF.
COUNTY CLONING FACILITY
HE WOULD RATHER DIE THAN LEAVE THE LABORATORY. HE ASKED FOR THE TRANSPLANT.
THUS, HE ESSENTIALLY LOST HIS LIFE A SECOND TIME.
BUT IT TURNED OUT HIS 60-YEAR-OLD BRAIN WAS QUITE PLEASED WITH HIS NEW 20-YEAR-OLD BODY.

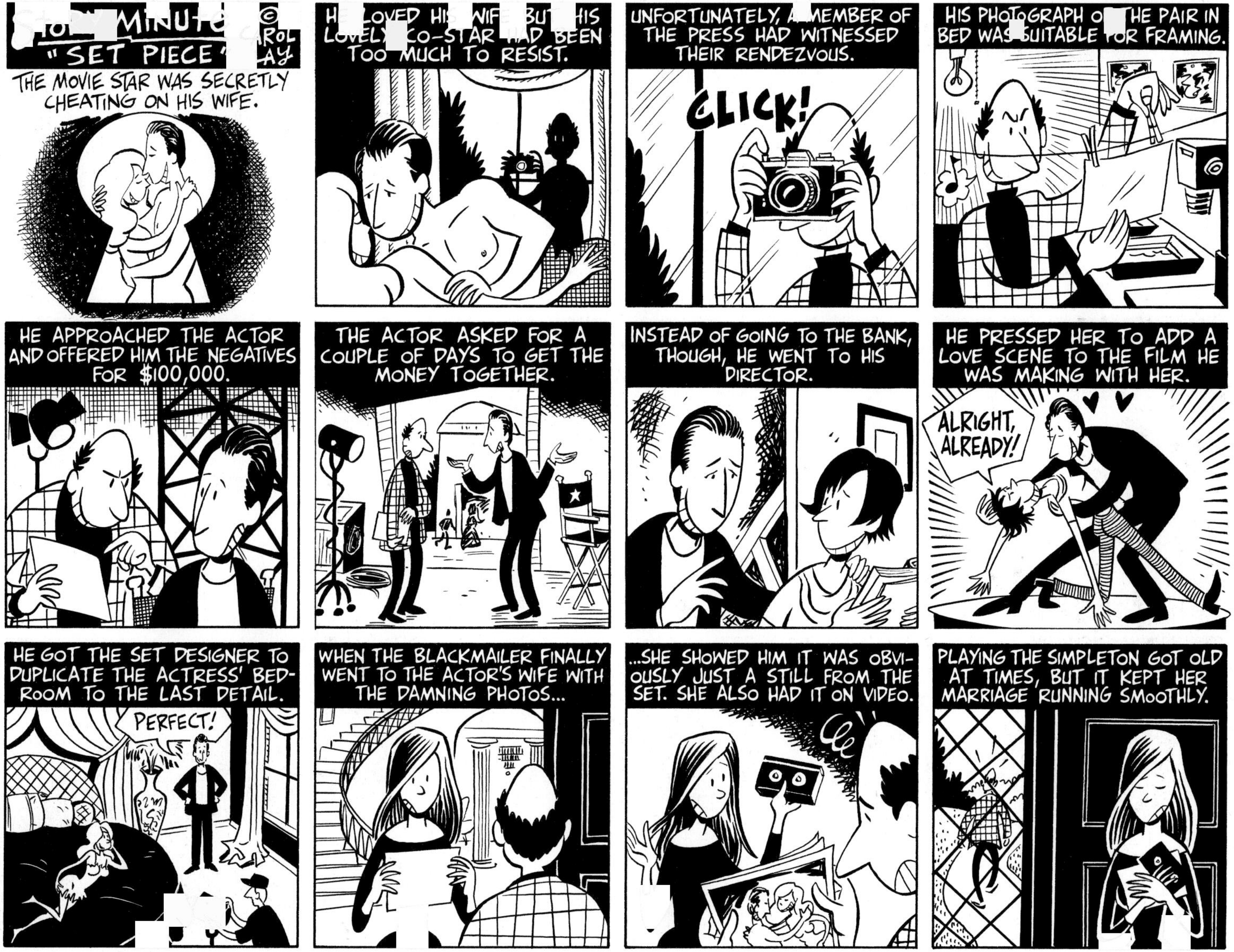
[redacted] MINUT[redacted] © [redacted] CAROL
"SET PIECE" [redacted]LAY
THE MOVIE STAR WAS SECRETLY CHEATING ON HIS WIFE.
HE LOVED HIS WIFE BUT HIS LOVELY CO-STAR HAD BEEN TOO MUCH TO RESIST.
UNFORTUNATELY, A MEMBER OF THE PRESS HAD WITNESSED THEIR RENDEZVOUS.
CLICK!
HIS PHOTOGRAPH OF THE PAIR IN BED WAS SUITABLE FOR FRAMING.
HE APPROACHED THE ACTOR AND OFFERED HIM THE NEGATIVES FOR $100,000.
THE ACTOR ASKED FOR A COUPLE OF DAYS TO GET THE MONEY TOGETHER.
INSTEAD OF GOING TO THE BANK, THOUGH, HE WENT TO HIS DIRECTOR.
HE PRESSED HER TO ADD A LOVE SCENE TO THE FILM HE WAS MAKING WITH HER.
ALRIGHT, ALREADY!
HE GOT THE SET DESIGNER TO DUPLICATE THE ACTRESS' BEDROOM TO THE LAST DETAIL.
PERFECT!
WHEN THE BLACKMAILER FINALLY WENT TO THE ACTOR'S WIFE WITH THE DAMNING PHOTOS...
...SHE SHOWED HIM IT WAS OBVIOUSLY JUST A STILL FROM THE SET. SHE ALSO HAD IT ON VIDEO.
PLAYING THE SIMPLETON GOT OLD AT TIMES, BUT IT KEPT HER MARRIAGE RUNNING SMOOTHLY.

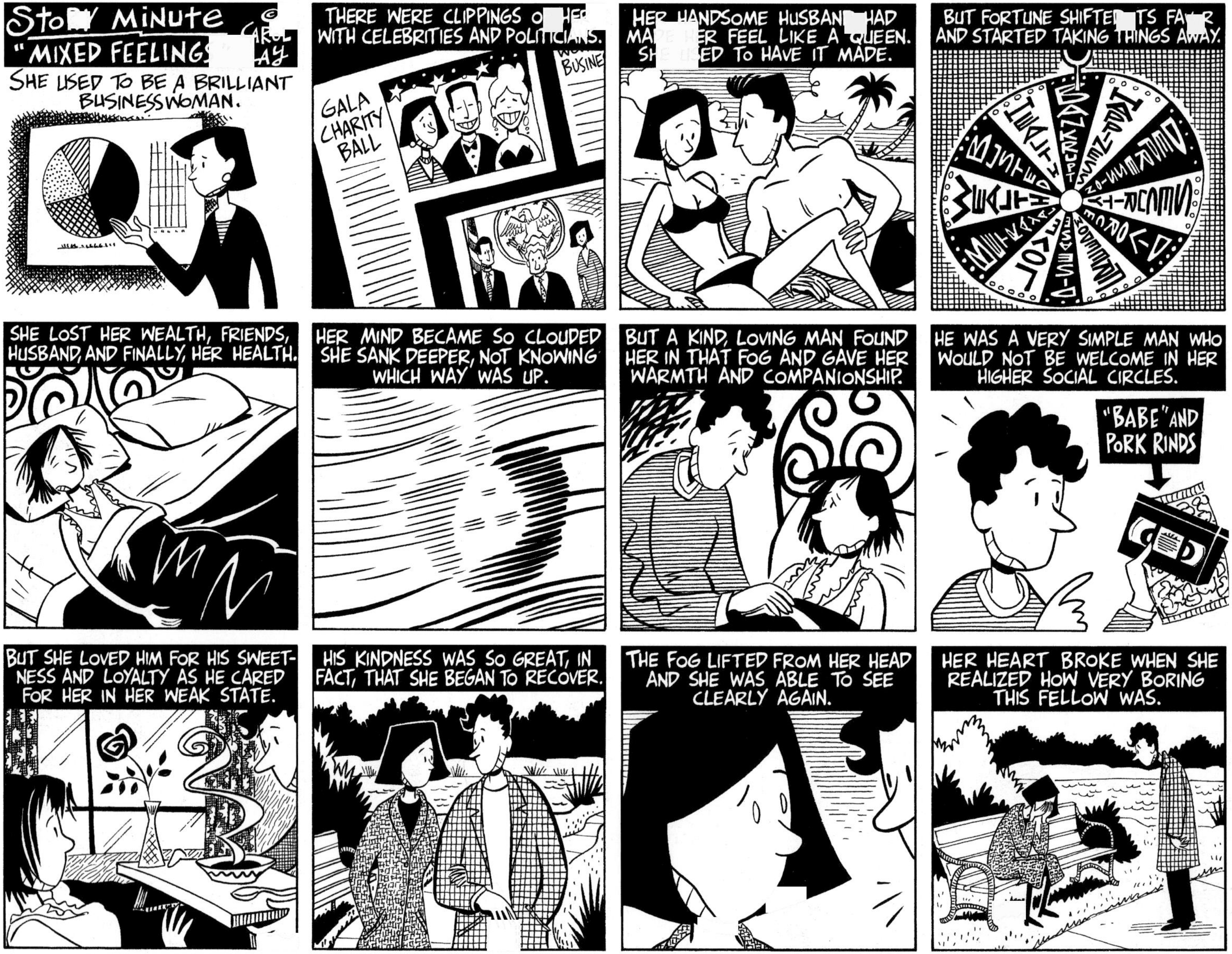
STO Y MINUTE
"MIXED FEELINGS
© AROL AY
SHE USED TO BE A BRILLIANT BUSINESSWOMAN.
THERE WERE CLIPPINGS O HE WITH CELEBRITIES AND POLITICIANS.
GALA CHARITY BALL
BUSINE
HER HANDSOME HUSBAN HAD MA E HER FEEL LIKE A QUEEN. S ED TO HAVE IT MADE.
BUT FORTUNE SHIFTE TS FA R AND STARTED TAKING THINGS AWAY.
BANKRUPT
SHE LOST HER WEALTH, FRIENDS, HUSBAND, AND FINALLY, HER HEALTH.
HER MIND BECAME SO CLOUDED SHE SANK DEEPER, NOT KNOWING WHICH WAY WAS UP.
BUT A KIND, LOVING MAN FOUND HER IN THAT FOG AND GAVE HER WARMTH AND COMPANIONSHIP.
HE WAS A VERY SIMPLE MAN WHO WOULD NOT BE WELCOME IN HER HIGHER SOCIAL CIRCLES.
"BABE" AND PORK RINDS
BUT SHE LOVED HIM FOR HIS SWEETNESS AND LOYALTY AS HE CARED FOR HER IN HER WEAK STATE.
HIS KINDNESS WAS SO GREAT, IN FACT, THAT SHE BEGAN TO RECOVER.
THE FOG LIFTED FROM HER HEAD AND SHE WAS ABLE TO SEE CLEARLY AGAIN.
HER HEART BROKE WHEN SHE REALIZED HOW VERY BORING THIS FELLOW WAS.

STORY MINUTE © CAROL LAY
"LIKE CLOCKWORK"

SHE RAN HER LIFE LIKE MUSSOLINI RAN TRAINS.

AND, ALTHOUGH HER TIME-LINES WERE BASED ON HER OWN EXPERIENCES...

SHE FELT THEY SHOULD APPLY TO HER BEST FRIEND, TOO.

BUT IT'S TOO EARLY FOR YOU TO START DATING AGAIN.

THE FRIEND TRIED TO TAKE THESE PRONOUNCEMENTS WITH GRAINS OF SALT.

HE SAID HE LOVES YOU?!

IT'S WAY TOO SOON FOR THAT!

BUT SHE WAS WARY. MAYBE THIS WOMAN KNEW SOMETHING.

RELATIONSHIPS DON'T LAST MORE THAN 4½ YEARS.

I KNOW BECAUSE THAT'S HOW LONG EACH OF MY THREE MARRIAGES LASTED.

THERE SEEMED TO BE A TIME-TABLE FOR EVERYTHING...

HE PROPOSED?!

YOU'VE ONLY KNOWN HIM SIX MONTHS!

...AND SHE NEVER FAILED TO MAKE A COMMENT.

YOU ONLY MAKE LOVE TWICE A WEEK?! YOU'RE TOO YOUNG FOR **THAT** YET!

THIS WENT ON FOR SOME TIME...

IT'S TOO EARLY FOR YOU TO BUY A PLACE TOGETHER.

...UNTIL THE FRIEND FINALLY HAD ALL SHE COULD TAKE.

I REALLY DON'T HAVE TIME FOR YOU ANYMORE.

THE WOMAN REGRETTED THE LOSS OF HER FRIEND AFTER SO LONG...

...AND THEN REALIZED THEY HAD KNOWN EACH OTHER EXACTLY 4½ YEARS.

I TOLD HER SO.

AUGUST

STORY MINUTE
"DO YOU COPY?"
© CAROL LAY
HE HAD KNOWN THERE WAS SOME-
THING PHONY ABOUT HER ALL
WE INTERRUPT THIS STRIP WITH
WORD FROM THE AUTHOR.
A FEW WEEKS AGO I WROTE TWO STRIPS ABOUT CLONING, WHICH WAS THEN STILL IN THE REALM OF SCIENCE FICTION.
SHORTLY AFTER I FINISHED THE STRIPS, A CLONED SHEEP BECAME BIG NEWS.
MISCONCEPTIONS ABOUT HUMAN CLONING WERE VOICED BY MANY.
SHORT PEOPLE WILL BECOME EXTINCT.
IT'S IMMORAL AND DISGUST-ING.
WE WON'T NEED MEN ANY-MORE.
THE SECOND COMING OF HITLER AND THE HARVESTING OF ORGANS BECAME COMMON CONCERNS.
THUMP
THUMP
MY OWN COMICS SUGGESTED THAT A CLONE MIGHT BE GROWN TO REPLACE A MURDER VICTIM.
THIS INVOLVED TRANSPLANTING THE VICTIM'S FROZEN BRAIN— STILL IN THE SPECULATIVE STAGE.
SQUOOSH
I DID NOT MEAN TO REINFORCE THE FALSE NOTION THAT CLONES MAY BE HARVESTED IN ANY WAY.
MY OWN CLONE, OF COURSE, WILL BE HER OWN PERSON WITH HER OWN MIND AND *RAISON d'ETRE.*
SHE WILL HAVE MY SAME ABIL-ITIES AND LIABILITIES, BUT IT'S GOOD TO KNOW WHAT TO EXPECT.
ARTY
TALL
NEAR-SIGHTED
SHY
PARANOID
DROLL
HONEST
HIGHLY COMPETITIVE
NAÏVE
I WOULD HAVE ABSOLUTELY NO RIGHT TO HARVEST ANY PART OF HER IDENTICAL BODY.
YOU MAY, HOWEVER, LOOK FORWARD TO SEEING THE STRIP COME OUT TWICE A WEEK BY THE YEAR 2015.

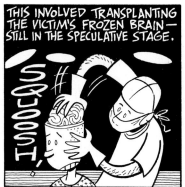

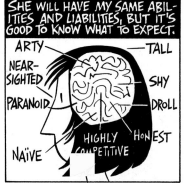

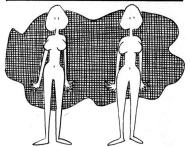

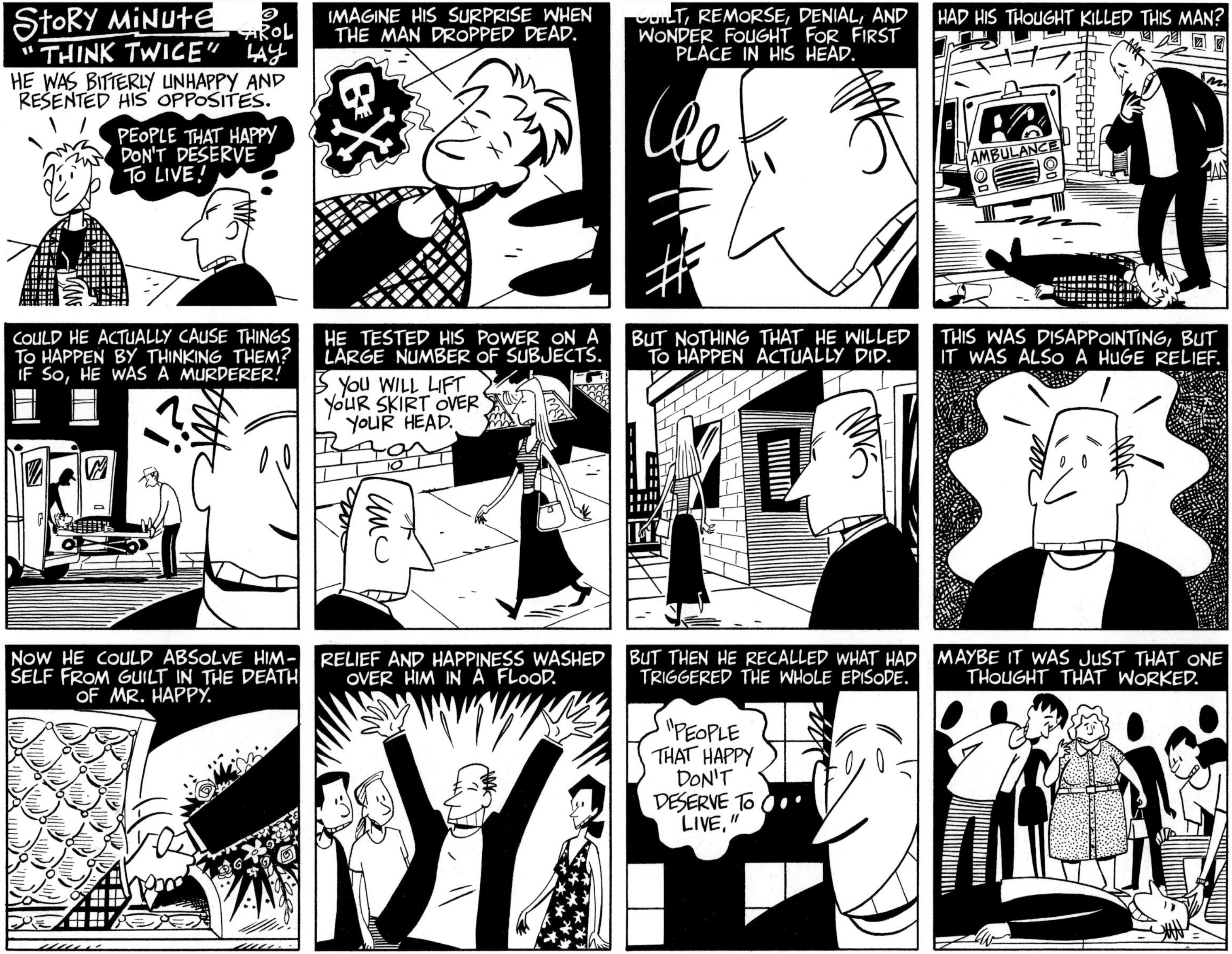
STORY MINUTE
© CAROL LAY
"THINK TWICE"
HE WAS BITTERLY UNHAPPY AND RESENTED HIS OPPOSITES.
PEOPLE THAT HAPPY DON'T DESERVE TO LIVE!
IMAGINE HIS SURPRISE WHEN THE MAN DROPPED DEAD.
GUILT, REMORSE, DENIAL, AND WONDER FOUGHT FOR FIRST PLACE IN HIS HEAD.
HAD HIS THOUGHT KILLED THIS MAN?
AMBULANCE
COULD HE ACTUALLY CAUSE THINGS TO HAPPEN BY THINKING THEM? IF SO, HE WAS A MURDERER!
!?
HE TESTED HIS POWER ON A LARGE NUMBER OF SUBJECTS.
YOU WILL LIFT YOUR SKIRT OVER YOUR HEAD.
BUT NOTHING THAT HE WILLED TO HAPPEN ACTUALLY DID.
THIS WAS DISAPPOINTING, BUT IT WAS ALSO A HUGE RELIEF.
NOW HE COULD ABSOLVE HIMSELF FROM GUILT IN THE DEATH OF MR. HAPPY.
RELIEF AND HAPPINESS WASHED OVER HIM IN A FLOOD.
BUT THEN HE RECALLED WHAT HAD TRIGGERED THE WHOLE EPISODE.
"PEOPLE THAT HAPPY DON'T DESERVE TO LIVE."
MAYBE IT WAS JUST THAT ONE THOUGHT THAT WORKED.

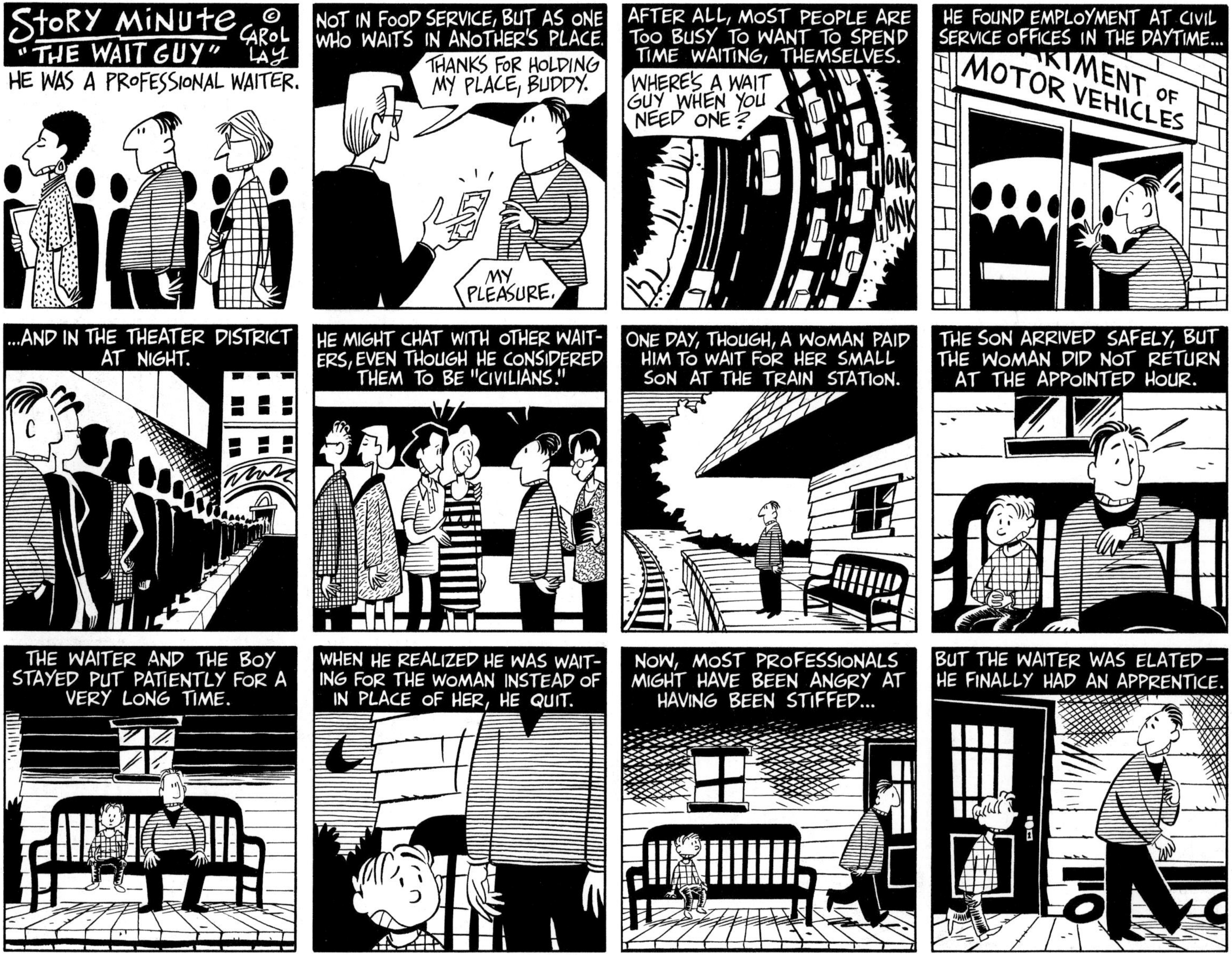
STORY MINUTE
"THE WAIT GUY"
© CAROL LAY
HE WAS A PROFESSIONAL WAITER.
NOT IN FOOD SERVICE, BUT AS ONE WHO WAITS IN ANOTHER'S PLACE.
THANKS FOR HOLDING MY PLACE, BUDDY.
MY PLEASURE.
AFTER ALL, MOST PEOPLE ARE TOO BUSY TO WANT TO SPEND TIME WAITING, THEMSELVES.
WHERE'S A WAIT GUY WHEN YOU NEED ONE?
HONK
HONK
HE FOUND EMPLOYMENT AT CIVIL SERVICE OFFICES IN THE DAYTIME...
MOTOR VEHICLES
...AND IN THE THEATER DISTRICT AT NIGHT.
HE MIGHT CHAT WITH OTHER WAITERS, EVEN THOUGH HE CONSIDERED THEM TO BE "CIVILIANS."
ONE DAY, THOUGH, A WOMAN PAID HIM TO WAIT FOR HER SMALL SON AT THE TRAIN STATION.
THE SON ARRIVED SAFELY, BUT THE WOMAN DID NOT RETURN AT THE APPOINTED HOUR.
THE WAITER AND THE BOY STAYED PUT PATIENTLY FOR A VERY LONG TIME.
WHEN HE REALIZED HE WAS WAITING FOR THE WOMAN INSTEAD OF IN PLACE OF HER, HE QUIT.
NOW, MOST PROFESSIONALS MIGHT HAVE BEEN ANGRY AT HAVING BEEN STIFFED...
BUT THE WAITER WAS ELATED— HE FINALLY HAD AN APPRENTICE.

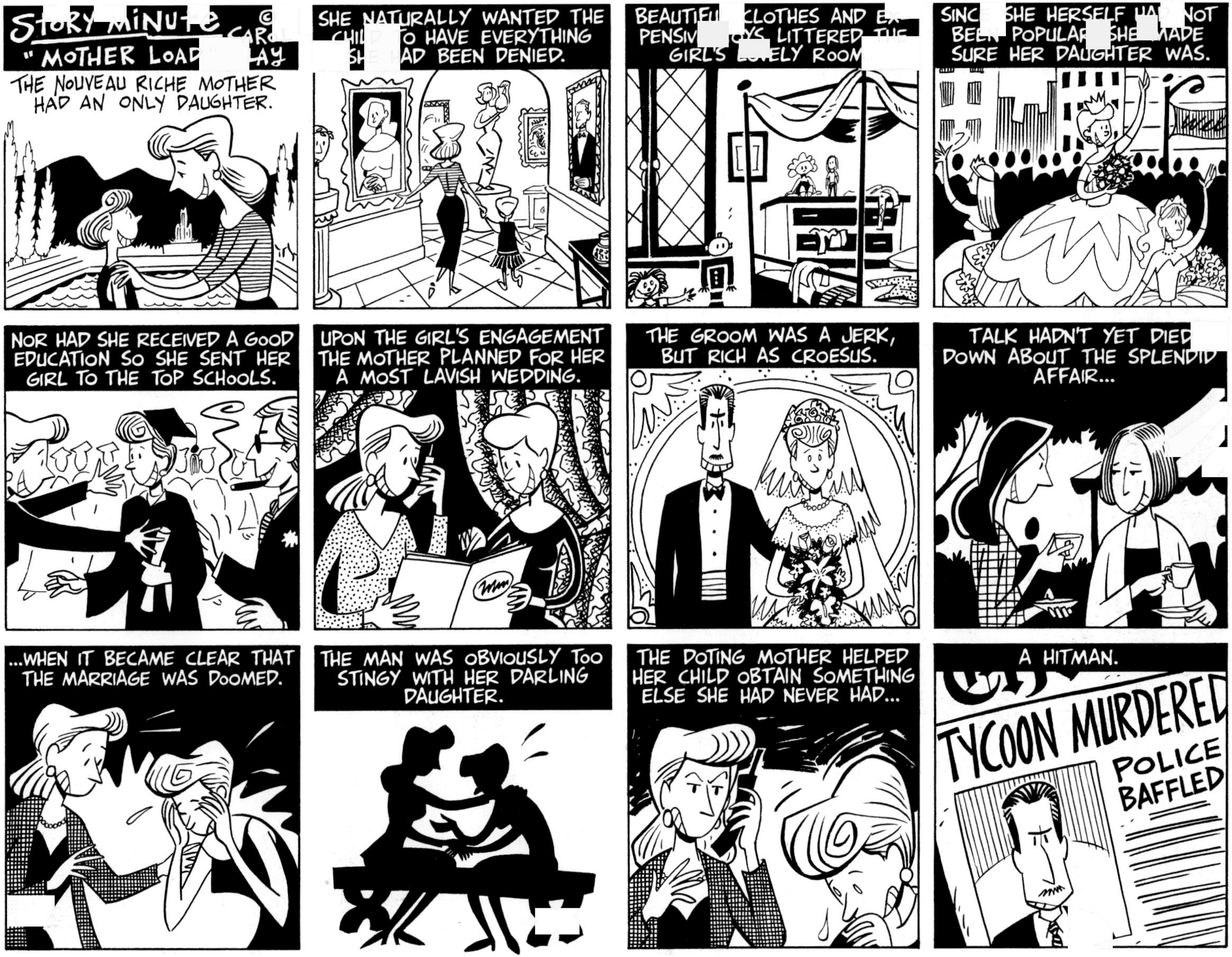

STORY MINUTE
"MOTHER LOAD
© CAR
LAY
THE NOUVEAU RICHE MOTHER HAD AN ONLY DAUGHTER.
SHE NATURALLY WANTED THE CHI O TO HAVE EVERYTHING HE AD BEEN DENIED.
BEAUTIFU CLOTHES AND EX- PENSIV LITTERED GIRL'S ROOM
SINC HE HERSELF HA NOT BEEN POPULAR SHE MADE SURE HER DAUGHTER WAS.
NOR HAD SHE RECEIVED A GOOD EDUCATION SO SHE SENT HER GIRL TO THE TOP SCHOOLS.
UPON THE GIRL'S ENGAGEMENT THE MOTHER PLANNED FOR HER A MOST LAVISH WEDDING.
THE GROOM WAS A JERK, BUT RICH AS CROESUS.
TALK HADN'T YET DIED DOWN ABOUT THE SPLENDID AFFAIR...
...WHEN IT BECAME CLEAR THAT THE MARRIAGE WAS DOOMED.
THE MAN WAS OBVIOUSLY TOO STINGY WITH HER DARLING DAUGHTER.
THE DOTING MOTHER HELPED HER CHILD OBTAIN SOMETHING ELSE SHE HAD NEVER HAD...
A HITMAN.
TYCOON MURDERED
POLICE BAFFLED

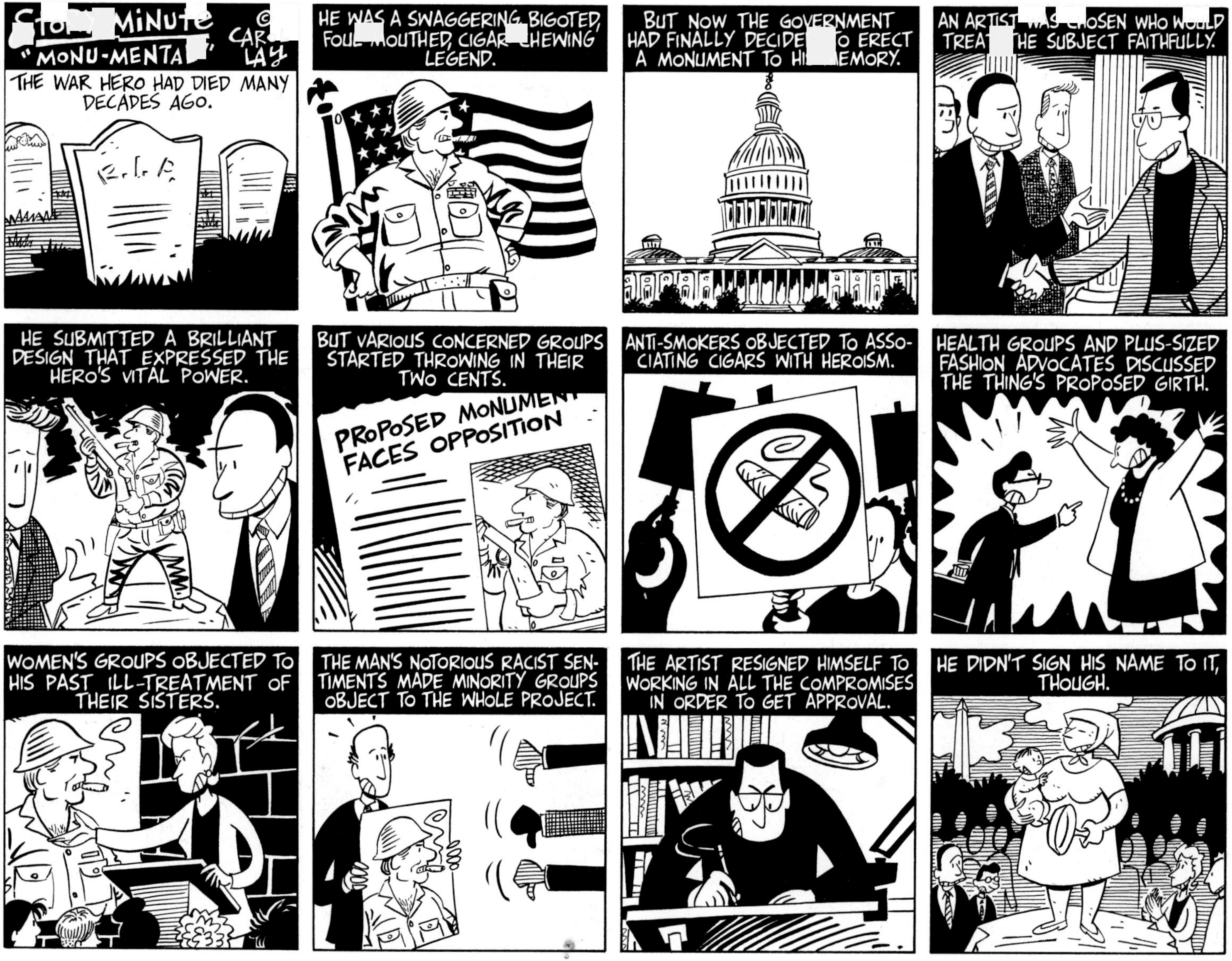

STO MINUTE
"MONU-MENTA
© CAR LAY
THE WAR HERO HAD DIED MANY DECADES AGO.
R.I.P.
HE WAS A SWAGGERING, BIGOTED, FOUL OUTHED, CIGAR HEWING LEGEND.
BUT NOW THE GOVERNMENT HAD FINALLY DECIDE O ERECT A MONUMENT TO HI EMORY.
AN ARTIST OSEN WHO W ULD TREA THE SUBJECT FAITHFULLY.
HE SUBMITTED A BRILLIANT DESIGN THAT EXPRESSED THE HERO'S VITAL POWER.
BUT VARIOUS CONCERNED GROUPS STARTED THROWING IN THEIR TWO CENTS.
PROPOSED MONUMENT FACES OPPOSITION
ANTI-SMOKERS OBJECTED TO ASSOCIATING CIGARS WITH HEROISM.
HEALTH GROUPS AND PLUS-SIZED FASHION ADVOCATES DISCUSSED THE THING'S PROPOSED GIRTH.
WOMEN'S GROUPS OBJECTED TO HIS PAST ILL-TREATMENT OF THEIR SISTERS.
THE MAN'S NOTORIOUS RACIST SENTIMENTS MADE MINORITY GROUPS OBJECT TO THE WHOLE PROJECT.
THE ARTIST RESIGNED HIMSELF TO WORKING IN ALL THE COMPROMISES IN ORDER TO GET APPROVAL.
HE DIDN'T SIGN HIS NAME TO IT, THOUGH.

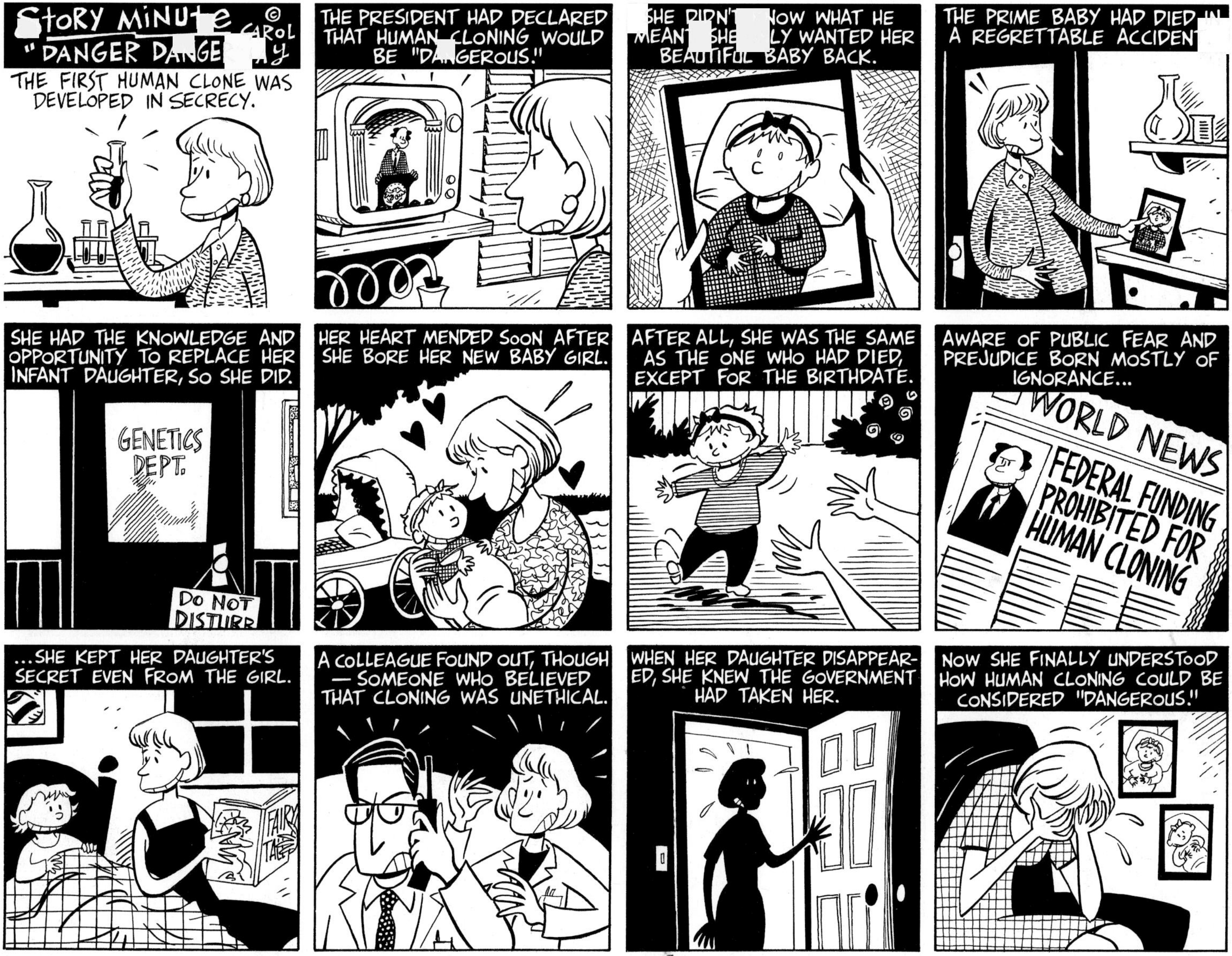
Story Minu e
"DANGER DANGE
© CAROL
THE FIRST HUMAN CLONE WAS DEVELOPED IN SECRECY.
THE PRESIDENT HAD DECLARED THAT HUMAN CLONING WOULD BE "D NGEROUS."
HE DIDN'T NOW WHAT HE MEAN SHE LY WANTED HER BEAUTIFUL BABY BACK.
THE PRIME BABY HAD DIED IN A REGRETTABLE ACCIDENT
SHE HAD THE KNOWLEDGE AND OPPORTUNITY TO REPLACE HER INFANT DAUGHTER, SO SHE DID.
GENETICS DEPT.
DO NOT
HER HEART MENDED SOON AFTER SHE BORE HER NEW BABY GIRL.
AFTER ALL, SHE WAS THE SAME AS THE ONE WHO HAD DIED, EXCEPT FOR THE BIRTHDATE.
AWARE OF PUBLIC FEAR AND PREJUDICE BORN MOSTLY OF IGNORANCE...
WORLD NEWS
FEDERAL FUNDING PROHIBITED FOR HUMAN CLONING
...SHE KEPT HER DAUGHTER'S SECRET EVEN FROM THE GIRL.
FAIRY TALE
A COLLEAGUE FOUND OUT, THOUGH — SOMEONE WHO BELIEVED THAT CLONING WAS UNETHICAL.
WHEN HER DAUGHTER DISAPPEARED, SHE KNEW THE GOVERNMENT HAD TAKEN HER.
NOW SHE FINALLY UNDERSTOOD HOW HUMAN CLONING COULD BE CONSIDERED "DANGEROUS."

STORY MINUTE © CAROL LAY
"MANIMORPHOSIS"
WHEN HE WOKE UP, HE HAD A NEW LEFT HAND.

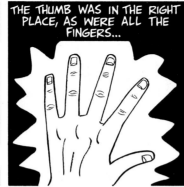

THE THUMB WAS IN THE RIGHT PLACE, AS WERE ALL THE FINGERS...

BUT HE KNEW THIS HAND NOT TO BE HIS OWN.

HE EXPERIMENTED. IN SOME WAYS THIS HAND WAS BETTER THAN THE OLD ONE.

HUH.

IT COULD PLAY THE PIANO— SOMETHING HIS RIGHT HAND COULDN'T DO.

BUT HIS WEDDING BAND WAS MISSING.

THERE WASN'T EVEN AN IMPRESSION OF A RING ON THAT FINGER.

HIS WIFE NOTICED AND ASKED ABOUT IT.

HE TRIED TO EXPLAIN ABOUT THE NEW HAND, BUT SHE DIDN'T BELIEVE HIM.

HIS LEFT HAND MADE A FIST. THEN IT RELAXED AND IT SLAPPED HER.

SHE WALKED OUT ON HIM TO THE TATTOO OF HIS FOREIGN FINGERS.

IT SEEMS THE NEW HAND DIDN'T LIKE TO BE MARRIED.

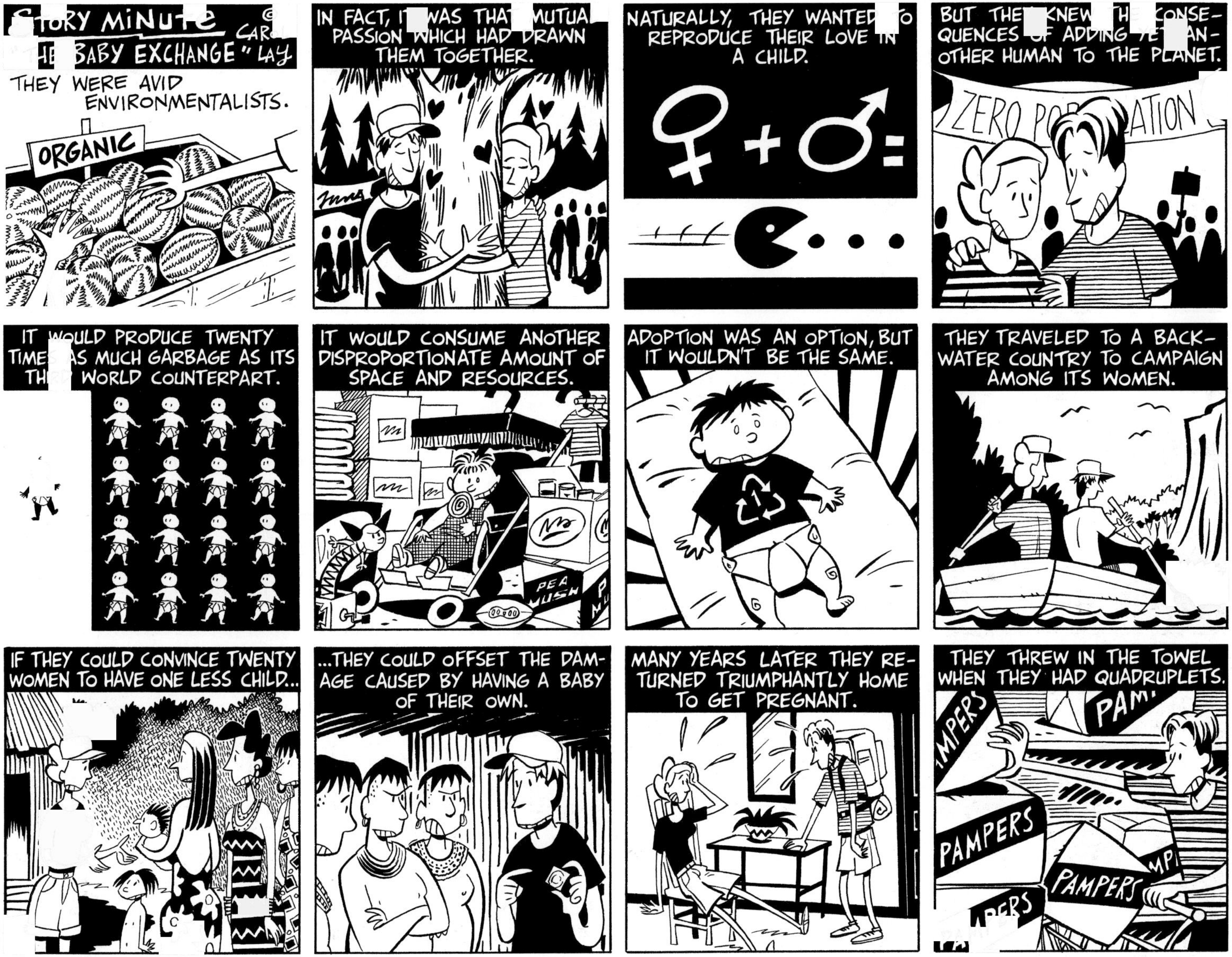

STORY MINUTE
"THE BABY EXCHANGE"
© CAROL LAY
THEY WERE AVID ENVIRONMENTALISTS.
ORGANIC
IN FACT, IT WAS THAT MUTUAL PASSION WHICH HAD DRAWN THEM TOGETHER.
NATURALLY, THEY WANTED TO REPRODUCE THEIR LOVE IN A CHILD.
BUT THEY KNEW THE CONSEQUENCES OF ADDING YET ANOTHER HUMAN TO THE PLANET.
ZERO POPULATION
IT WOULD PRODUCE TWENTY TIMES AS MUCH GARBAGE AS ITS THIRD WORLD COUNTERPART.
IT WOULD CONSUME ANOTHER DISPROPORTIONATE AMOUNT OF SPACE AND RESOURCES.
PEA MUSH
ADOPTION WAS AN OPTION, BUT IT WOULDN'T BE THE SAME.
THEY TRAVELED TO A BACKWATER COUNTRY TO CAMPAIGN AMONG ITS WOMEN.
IF THEY COULD CONVINCE TWENTY WOMEN TO HAVE ONE LESS CHILD...
...THEY COULD OFFSET THE DAMAGE CAUSED BY HAVING A BABY OF THEIR OWN.
MANY YEARS LATER THEY RETURNED TRIUMPHANTLY HOME TO GET PREGNANT.
THEY THREW IN THE TOWEL WHEN THEY HAD QUADRUPLETS.
PAMPERS
PAMPERS
PAMPERS

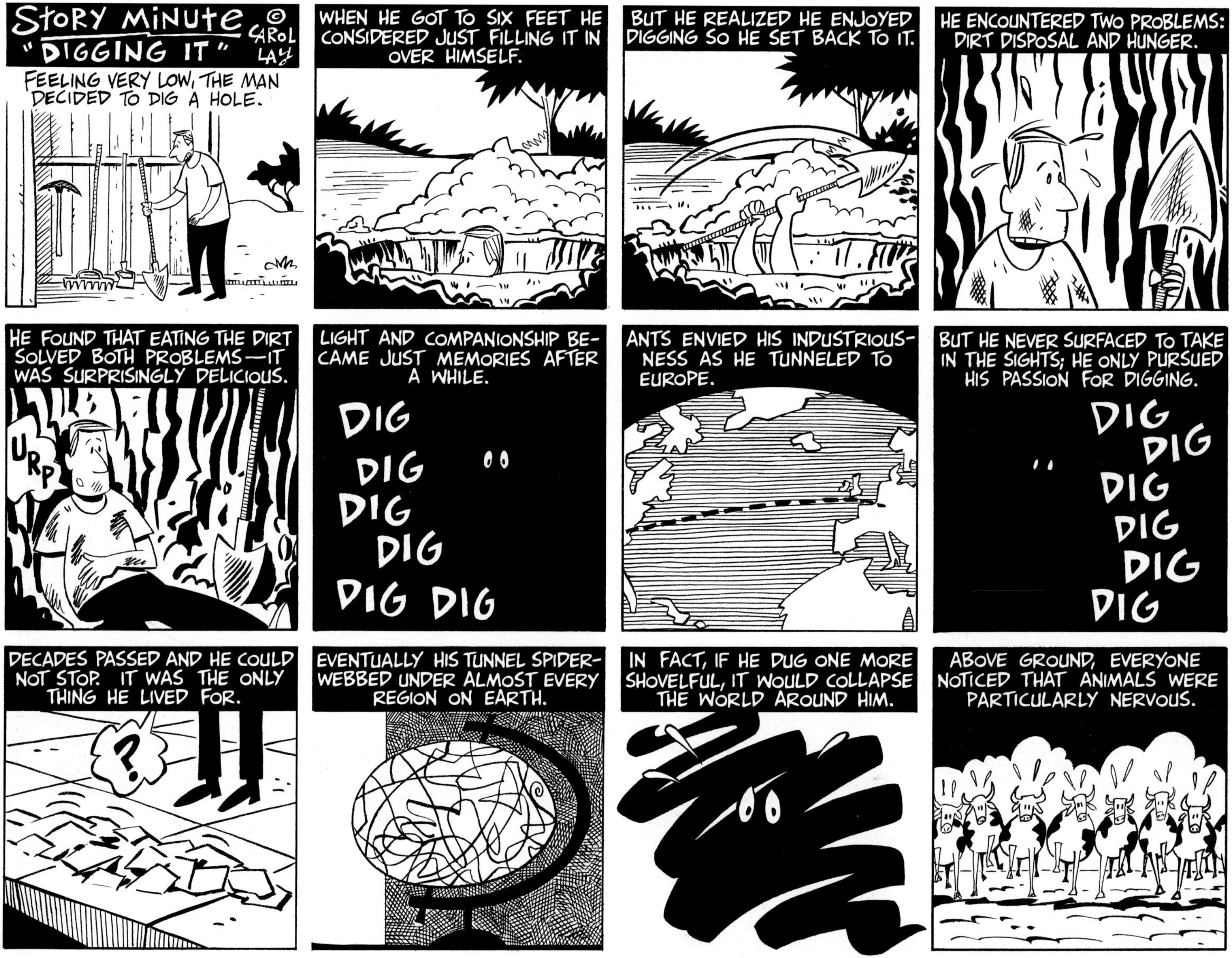
STORY MINUTE
"DIGGING IT"
© CAROL LAY
FEELING VERY LOW, THE MAN DECIDED TO DIG A HOLE.
WHEN HE GOT TO SIX FEET HE CONSIDERED JUST FILLING IT IN OVER HIMSELF.
BUT HE REALIZED HE ENJOYED DIGGING SO HE SET BACK TO IT.
HE ENCOUNTERED TWO PROBLEMS: DIRT DISPOSAL AND HUNGER.
HE FOUND THAT EATING THE DIRT SOLVED BOTH PROBLEMS—IT WAS SURPRISINGLY DELICIOUS.
URP
LIGHT AND COMPANIONSHIP BECAME JUST MEMORIES AFTER A WHILE.
DIG DIG DIG DIG DIG DIG
ANTS ENVIED HIS INDUSTRIOUSNESS AS HE TUNNELED TO EUROPE.
BUT HE NEVER SURFACED TO TAKE IN THE SIGHTS; HE ONLY PURSUED HIS PASSION FOR DIGGING.
DIG DIG DIG DIG DIG DIG
DECADES PASSED AND HE COULD NOT STOP. IT WAS THE ONLY THING HE LIVED FOR.
?
EVENTUALLY HIS TUNNEL SPIDERWEBBED UNDER ALMOST EVERY REGION ON EARTH.
IN FACT, IF HE DUG ONE MORE SHOVELFUL, IT WOULD COLLAPSE THE WORLD AROUND HIM.
ABOVE GROUND, EVERYONE NOTICED THAT ANIMALS WERE PARTICULARLY NERVOUS.

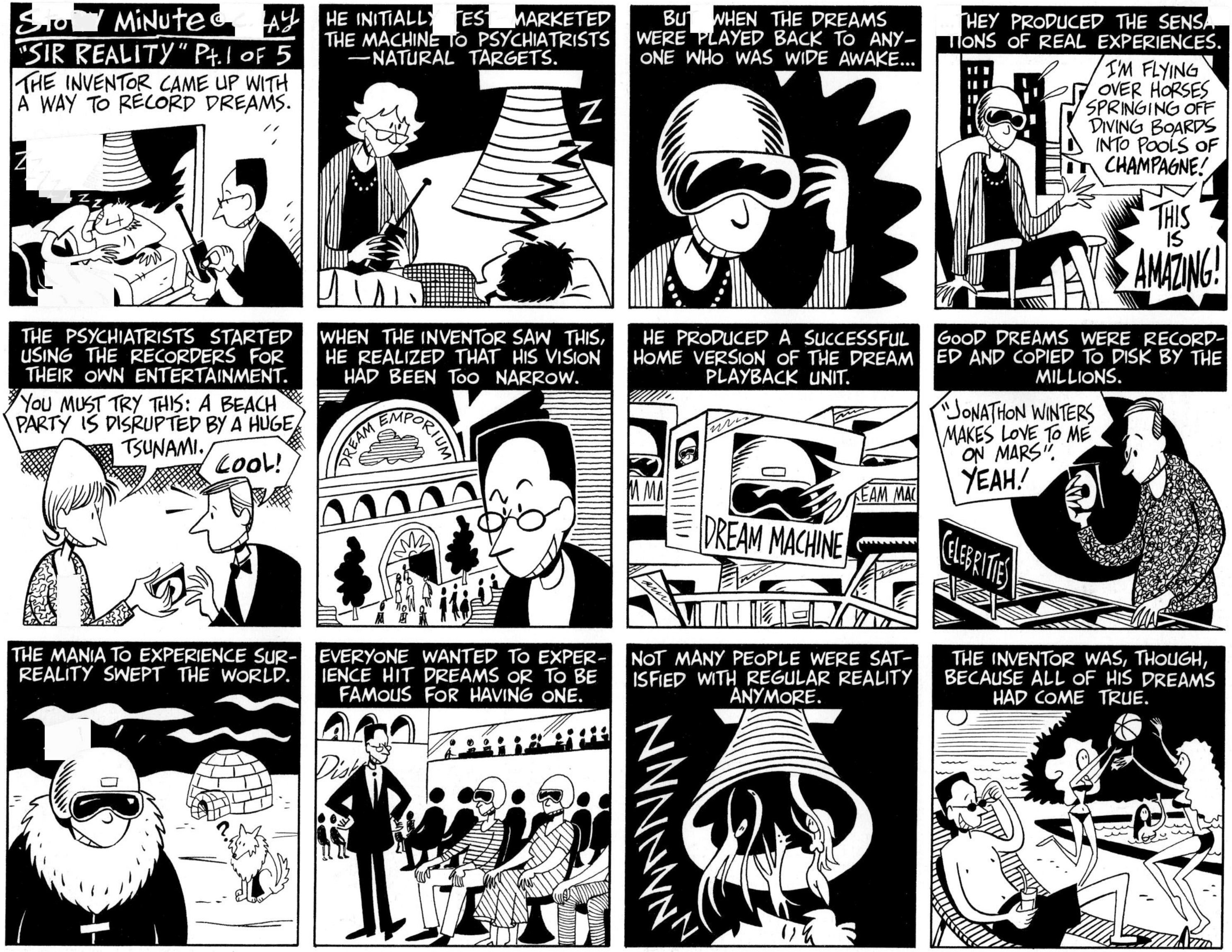

Minute ©
"SIR REALITY" Pt. I of 5
THE INVENTOR CAME UP WITH A WAY TO RECORD DREAMS.
HE INITIALLY TES MARKETED THE MACHINE TO PSYCHIATRISTS —NATURAL TARGETS.
Z
BU WHEN THE DREAMS WERE PLAYED BACK TO ANYONE WHO WAS WIDE AWAKE…
HEY PRODUCED THE SENSA IONS OF REAL EXPERIENCES.
I'M FLYING OVER HORSES SPRINGING OFF DIVING BOARDS INTO POOLS OF CHAMPAGNE!
THIS IS AMAZING!
THE PSYCHIATRISTS STARTED USING THE RECORDERS FOR THEIR OWN ENTERTAINMENT.
YOU MUST TRY THIS: A BEACH PARTY IS DISRUPTED BY A HUGE TSUNAMI.
COOL!
WHEN THE INVENTOR SAW THIS, HE REALIZED THAT HIS VISION HAD BEEN TOO NARROW.
DREAM EMPORIUM
HE PRODUCED A SUCCESSFUL HOME VERSION OF THE DREAM PLAYBACK UNIT.
DREAM MACHINE
GOOD DREAMS WERE RECORDED AND COPIED TO DISK BY THE MILLIONS.
"JONATHON WINTERS MAKES LOVE TO ME ON MARS". YEAH!
CELEBRITIES
THE MANIA TO EXPERIENCE SURREALITY SWEPT THE WORLD.
?
EVERYONE WANTED TO EXPERIENCE HIT DREAMS OR TO BE FAMOUS FOR HAVING ONE.
NOT MANY PEOPLE WERE SATISFIED WITH REGULAR REALITY ANYMORE.
THE INVENTOR WAS, THOUGH, BECAUSE ALL OF HIS DREAMS HAD COME TRUE.

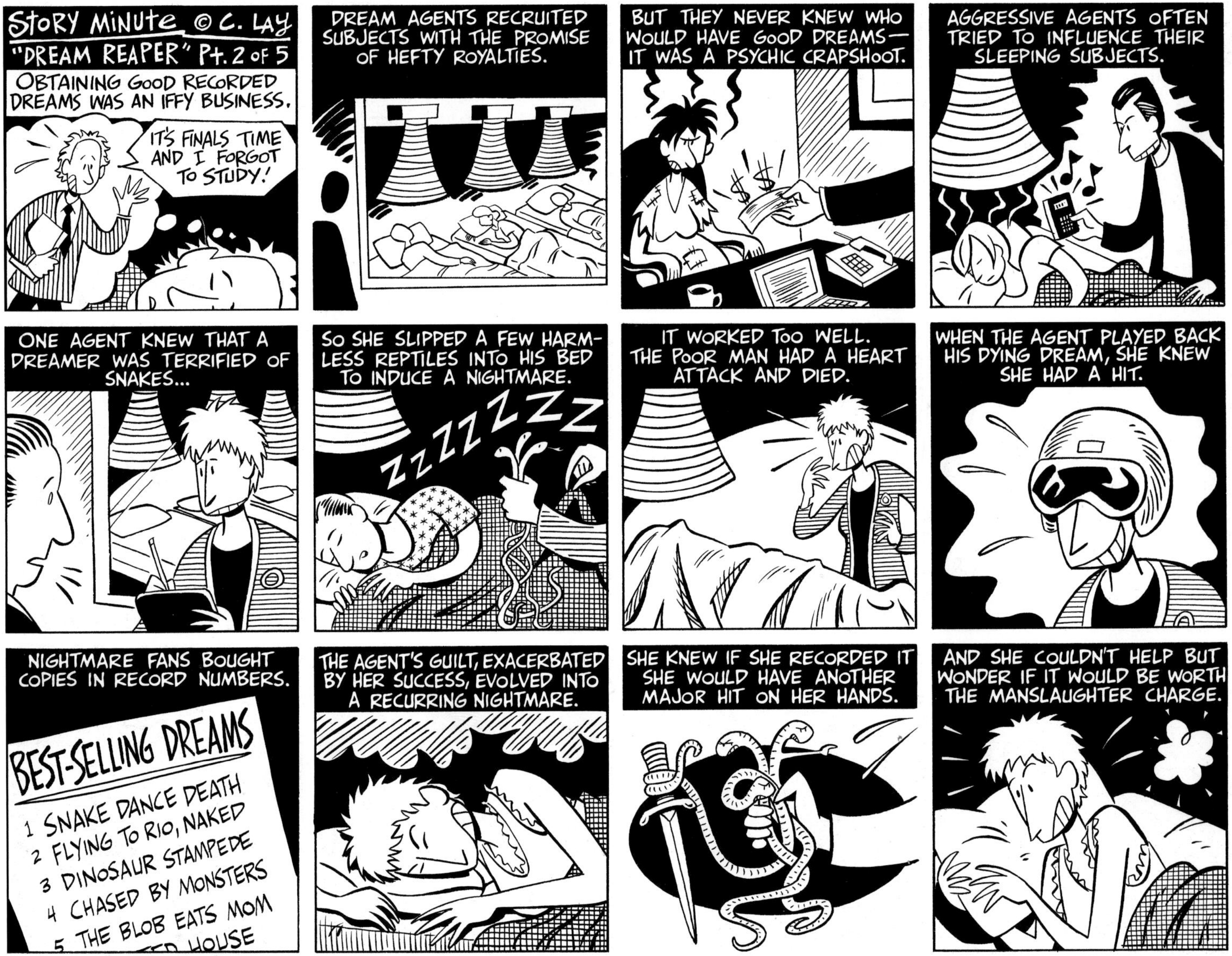

STORY MINUTE © C. LAY
"DREAM REAPER" Pt. 2 OF 5
OBTAINING GOOD RECORDED DREAMS WAS AN IFFY BUSINESS.
IT'S FINALS TIME AND I FORGOT TO STUDY!
DREAM AGENTS RECRUITED SUBJECTS WITH THE PROMISE OF HEFTY ROYALTIES.
BUT THEY NEVER KNEW WHO WOULD HAVE GOOD DREAMS— IT WAS A PSYCHIC CRAPSHOOT.
AGGRESSIVE AGENTS OFTEN TRIED TO INFLUENCE THEIR SLEEPING SUBJECTS.
ONE AGENT KNEW THAT A DREAMER WAS TERRIFIED OF SNAKES...
SO SHE SLIPPED A FEW HARMLESS REPTILES INTO HIS BED TO INDUCE A NIGHTMARE.
ZZZZZZZZ
IT WORKED TOO WELL. THE POOR MAN HAD A HEART ATTACK AND DIED.
WHEN THE AGENT PLAYED BACK HIS DYING DREAM, SHE KNEW SHE HAD A HIT.
NIGHTMARE FANS BOUGHT COPIES IN RECORD NUMBERS.
BEST-SELLING DREAMS
1 SNAKE DANCE DEATH
2 FLYING TO RIO, NAKED
3 DINOSAUR STAMPEDE
4 CHASED BY MONSTERS
5 THE BLOB EATS MOM
THE AGENT'S GUILT, EXACERBATED BY HER SUCCESS, EVOLVED INTO A RECURRING NIGHTMARE.
SHE KNEW IF SHE RECORDED IT SHE WOULD HAVE ANOTHER MAJOR HIT ON HER HANDS.
AND SHE COULDN'T HELP BUT WONDER IF IT WOULD BE WORTH THE MANSLAUGHTER CHARGE.

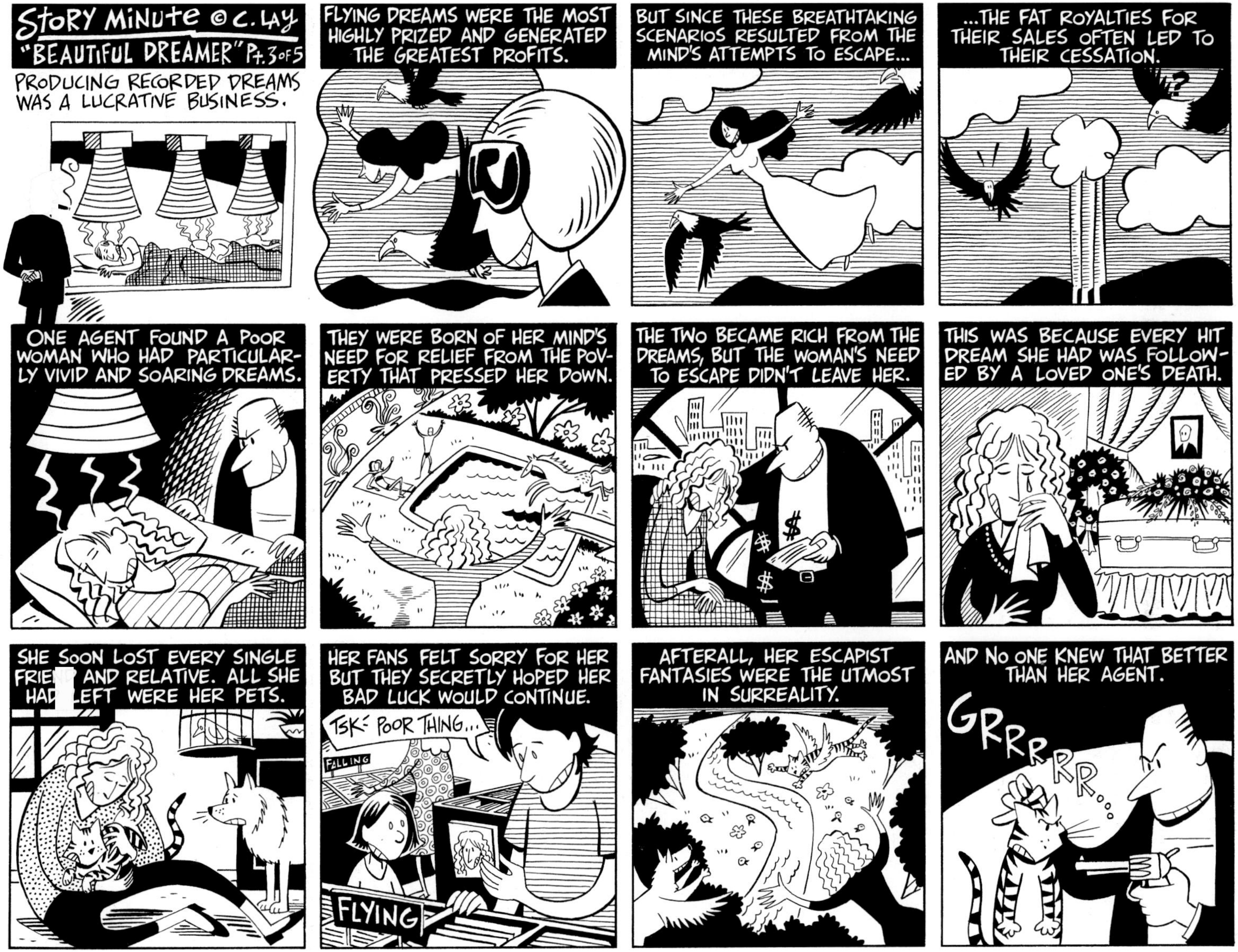
STORY MINUTE © C. LAY
"BEAUTIFUL DREAMER" Pt. 3 of 5
PRODUCING RECORDED DREAMS WAS A LUCRATIVE BUSINESS.
FLYING DREAMS WERE THE MOST HIGHLY PRIZED AND GENERATED THE GREATEST PROFITS.
BUT SINCE THESE BREATHTAKING SCENARIOS RESULTED FROM THE MIND'S ATTEMPTS TO ESCAPE...
...THE FAT ROYALTIES FOR THEIR SALES OFTEN LED TO THEIR CESSATION.
?
ONE AGENT FOUND A POOR WOMAN WHO HAD PARTICULARLY VIVID AND SOARING DREAMS.
THEY WERE BORN OF HER MIND'S NEED FOR RELIEF FROM THE POVERTY THAT PRESSED HER DOWN.
THE TWO BECAME RICH FROM THE DREAMS, BUT THE WOMAN'S NEED TO ESCAPE DIDN'T LEAVE HER.
$
$
$
THIS WAS BECAUSE EVERY HIT DREAM SHE HAD WAS FOLLOWED BY A LOVED ONE'S DEATH.
SHE SOON LOST EVERY SINGLE FRIE AND RELATIVE. ALL SHE HA EFT WERE HER PETS.
HER FANS FELT SORRY FOR HER BUT THEY SECRETLY HOPED HER BAD LUCK WOULD CONTINUE.
TSK: POOR THING...
FALLING
FLYING
AFTERALL, HER ESCAPIST FANTASIES WERE THE UTMOST IN SURREALITY.
AND NO ONE KNEW THAT BETTER THAN HER AGENT.
GRRRRR...

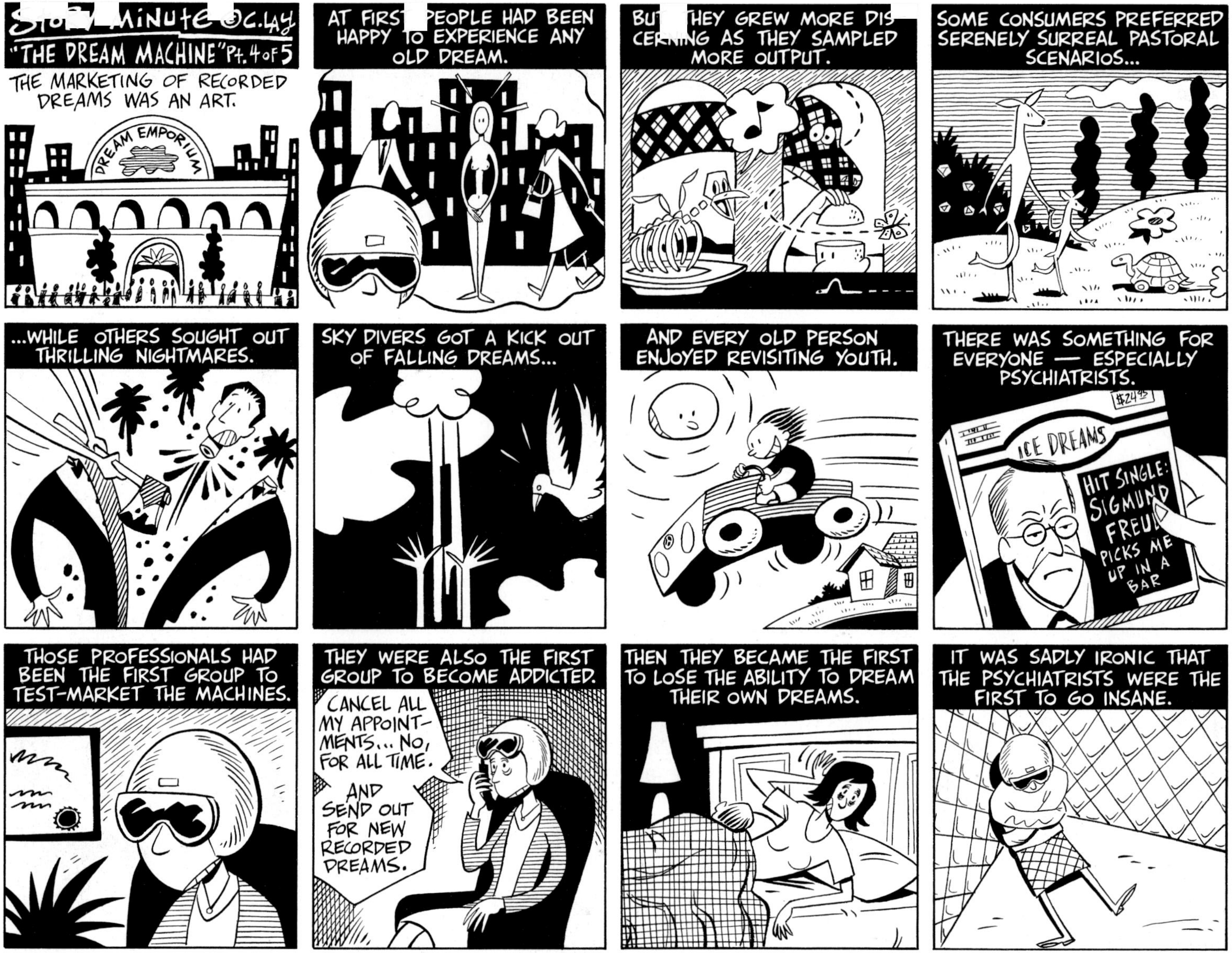
STORY MINUTE ©C.LAY
"THE DREAM MACHINE" Pt. 4 of 5
THE MARKETING OF RECORDED DREAMS WAS AN ART.
DREAM EMPORIUM
AT FIRST PEOPLE HAD BEEN HAPPY TO EXPERIENCE ANY OLD DREAM.
BUT THEY GREW MORE DISCERNING AS THEY SAMPLED MORE OUTPUT.
SOME CONSUMERS PREFERRED SERENELY SURREAL PASTORAL SCENARIOS...
...WHILE OTHERS SOUGHT OUT THRILLING NIGHTMARES.
SKY DIVERS GOT A KICK OUT OF FALLING DREAMS...
AND EVERY OLD PERSON ENJOYED REVISITING YOUTH.
THERE WAS SOMETHING FOR EVERYONE — ESPECIALLY PSYCHIATRISTS.
$24.95
ICE DREAMS
HIT SINGLE: SIGMUND FREUD PICKS ME UP IN A BAR
THOSE PROFESSIONALS HAD BEEN THE FIRST GROUP TO TEST-MARKET THE MACHINES.
THEY WERE ALSO THE FIRST GROUP TO BECOME ADDICTED.
CANCEL ALL MY APPOINTMENTS... NO, FOR ALL TIME.
AND SEND OUT FOR NEW RECORDED DREAMS.
THEN THEY BECAME THE FIRST TO LOSE THE ABILITY TO DREAM THEIR OWN DREAMS.
IT WAS SADLY IRONIC THAT THE PSYCHIATRISTS WERE THE FIRST TO GO INSANE.

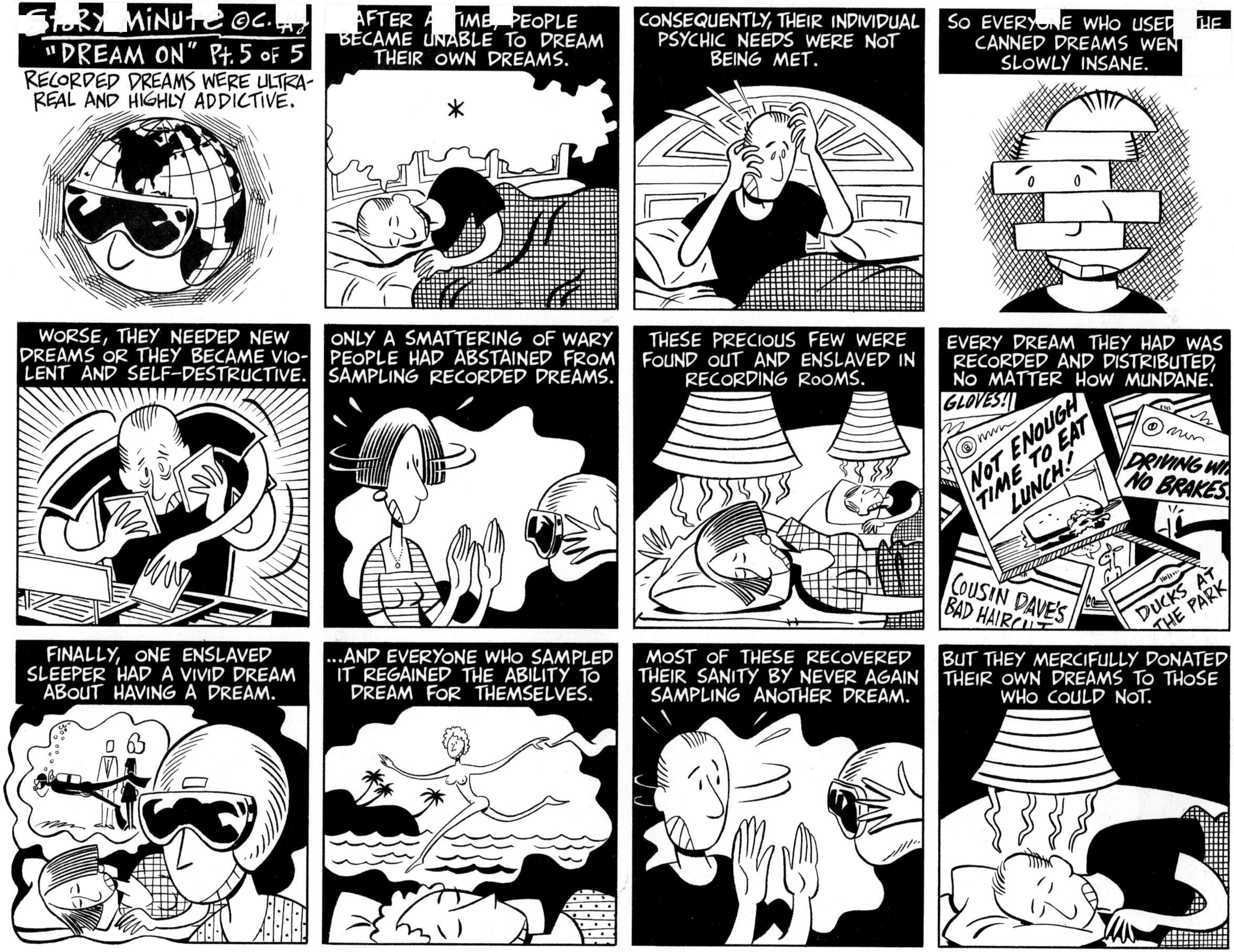
MINUTE ©C.
"DREAM ON" Pt. 5 of 5
RECORDED DREAMS WERE ULTRA-REAL AND HIGHLY ADDICTIVE.
AFTER A TIME, PEOPLE BECAME UNABLE TO DREAM THEIR OWN DREAMS.
CONSEQUENTLY, THEIR INDIVIDUAL PSYCHIC NEEDS WERE NOT BEING MET.
SO EVERYONE WHO USED THE CANNED DREAMS WENT SLOWLY INSANE.
WORSE, THEY NEEDED NEW DREAMS OR THEY BECAME VIOLENT AND SELF-DESTRUCTIVE.
ONLY A SMATTERING OF WARY PEOPLE HAD ABSTAINED FROM SAMPLING RECORDED DREAMS.
THESE PRECIOUS FEW WERE FOUND OUT AND ENSLAVED IN RECORDING ROOMS.
EVERY DREAM THEY HAD WAS RECORDED AND DISTRIBUTED, NO MATTER HOW MUNDANE.
GLOVES!!
NOT ENOUGH TIME TO EAT LUNCH!
DRIVING WITH NO BRAKES!
COUSIN DAVE'S BAD HAIRCUT
DUCKS AT THE PARK
FINALLY, ONE ENSLAVED SLEEPER HAD A VIVID DREAM ABOUT HAVING A DREAM.
...AND EVERYONE WHO SAMPLED IT REGAINED THE ABILITY TO DREAM FOR THEMSELVES.
MOST OF THESE RECOVERED THEIR SANITY BY NEVER AGAIN SAMPLING ANOTHER DREAM.
BUT THEY MERCIFULLY DONATED THEIR OWN DREAMS TO THOSE WHO COULD NOT.

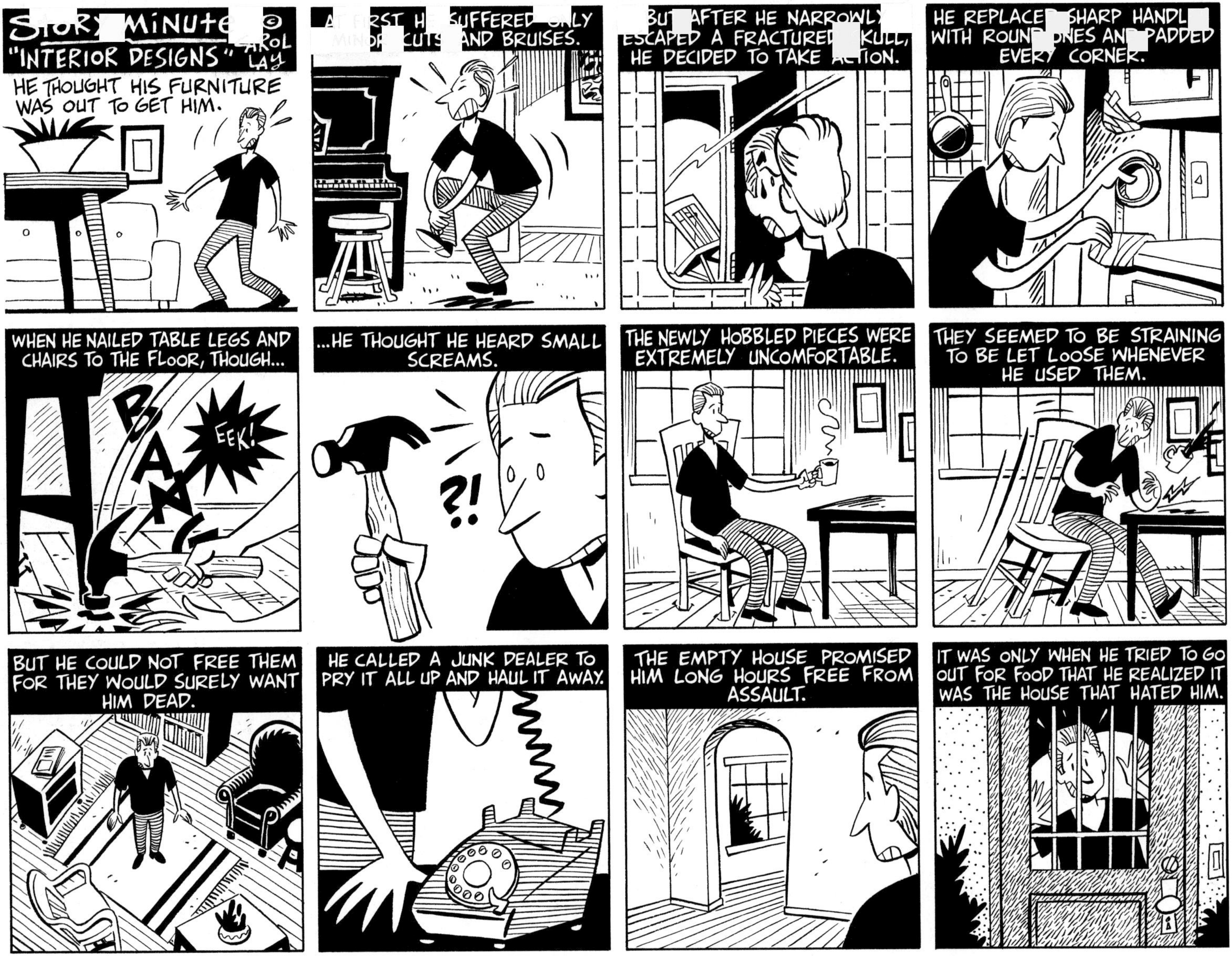
STOR MINUTE ©
"INTERIOR DESIGNS" CAROL LAY
HE THOUGHT HIS FURNITURE WAS OUT TO GET HIM.
AT FIRST HE SUFFERED ONLY MINO CUTS AND BRUISES.
BUT AFTER HE NARROWLY ESCAPED A FRACTURED KULL, HE DECIDED TO TAKE ACTION.
HE REPLACED SHARP HANDL WITH ROUND ONES AND PADDED EVERY CORNER.
WHEN HE NAILED TABLE LEGS AND CHAIRS TO THE FLOOR, THOUGH...
BAM!
EEK!
...HE THOUGHT HE HEARD SMALL SCREAMS.
?!
THE NEWLY HOBBLED PIECES WERE EXTREMELY UNCOMFORTABLE.
THEY SEEMED TO BE STRAINING TO BE LET LOOSE WHENEVER HE USED THEM.
BUT HE COULD NOT FREE THEM FOR THEY WOULD SURELY WANT HIM DEAD.
HE CALLED A JUNK DEALER TO PRY IT ALL UP AND HAUL IT AWAY.
THE EMPTY HOUSE PROMISED HIM LONG HOURS FREE FROM ASSAULT.
IT WAS ONLY WHEN HE TRIED TO GO OUT FOR FOOD THAT HE REALIZED IT WAS THE HOUSE THAT HATED HIM.

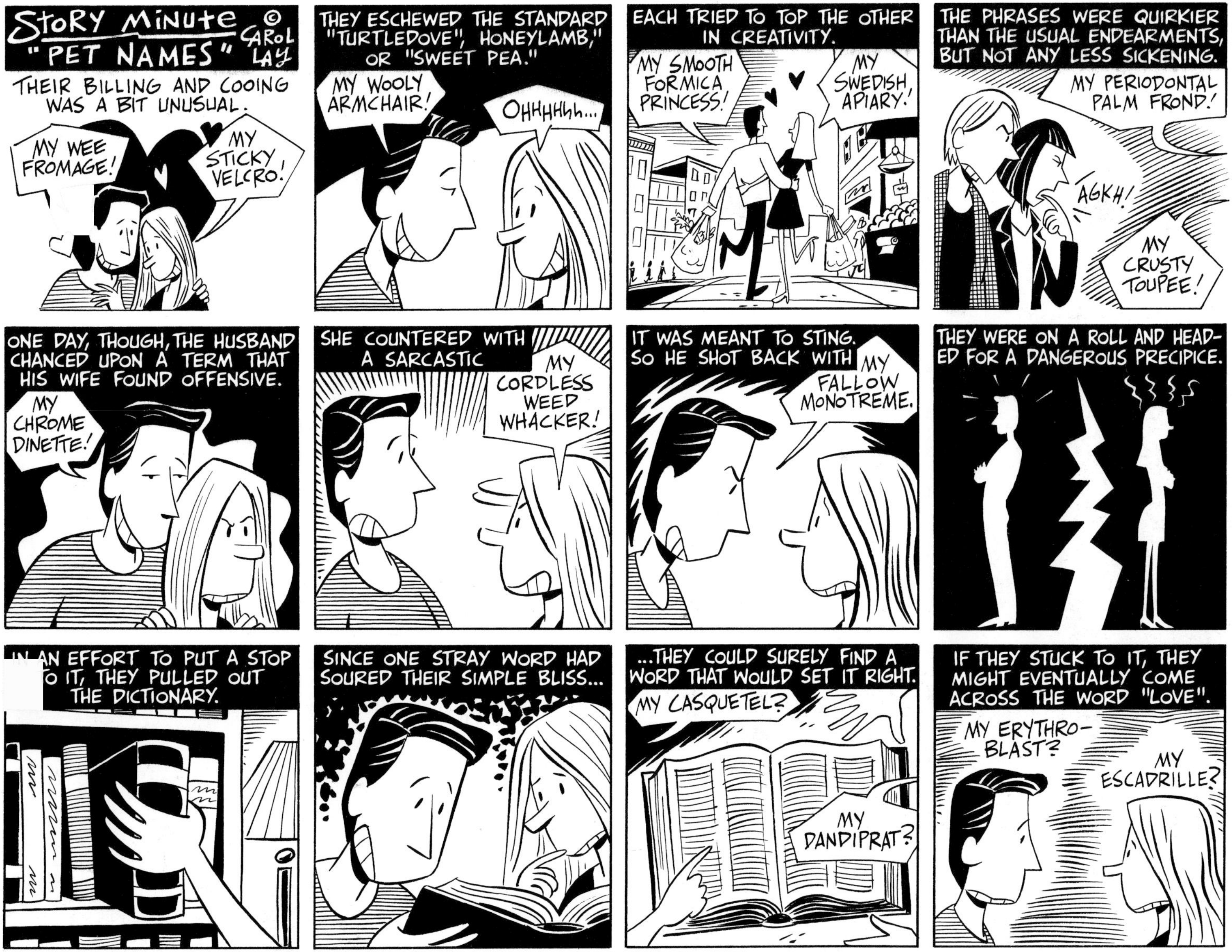
STORY MINUTE "PET NAMES" © CAROL LAY
THEIR BILLING AND COOING WAS A BIT UNUSUAL.
MY WEE FROMAGE!
MY STICKY VELCRO!
THEY ESCHEWED THE STANDARD "TURTLEDOVE", HONEYLAMB," OR "SWEET PEA."
MY WOOLY ARMCHAIR!
OHHHHHH...
EACH TRIED TO TOP THE OTHER IN CREATIVITY.
MY SMOOTH FORMICA PRINCESS!
MY SWEDISH APIARY!
THE PHRASES WERE QUIRKIER THAN THE USUAL ENDEARMENTS, BUT NOT ANY LESS SICKENING.
MY PERIODONTAL PALM FROND!
AGKH!
MY CRUSTY TOUPEE!
ONE DAY, THOUGH, THE HUSBAND CHANCED UPON A TERM THAT HIS WIFE FOUND OFFENSIVE.
MY CHROME DINETTE!
SHE COUNTERED WITH A SARCASTIC
MY CORDLESS WEED WHACKER!
IT WAS MEANT TO STING. SO HE SHOT BACK WITH
MY FALLOW MONOTREME.
THEY WERE ON A ROLL AND HEADED FOR A DANGEROUS PRECIPICE.
IN AN EFFORT TO PUT A STOP TO IT, THEY PULLED OUT THE DICTIONARY.
SINCE ONE STRAY WORD HAD SOURED THEIR SIMPLE BLISS...
...THEY COULD SURELY FIND A WORD THAT WOULD SET IT RIGHT.
MY CASQUETEL?
MY DANDIPRAT?
IF THEY STUCK TO IT, THEY MIGHT EVENTUALLY COME ACROSS THE WORD "LOVE".
MY ERYTHROBLAST?
MY ESCADRILLE?

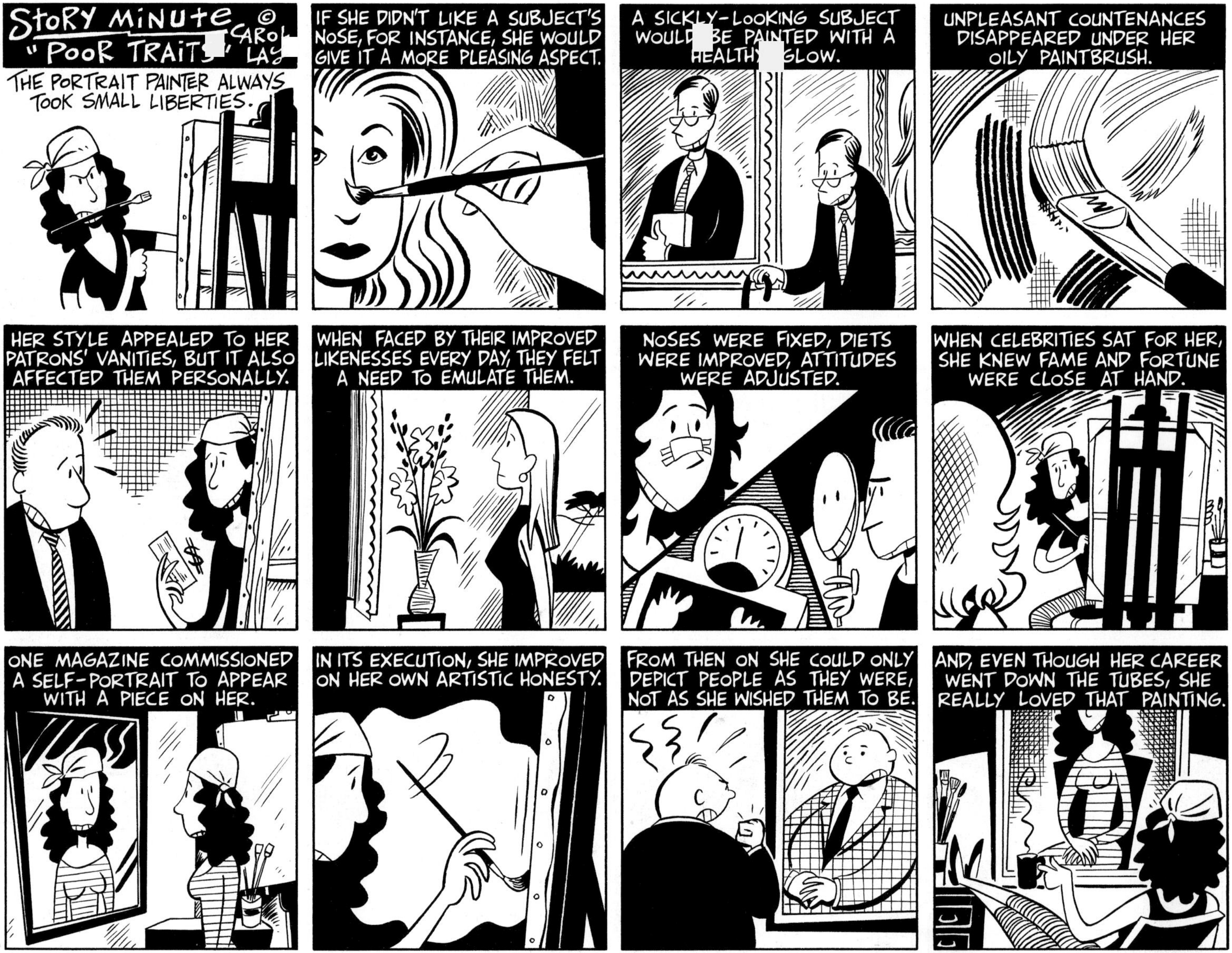
STORY MINUTE ©
"POOR TRAITS" CAROL LAY
THE PORTRAIT PAINTER ALWAYS TOOK SMALL LIBERTIES.
IF SHE DIDN'T LIKE A SUBJECT'S NOSE, FOR INSTANCE, SHE WOULD GIVE IT A MORE PLEASING ASPECT.
A SICKLY-LOOKING SUBJECT WOULD BE PAINTED WITH A HEALTHY GLOW.
UNPLEASANT COUNTENANCES DISAPPEARED UNDER HER OILY PAINTBRUSH.
HER STYLE APPEALED TO HER PATRONS' VANITIES, BUT IT ALSO AFFECTED THEM PERSONALLY.
WHEN FACED BY THEIR IMPROVED LIKENESSES EVERY DAY, THEY FELT A NEED TO EMULATE THEM.
NOSES WERE FIXED, DIETS WERE IMPROVED, ATTITUDES WERE ADJUSTED.
WHEN CELEBRITIES SAT FOR HER, SHE KNEW FAME AND FORTUNE WERE CLOSE AT HAND.
ONE MAGAZINE COMMISSIONED A SELF-PORTRAIT TO APPEAR WITH A PIECE ON HER.
IN ITS EXECUTION, SHE IMPROVED ON HER OWN ARTISTIC HONESTY.
FROM THEN ON SHE COULD ONLY DEPICT PEOPLE AS THEY WERE, NOT AS SHE WISHED THEM TO BE.
AND, EVEN THOUGH HER CAREER WENT DOWN THE TUBES, SHE REALLY LOVED THAT PAINTING.

STORY MINUTE © CAROL LAY
"WALLFLOWER"

SHE WAS REALLY QUITE POPULAR, BUT SHE RARELY WENT OUT.

IT STARTED BECAUSE SHE WAS JUST TOO BUSY TO ATTEND ALL THOSE OPENINGS AND PARTIES.

THEN PEOPLE ASSUMED SHE WAS SNUBBING THEM SO THE INVITATIONS DRIED UP.

FINALLY THEY FORGOT ABOUT HER BECAUSE SHE NEVER SHOWED UP ANYWHERE.

WHEN NO ONE WAS LOOKING, SHE MOVED TO ANOTHER TOWN.

YEARS WENT BY BEFORE ANYONE IN THE FIRST TOWN SENT HER AN INVITATION.

IT WAS RETURNED TO THE SENDER—"ADDRESS UNKNOWN!"

THE SENDER ASKED ALL AROUND TOWN. NO ONE HAD SEEN HER IN AGES.

SHE MUST HAVE DIED, THEY FIGURED. THAT'S WHY SHE NEVER SHOWED UP ANYWHERE.

"I NEVER GET OUT ANYMORE"

THE TOWN THREW HER A WAKE. IT TURNED OUT TO BE THE EVENT OF THE SEASON.

MEMORIAL

PEOPLE LAUGHED, MOURNED, TOLD STORIES, AND WHISPERED REGRETS TO HER MEMORY.

AND IT'S JUST AS WELL THAT SHE DIDN'T HEAR ABOUT HER WAKE. IT WAS SHAMPOO NIGHT.

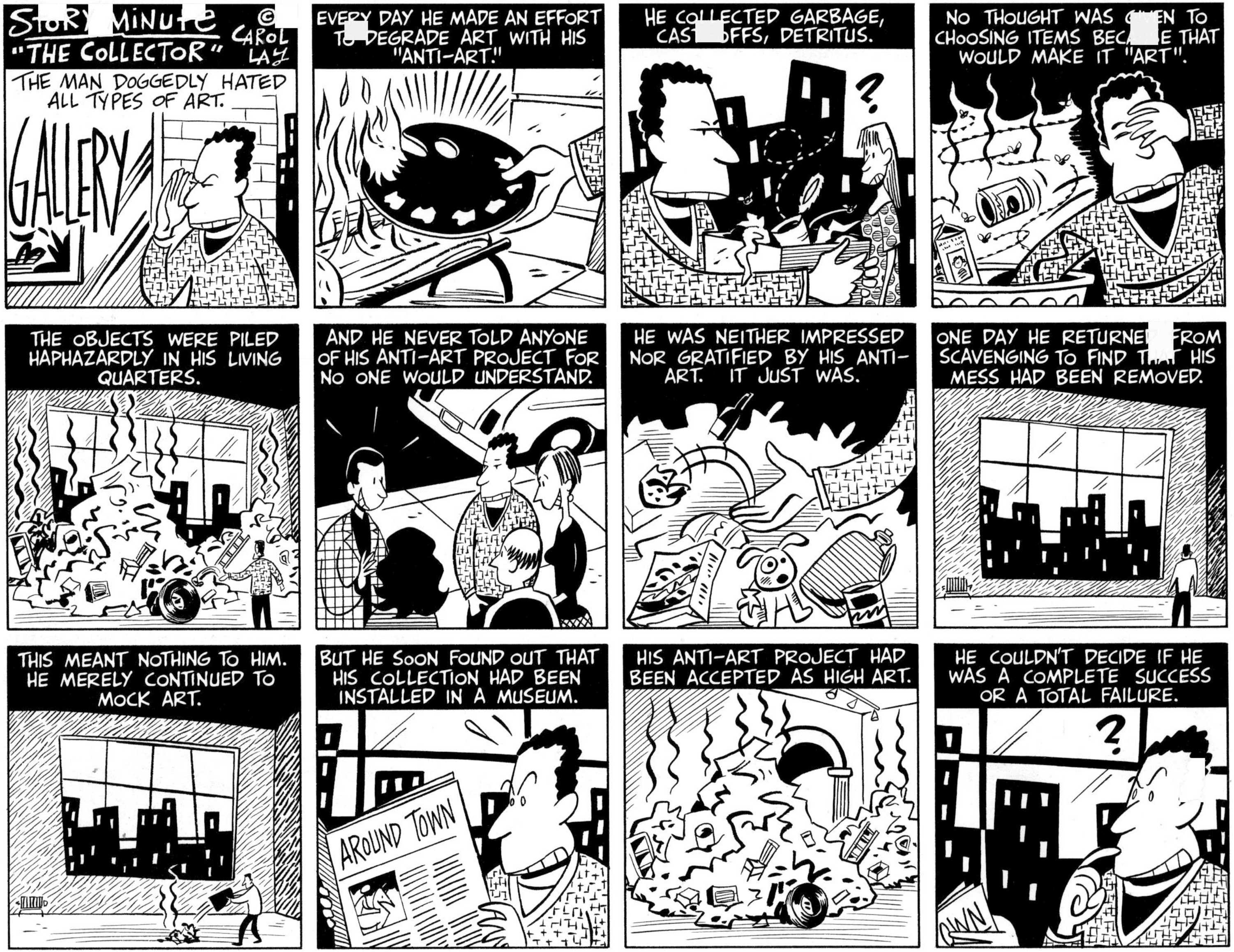
STORY MINUTE
"THE COLLECTOR"
© CAROL LAY
THE MAN DOGGEDLY HATED ALL TYPES OF ART.
GALLERY
EVERY DAY HE MADE AN EFFORT TO DEGRADE ART WITH HIS "ANTI-ART."
HE COLLECTED GARBAGE, CAST-OFFS, DETRITUS.
?
NO THOUGHT WAS GIVEN TO CHOOSING ITEMS BECAUSE THAT WOULD MAKE IT "ART".
THE OBJECTS WERE PILED HAPHAZARDLY IN HIS LIVING QUARTERS.
AND HE NEVER TOLD ANYONE OF HIS ANTI-ART PROJECT FOR NO ONE WOULD UNDERSTAND.
HE WAS NEITHER IMPRESSED NOR GRATIFIED BY HIS ANTI-ART. IT JUST WAS.
ONE DAY HE RETURNED FROM SCAVENGING TO FIND THAT HIS MESS HAD BEEN REMOVED.
THIS MEANT NOTHING TO HIM. HE MERELY CONTINUED TO MOCK ART.
BUT HE SOON FOUND OUT THAT HIS COLLECTION HAD BEEN INSTALLED IN A MUSEUM.
AROUND TOWN
HIS ANTI-ART PROJECT HAD BEEN ACCEPTED AS HIGH ART.
HE COULDN'T DECIDE IF HE WAS A COMPLETE SUCCESS OR A TOTAL FAILURE.
?

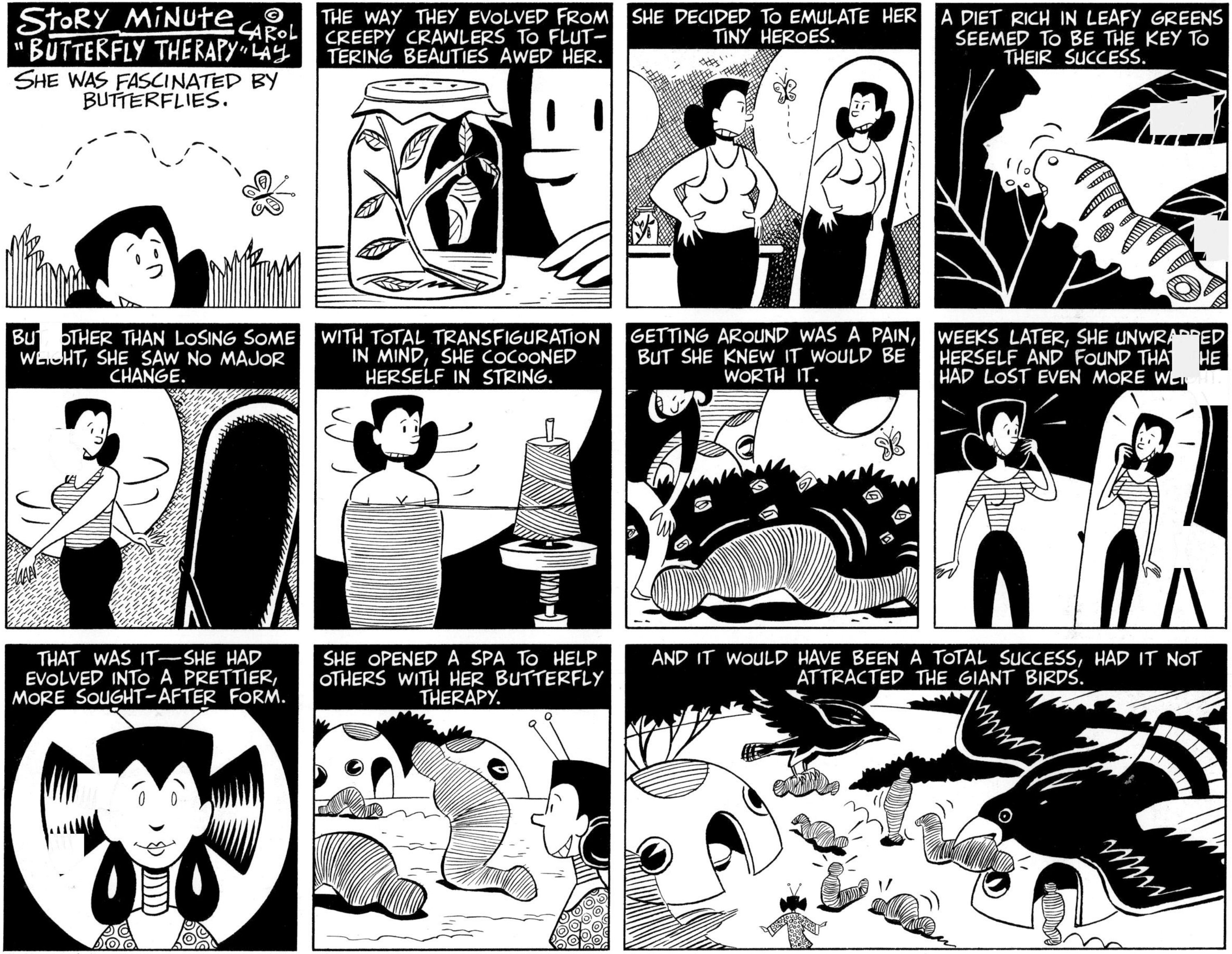
STORY MINUTE
"BUTTERFLY THERAPY"
© CAROL LAY
SHE WAS FASCINATED BY BUTTERFLIES.
THE WAY THEY EVOLVED FROM CREEPY CRAWLERS TO FLUTTERING BEAUTIES AWED HER.
SHE DECIDED TO EMULATE HER TINY HEROES.
A DIET RICH IN LEAFY GREENS SEEMED TO BE THE KEY TO THEIR SUCCESS.
BUT OTHER THAN LOSING SOME WEIGHT, SHE SAW NO MAJOR CHANGE.
WITH TOTAL TRANSFIGURATION IN MIND, SHE COCOONED HERSELF IN STRING.
GETTING AROUND WAS A PAIN, BUT SHE KNEW IT WOULD BE WORTH IT.
WEEKS LATER, SHE UNWRAPPED HERSELF AND FOUND THAT SHE HAD LOST EVEN MORE WEIGHT.
THAT WAS IT—SHE HAD EVOLVED INTO A PRETTIER, MORE SOUGHT-AFTER FORM.
SHE OPENED A SPA TO HELP OTHERS WITH HER BUTTERFLY THERAPY.
AND IT WOULD HAVE BEEN A TOTAL SUCCESS, HAD IT NOT ATTRACTED THE GIANT BIRDS.

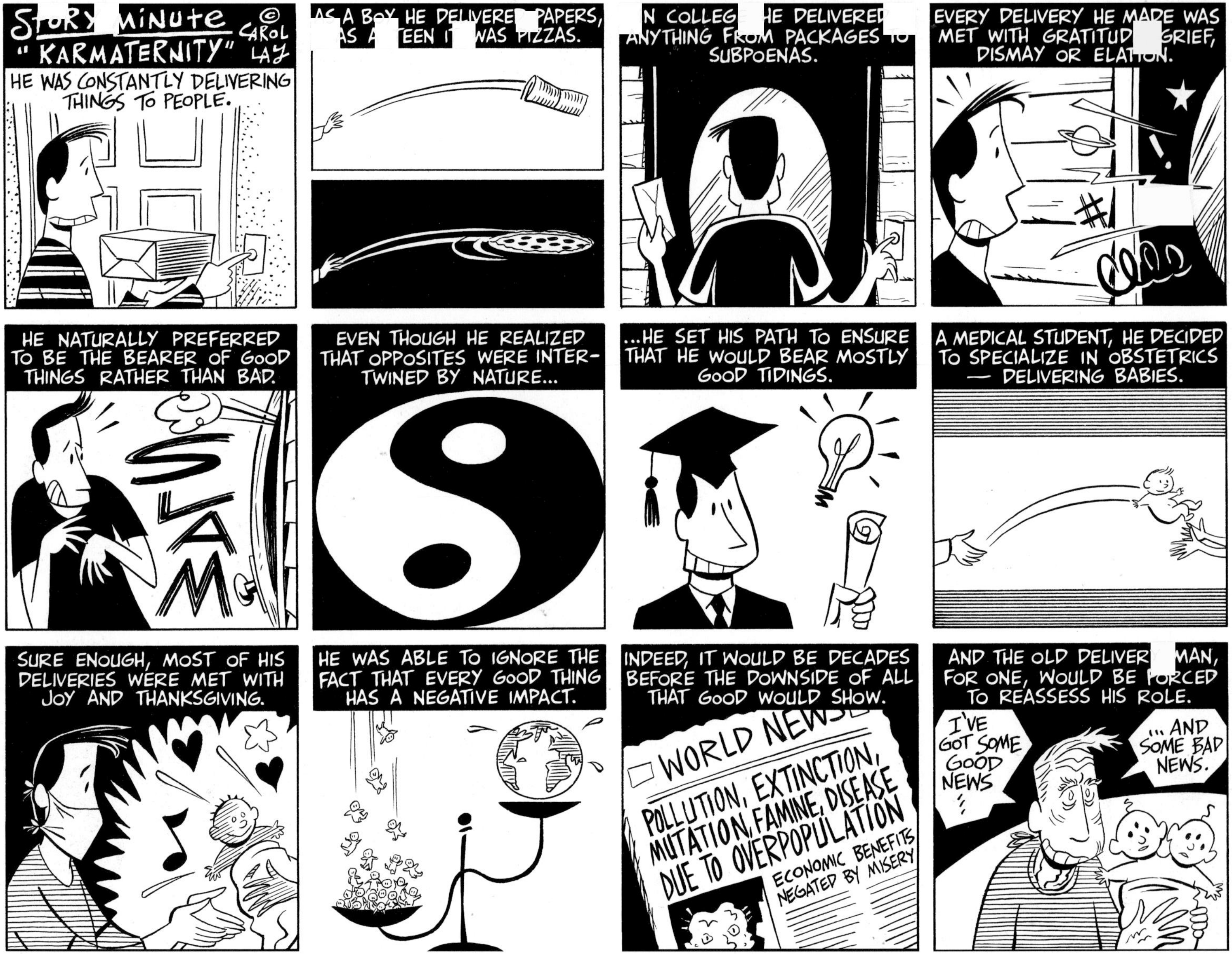
STORY MINUTE
"KARMATERNITY"
© CAROL LAY
HE WAS CONSTANTLY DELIVERING THINGS TO PEOPLE.
AS A BOY HE DELIVERED PAPERS, AS A TEEN IT WAS PIZZAS.
IN COLLEGE HE DELIVERED ANYTHING FROM PACKAGES TO SUBPOENAS.
EVERY DELIVERY HE MADE WAS MET WITH GRATITUDE, GRIEF, DISMAY OR ELATION.
HE NATURALLY PREFERRED TO BE THE BEARER OF GOOD THINGS RATHER THAN BAD.
SLAM
EVEN THOUGH HE REALIZED THAT OPPOSITES WERE INTERTWINED BY NATURE...
...HE SET HIS PATH TO ENSURE THAT HE WOULD BEAR MOSTLY GOOD TIDINGS.
A MEDICAL STUDENT, HE DECIDED TO SPECIALIZE IN OBSTETRICS — DELIVERING BABIES.
SURE ENOUGH, MOST OF HIS DELIVERIES WERE MET WITH JOY AND THANKSGIVING.
HE WAS ABLE TO IGNORE THE FACT THAT EVERY GOOD THING HAS A NEGATIVE IMPACT.
INDEED, IT WOULD BE DECADES BEFORE THE DOWNSIDE OF ALL THAT GOOD WOULD SHOW.
WORLD NEWS
POLLUTION, EXTINCTION, MUTATION, FAMINE, DISEASE DUE TO OVERPOPULATION
ECONOMIC BENEFITS NEGATED BY MISERY
AND THE OLD DELIVERY MAN, FOR ONE, WOULD BE FORCED TO REASSESS HIS ROLE.
I'VE GOT SOME GOOD NEWS
...AND SOME BAD NEWS.

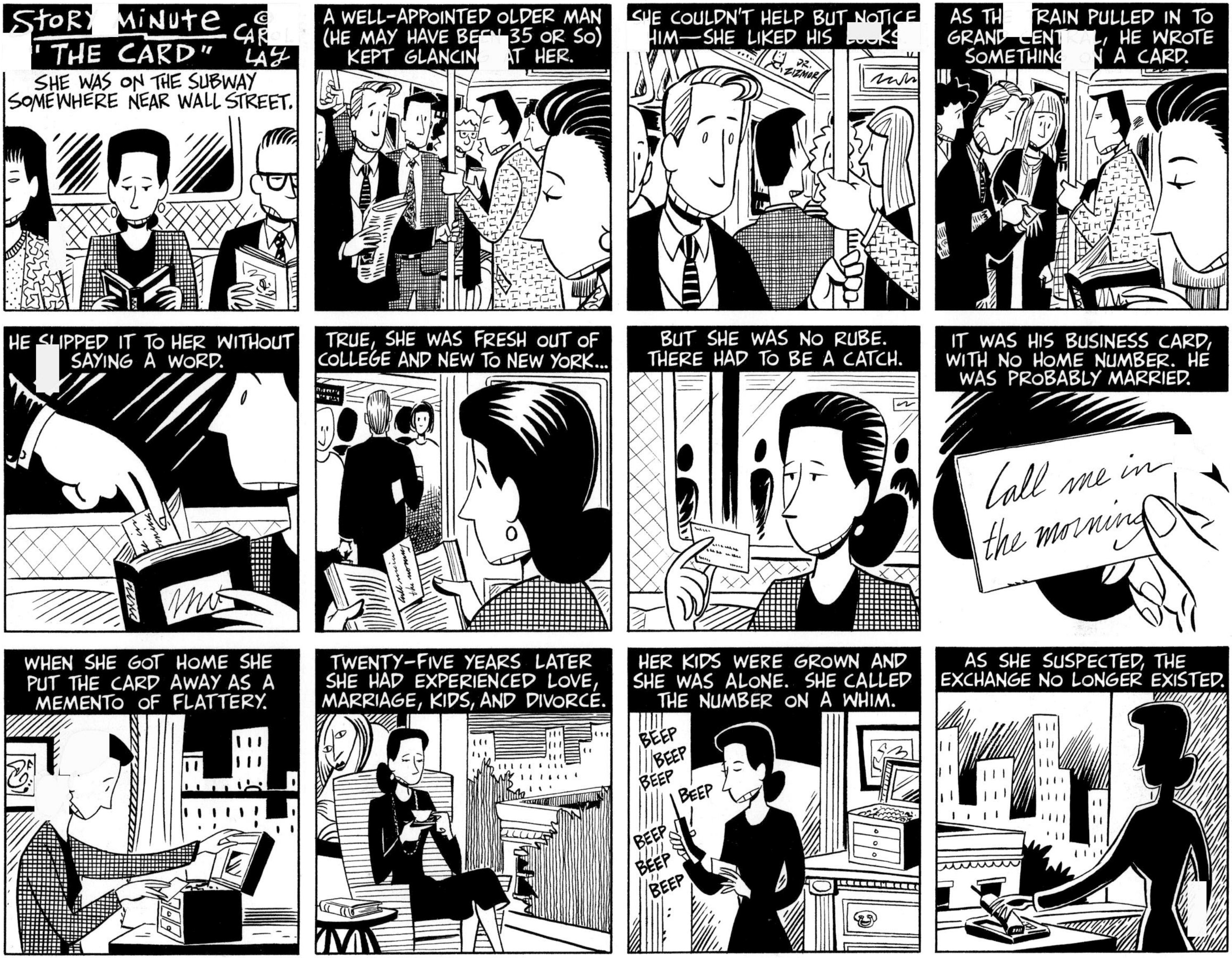

STORY MINUTE
"THE CARD"
© CAROL LAY
SHE WAS ON THE SUBWAY SOMEWHERE NEAR WALL STREET.
A WELL-APPOINTED OLDER MAN (HE MAY HAVE BEEN 35 OR SO) KEPT GLANCING AT HER.
SHE COULDN'T HELP BUT NOTICE HIM—SHE LIKED HIS LOOKS.
DR. ZIZMOR
AS THE TRAIN PULLED IN TO GRAND CENTRAL, HE WROTE SOMETHING ON A CARD.
HE SLIPPED IT TO HER WITHOUT SAYING A WORD.
TRUE, SHE WAS FRESH OUT OF COLLEGE AND NEW TO NEW YORK...
BUT SHE WAS NO RUBE. THERE HAD TO BE A CATCH.
IT WAS HIS BUSINESS CARD, WITH NO HOME NUMBER. HE WAS PROBABLY MARRIED.
Call me in the morning
WHEN SHE GOT HOME SHE PUT THE CARD AWAY AS A MEMENTO OF FLATTERY.
TWENTY-FIVE YEARS LATER SHE HAD EXPERIENCED LOVE, MARRIAGE, KIDS, AND DIVORCE.
HER KIDS WERE GROWN AND SHE WAS ALONE. SHE CALLED THE NUMBER ON A WHIM.
BEEP BEEP BEEP BEEP
BEEP BEEP BEEP
AS SHE SUSPECTED, THE EXCHANGE NO LONGER EXISTED.

STORY MINUTE © CAROL LAY
"THE BEST REVENGE"

THE ROAD TO SUCCESS HAD BEEN RIFE WITH POTHOLES.

FRIENDS, LOVERS, AND PARTNERS HAD BETRAYED HER AT KEY POINTS IN HER LIFE.

BZZ!

BUT NOW SHE WAS ON TOP. SHE HAD SCADS OF MONEY AND A YOUNG TROPHY HUSBAND.

YOUR HUSBAND TO SEE YOU.

SEND HIM IN.

IT WAS TIME TO GLOAT IN THE FACES OF THOSE WHO HAD DONE HER WRONG.

MY DEAR, YOU LOOK RAVISHING!

WRONG TIE, IDIOT!

LET'S GO!

FIRST THERE WAS HER FORMER "BEST FRIEND" WHO HAD STOLEN HER HIGH SCHOOL SWEETHEART.

SAY, WHY DON'T YOU AND I...?

SORRY, BUT I LOVE MY BEAUTIFUL WIFE!

NEXT THERE WAS THE FORMER LOVER WHO HAD JILTED HER FOR HER BUSINESS PARTNER.

IT WAS PLAIN TO HIM THAT SHE HAD SCORED FINANCIALLY AND ROMANTICALLY.

AND HER FORMER PARTNER REGRETTED THEIR FALLING-OUT AND HER OWN POOR CHOICES.

IT WORKED. LIVING WELL **WAS** THE BEST REVENGE.

THE SHOW'S OVER. QUIT TOUCHING ME.

YES, DEAR.

AND WHEN THE BITTER OLD THING FINALLY DROPPED DEAD...

...THAT'S EXACTLY WHAT THE HANDSOME YOUNG WIDOWER FOUND OUT.

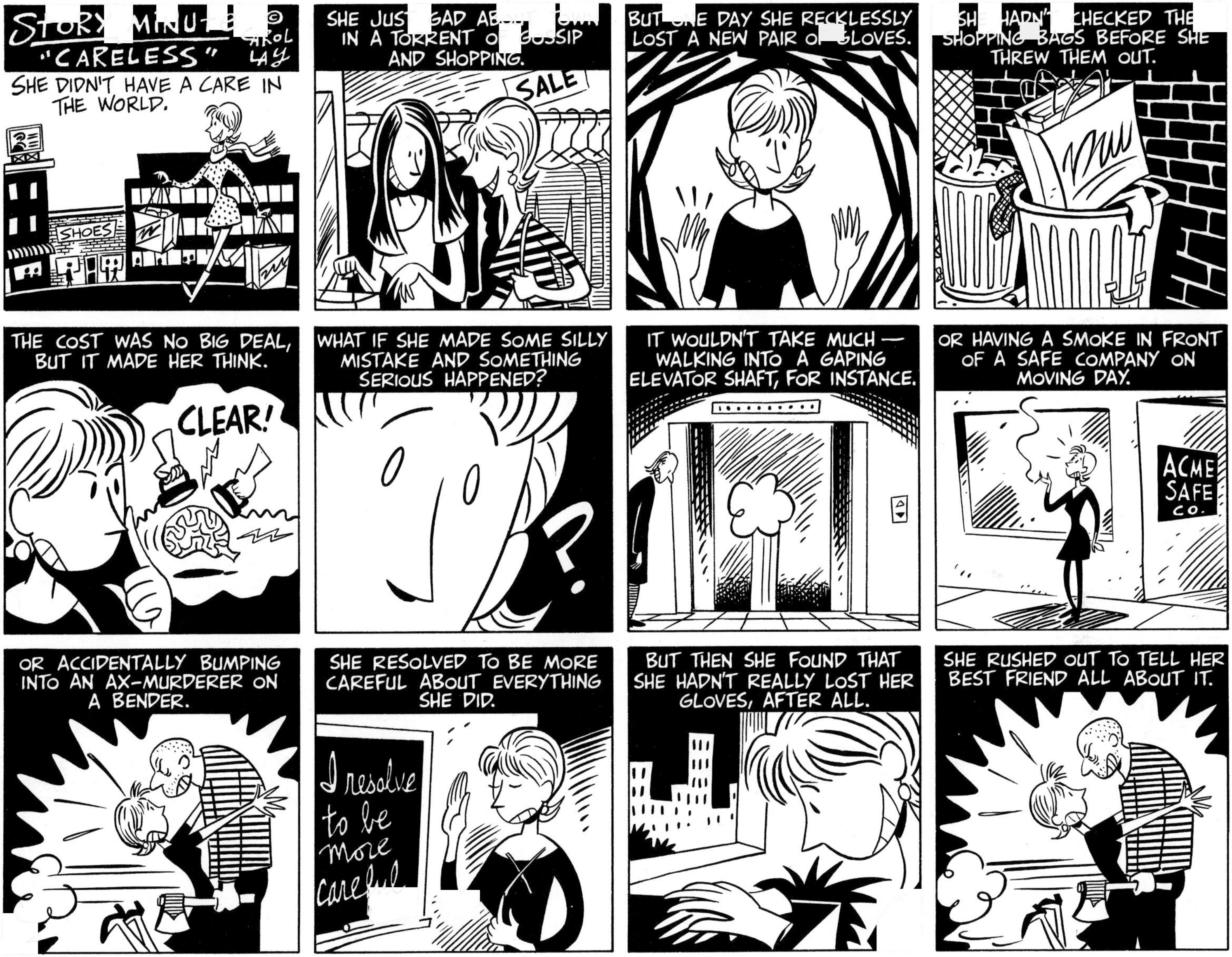
STORY MINUTE © CAROL LAY
"CARELESS"
SHE DIDN'T HAVE A CARE IN THE WORLD.
SHOES
SHE JUST GAD ABOUT TOWN IN A TORRENT OF GOSSIP AND SHOPPING.
SALE
BUT ONE DAY SHE RECKLESSLY LOST A NEW PAIR OF GLOVES.
SHE HADN'T CHECKED THE SHOPPING BAGS BEFORE SHE THREW THEM OUT.
THE COST WAS NO BIG DEAL, BUT IT MADE HER THINK.
CLEAR!
WHAT IF SHE MADE SOME SILLY MISTAKE AND SOMETHING SERIOUS HAPPENED?
?
IT WOULDN'T TAKE MUCH — WALKING INTO A GAPING ELEVATOR SHAFT, FOR INSTANCE.
OR HAVING A SMOKE IN FRONT OF A SAFE COMPANY ON MOVING DAY.
ACME SAFE CO.
OR ACCIDENTALLY BUMPING INTO AN AX-MURDERER ON A BENDER.
SHE RESOLVED TO BE MORE CAREFUL ABOUT EVERYTHING SHE DID.
I resolve to be more careful
BUT THEN SHE FOUND THAT SHE HADN'T REALLY LOST HER GLOVES, AFTER ALL.
SHE RUSHED OUT TO TELL HER BEST FRIEND ALL ABOUT IT.

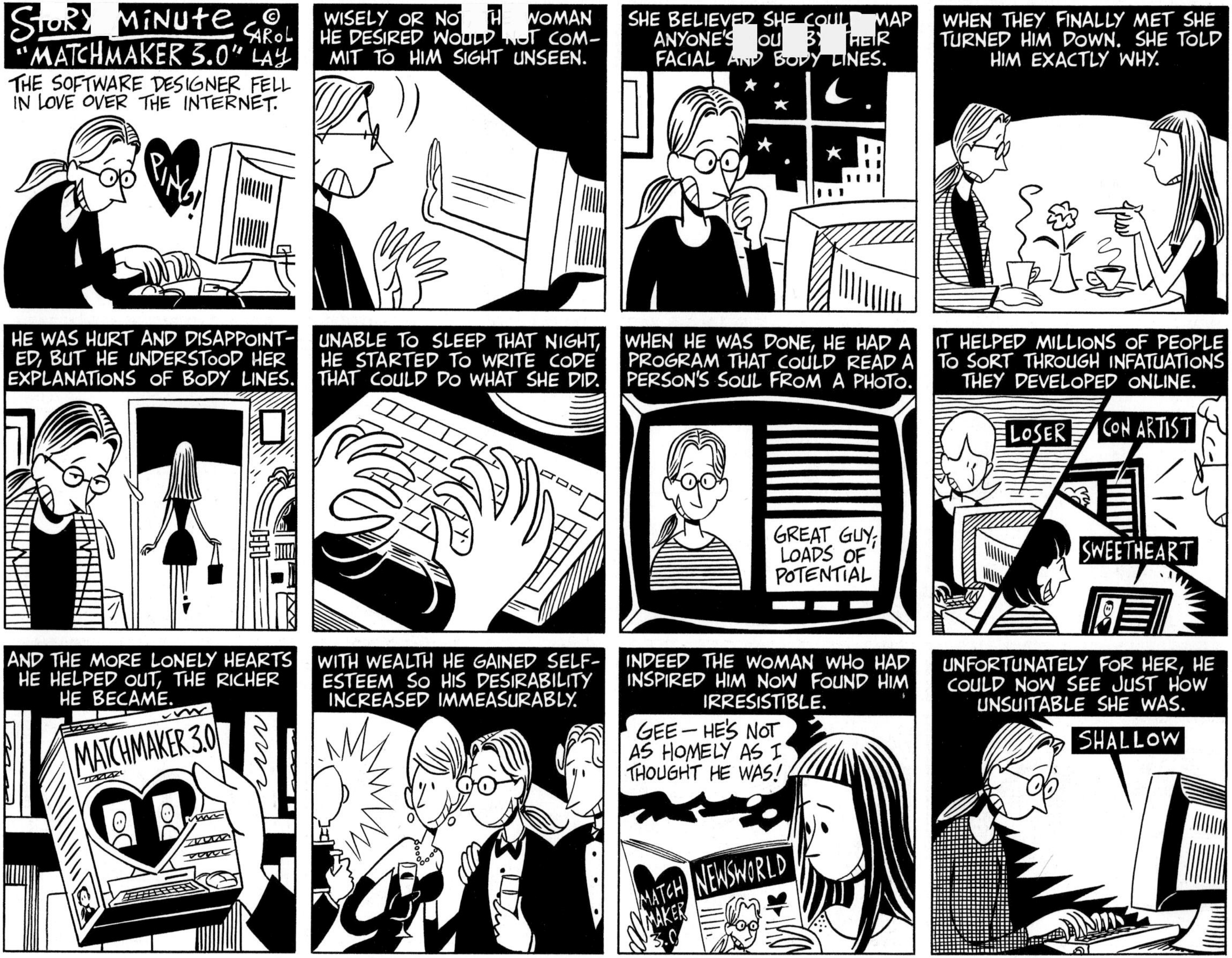
STORY[redacted]MINUTE
© CAROL LAY
"MATCHMAKER 3.0"
THE SOFTWARE DESIGNER FELL IN LOVE OVER THE INTERNET.
PING!
WISELY OR NOT[redacted]HE WOMAN HE DESIRED WOULD[redacted]COMMIT TO HIM SIGHT UNSEEN.
SHE BELIEVED SHE COUL[redacted]MAP ANYONE'S[redacted]OU[redacted]B[redacted]HEIR FACIAL AND BODY LINES.
WHEN THEY FINALLY MET SHE TURNED HIM DOWN. SHE TOLD HIM EXACTLY WHY.
HE WAS HURT AND DISAPPOINTED, BUT HE UNDERSTOOD HER EXPLANATIONS OF BODY LINES.
UNABLE TO SLEEP THAT NIGHT, HE STARTED TO WRITE CODE THAT COULD DO WHAT SHE DID.
WHEN HE WAS DONE, HE HAD A PROGRAM THAT COULD READ A PERSON'S SOUL FROM A PHOTO.
GREAT GUY; LOADS OF POTENTIAL
IT HELPED MILLIONS OF PEOPLE TO SORT THROUGH INFATUATIONS THEY DEVELOPED ONLINE.
LOSER
CON ARTIST
SWEETHEART
AND THE MORE LONELY HEARTS HE HELPED OUT, THE RICHER HE BECAME.
MATCHMAKER 3.0
WITH WEALTH HE GAINED SELF-ESTEEM SO HIS DESIRABILITY INCREASED IMMEASURABLY.
INDEED THE WOMAN WHO HAD INSPIRED HIM NOW FOUND HIM IRRESISTIBLE.
GEE — HE'S NOT AS HOMELY AS I THOUGHT HE WAS!
MATCH MAKER 3.0
NEWSWORLD
UNFORTUNATELY FOR HER, HE COULD NOW SEE JUST HOW UNSUITABLE SHE WAS.
SHALLOW

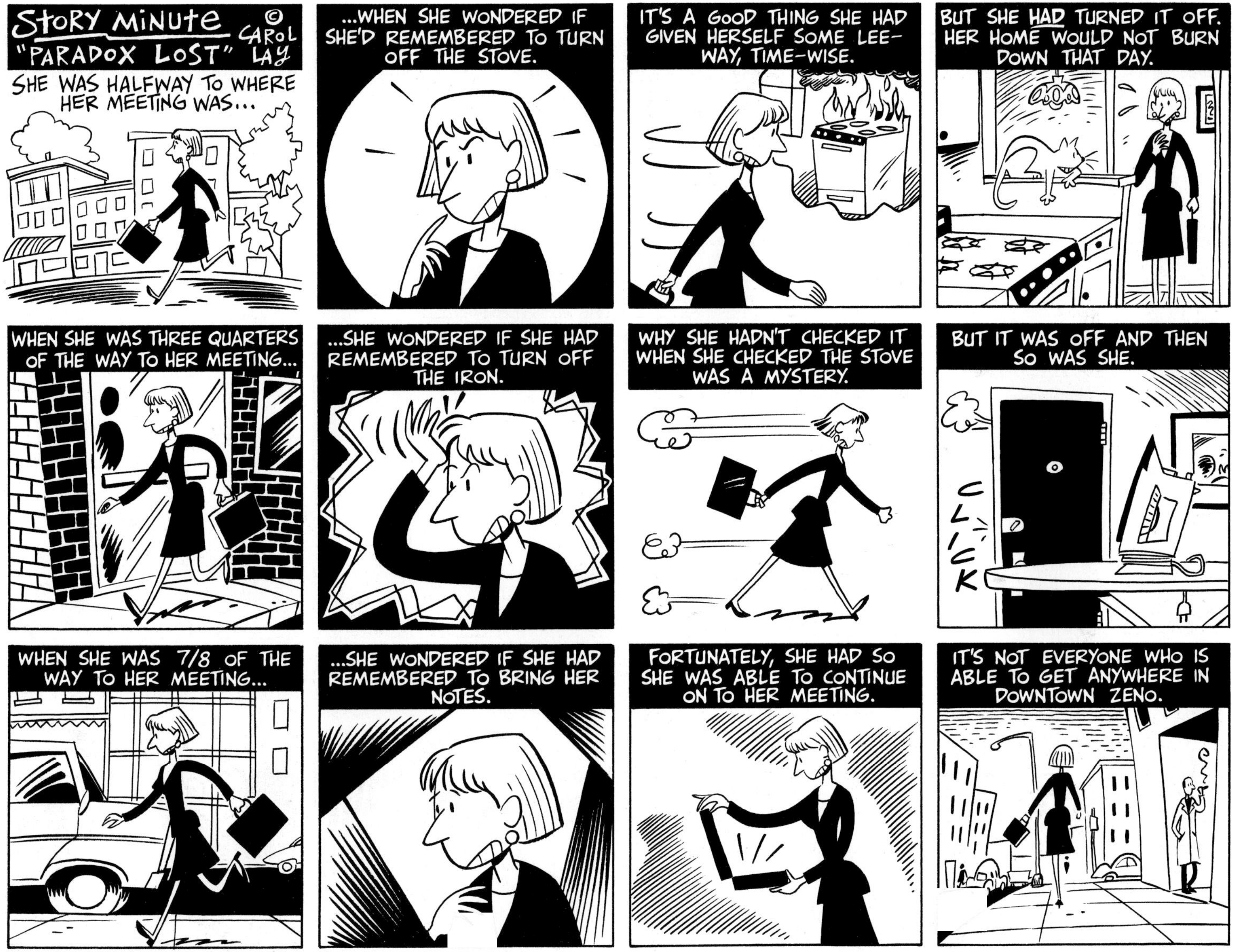
STORY MINUTE
"PARADOX LOST"
© CAROL LAY
SHE WAS HALFWAY TO WHERE HER MEETING WAS...
...WHEN SHE WONDERED IF SHE'D REMEMBERED TO TURN OFF THE STOVE.
IT'S A GOOD THING SHE HAD GIVEN HERSELF SOME LEE-WAY, TIME-WISE.
BUT SHE HAD TURNED IT OFF. HER HOME WOULD NOT BURN DOWN THAT DAY.
WHEN SHE WAS THREE QUARTERS OF THE WAY TO HER MEETING...
...SHE WONDERED IF SHE HAD REMEMBERED TO TURN OFF THE IRON.
WHY SHE HADN'T CHECKED IT WHEN SHE CHECKED THE STOVE WAS A MYSTERY.
BUT IT WAS OFF AND THEN SO WAS SHE.
CLICK
WHEN SHE WAS 7/8 OF THE WAY TO HER MEETING...
...SHE WONDERED IF SHE HAD REMEMBERED TO BRING HER NOTES.
FORTUNATELY, SHE HAD SO SHE WAS ABLE TO CONTINUE ON TO HER MEETING.
IT'S NOT EVERYONE WHO IS ABLE TO GET ANYWHERE IN DOWNTOWN ZENO.

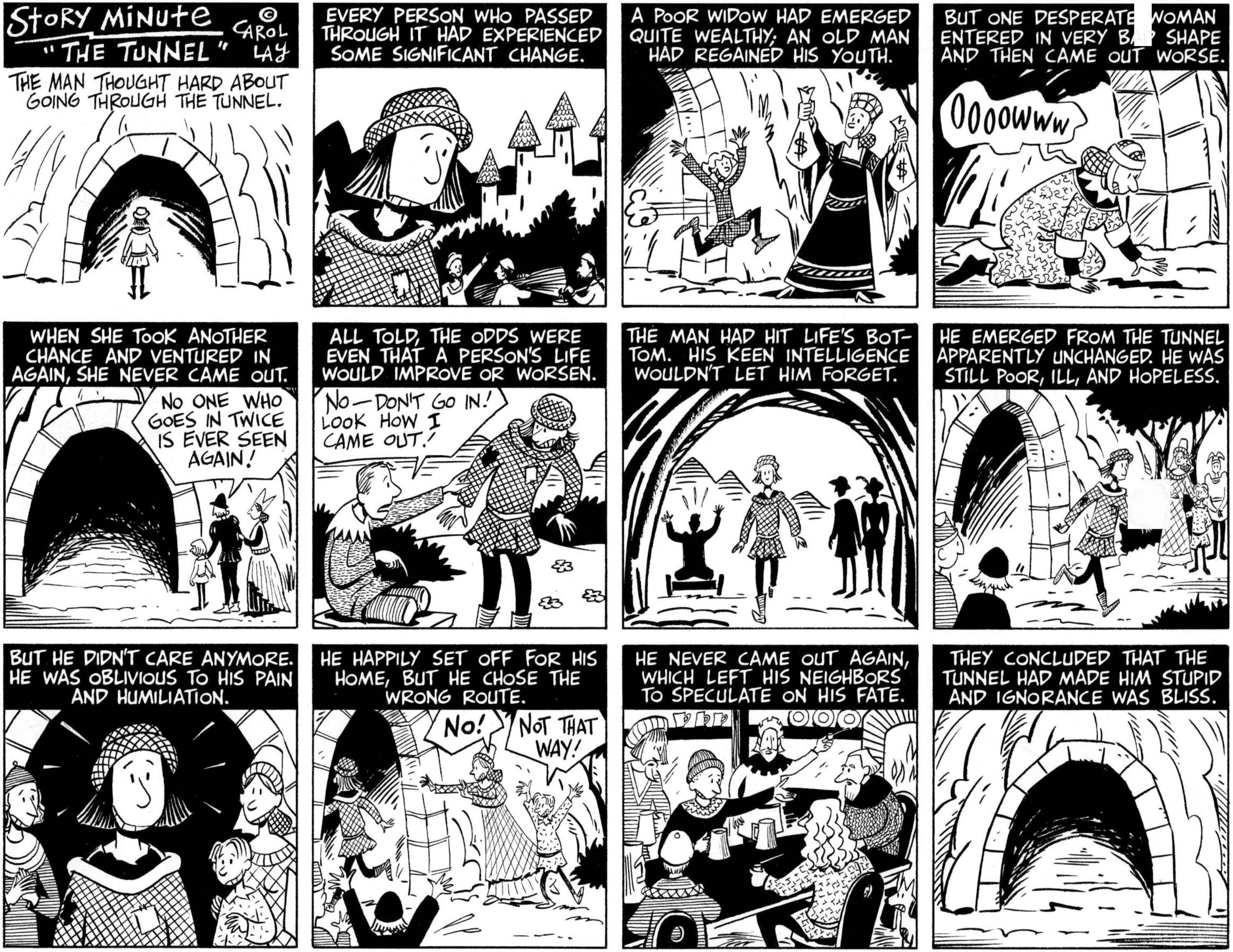
STORY MINUTE
"THE TUNNEL"
© CAROL LAY
THE MAN THOUGHT HARD ABOUT GOING THROUGH THE TUNNEL.
EVERY PERSON WHO PASSED THROUGH IT HAD EXPERIENCED SOME SIGNIFICANT CHANGE.
A POOR WIDOW HAD EMERGED QUITE WEALTHY; AN OLD MAN HAD REGAINED HIS YOUTH.
BUT ONE DESPERATE WOMAN ENTERED IN VERY BAD SHAPE AND THEN CAME OUT WORSE.
OOOOWWW
WHEN SHE TOOK ANOTHER CHANCE AND VENTURED IN AGAIN, SHE NEVER CAME OUT.
NO ONE WHO GOES IN TWICE IS EVER SEEN AGAIN!
ALL TOLD, THE ODDS WERE EVEN THAT A PERSON'S LIFE WOULD IMPROVE OR WORSEN.
NO—DON'T GO IN! LOOK HOW I CAME OUT!
THE MAN HAD HIT LIFE'S BOTTOM. HIS KEEN INTELLIGENCE WOULDN'T LET HIM FORGET.
HE EMERGED FROM THE TUNNEL APPARENTLY UNCHANGED. HE WAS STILL POOR, ILL, AND HOPELESS.
BUT HE DIDN'T CARE ANYMORE. HE WAS OBLIVIOUS TO HIS PAIN AND HUMILIATION.
HE HAPPILY SET OFF FOR HIS HOME, BUT HE CHOSE THE WRONG ROUTE.
NO!
NOT THAT WAY!
HE NEVER CAME OUT AGAIN, WHICH LEFT HIS NEIGHBORS TO SPECULATE ON HIS FATE.
THEY CONCLUDED THAT THE TUNNEL HAD MADE HIM STUPID AND IGNORANCE WAS BLISS.

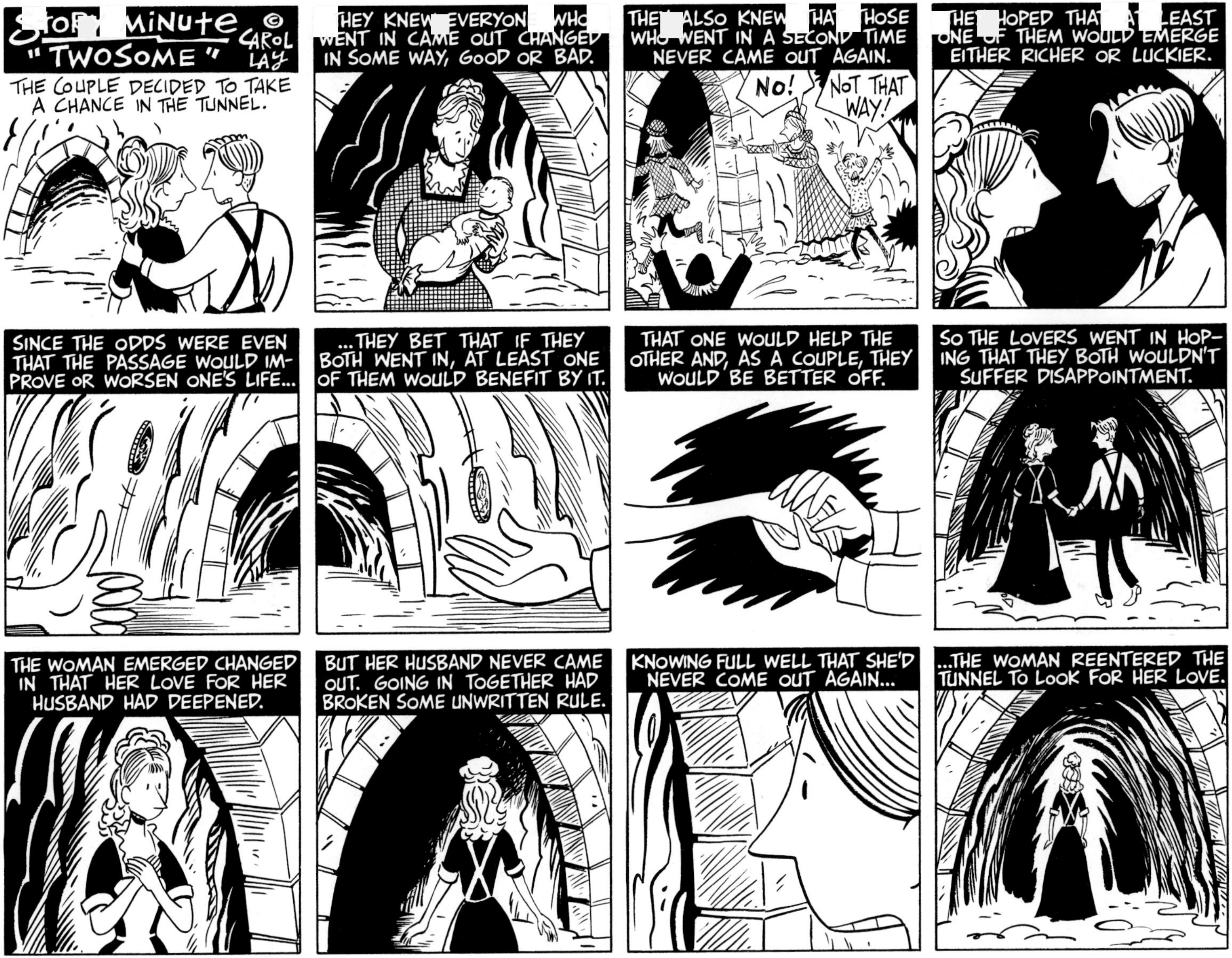
STORY MINUTE
"TWOSOME"
© CAROL LAY
THE COUPLE DECIDED TO TAKE A CHANCE IN THE TUNNEL.
THEY KNEW EVERYONE WHO WENT IN CAME OUT CHANGED IN SOME WAY, GOOD OR BAD.
THEY ALSO KNEW THAT THOSE WHO WENT IN A SECOND TIME NEVER CAME OUT AGAIN.
NO!
NOT THAT WAY!
THEY HOPED THAT AT LEAST ONE OF THEM WOULD EMERGE EITHER RICHER OR LUCKIER.
SINCE THE ODDS WERE EVEN THAT THE PASSAGE WOULD IMPROVE OR WORSEN ONE'S LIFE...
...THEY BET THAT IF THEY BOTH WENT IN, AT LEAST ONE OF THEM WOULD BENEFIT BY IT.
THAT ONE WOULD HELP THE OTHER AND, AS A COUPLE, THEY WOULD BE BETTER OFF.
SO THE LOVERS WENT IN HOPING THAT THEY BOTH WOULDN'T SUFFER DISAPPOINTMENT.
THE WOMAN EMERGED CHANGED IN THAT HER LOVE FOR HER HUSBAND HAD DEEPENED.
BUT HER HUSBAND NEVER CAME OUT. GOING IN TOGETHER HAD BROKEN SOME UNWRITTEN RULE.
KNOWING FULL WELL THAT SHE'D NEVER COME OUT AGAIN...
...THE WOMAN REENTERED THE TUNNEL TO LOOK FOR HER LOVE.

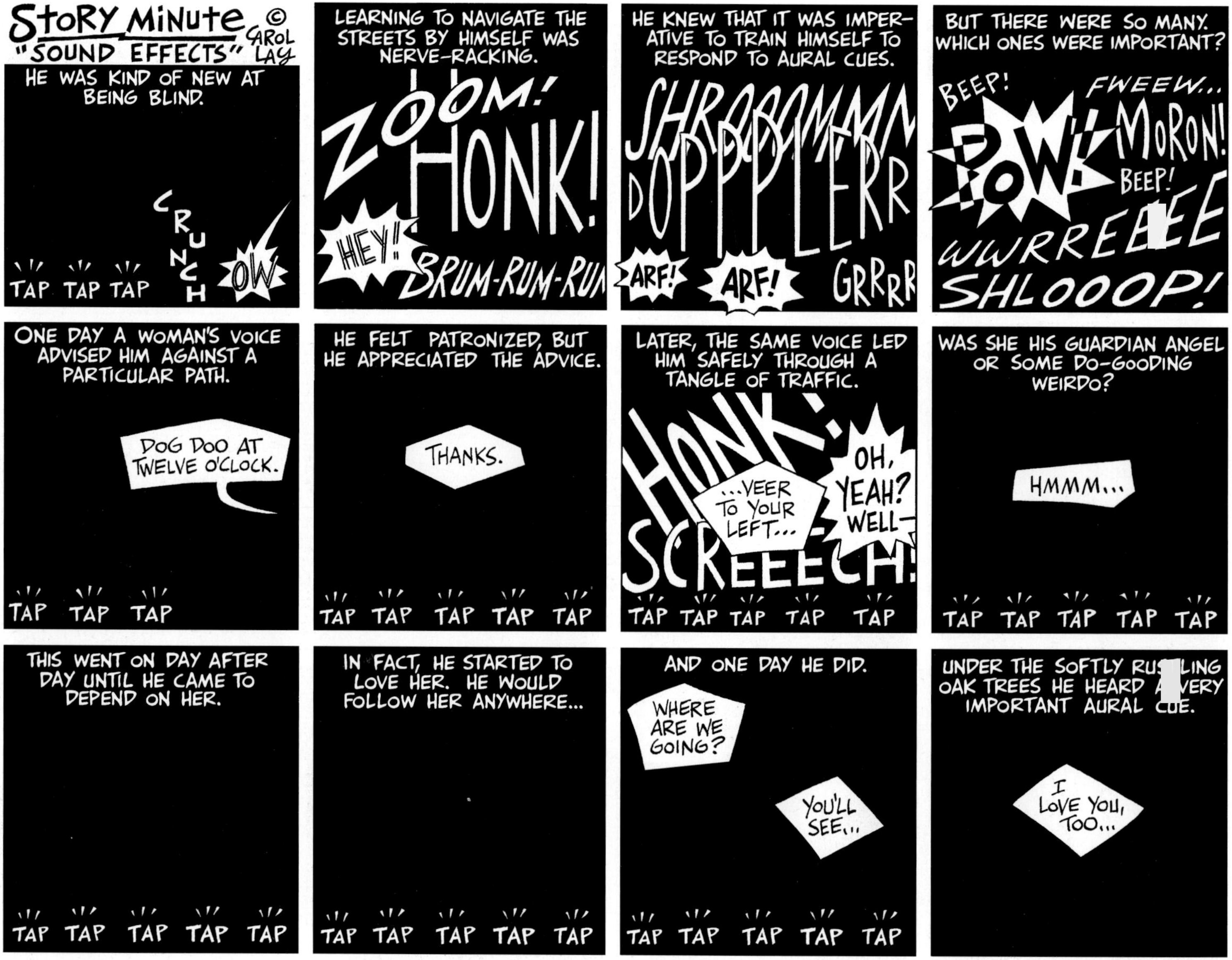
STORY MINUTE ©
CAROL LAY
"SOUND EFFECTS"
HE WAS KIND OF NEW AT BEING BLIND.
CRUNCH
OW
TAP TAP TAP
LEARNING TO NAVIGATE THE STREETS BY HIMSELF WAS NERVE-RACKING.
ZOOM!
HONK!
HEY!
BRUM-RUM-RUM
HE KNEW THAT IT WAS IMPERATIVE TO TRAIN HIMSELF TO RESPOND TO AURAL CUES.
SHROOOMMM
DOPPPLERR
ARF!
ARF!
GRRRR
BUT THERE WERE SO MANY. WHICH ONES WERE IMPORTANT?
BEEP!
FWEEW...
POW!
MORON!
BEEP!
WWRREEEEE
SHLOOOP!
ONE DAY A WOMAN'S VOICE ADVISED HIM AGAINST A PARTICULAR PATH.
DOG DOO AT TWELVE O'CLOCK.
TAP TAP TAP
HE FELT PATRONIZED, BUT HE APPRECIATED THE ADVICE.
THANKS.
TAP TAP TAP TAP TAP
LATER, THE SAME VOICE LED HIM SAFELY THROUGH A TANGLE OF TRAFFIC.
HONK!
...VEER TO YOUR LEFT...
OH, YEAH? WELL—
SCREEECH!
TAP TAP TAP TAP TAP
WAS SHE HIS GUARDIAN ANGEL OR SOME DO-GOODING WEIRDO?
HMMM...
TAP TAP TAP TAP TAP
THIS WENT ON DAY AFTER DAY UNTIL HE CAME TO DEPEND ON HER.
TAP TAP TAP TAP TAP
IN FACT, HE STARTED TO LOVE HER. HE WOULD FOLLOW HER ANYWHERE...
TAP TAP TAP TAP TAP
AND ONE DAY HE DID.
WHERE ARE WE GOING?
YOU'LL SEE...
TAP TAP TAP TAP TAP
UNDER THE SOFTLY RUSTLING OAK TREES HE HEARD A VERY IMPORTANT AURAL CUE.
I LOVE YOU, TOO...

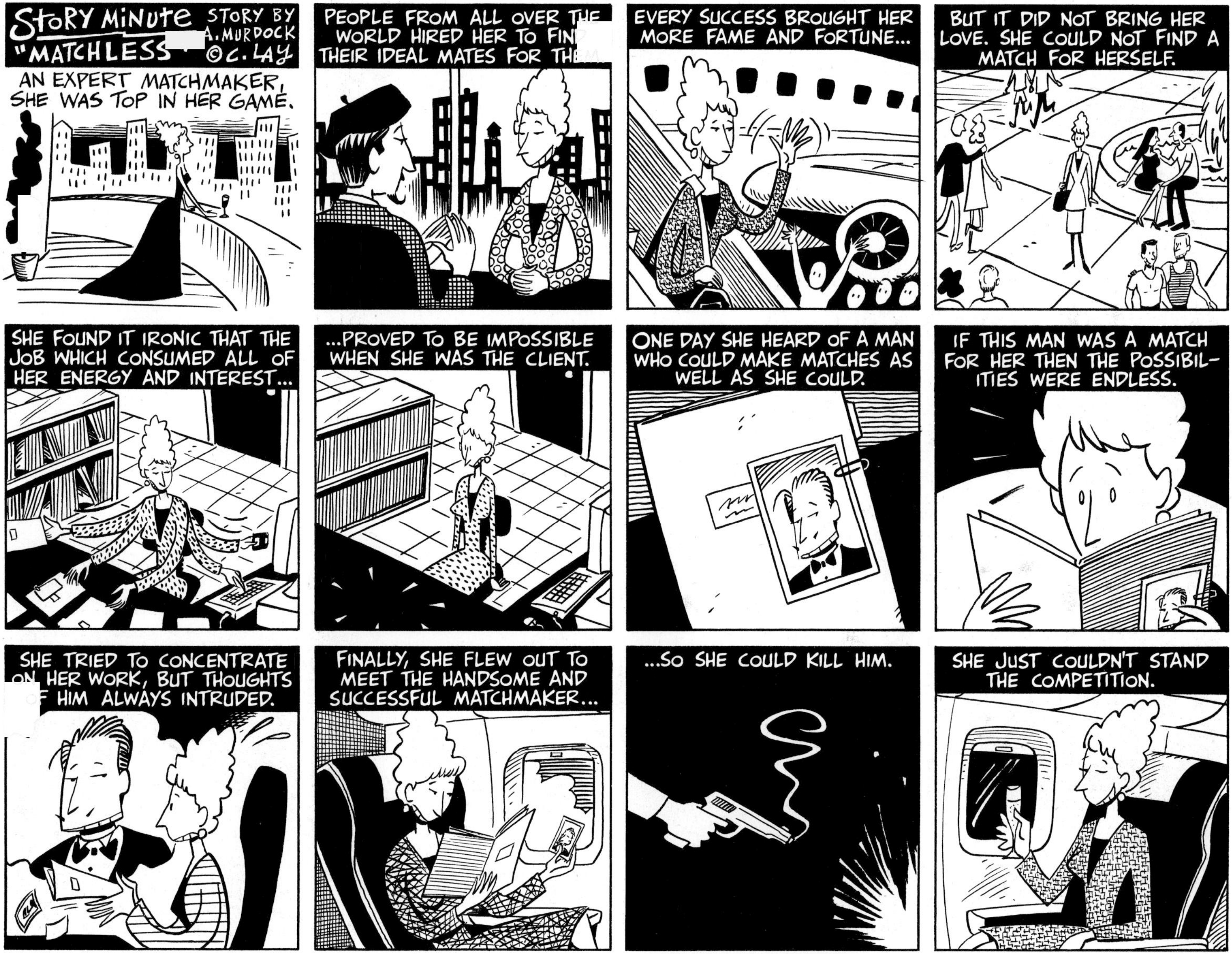
STORY MINUTE
"MATCHLESS"
STORY BY A. MURDOCK ©C. LAY
AN EXPERT MATCHMAKER, SHE WAS TOP IN HER GAME.
PEOPLE FROM ALL OVER THE WORLD HIRED HER TO FIND THEIR IDEAL MATES FOR THEM.
EVERY SUCCESS BROUGHT HER MORE FAME AND FORTUNE...
BUT IT DID NOT BRING HER LOVE. SHE COULD NOT FIND A MATCH FOR HERSELF.
SHE FOUND IT IRONIC THAT THE JOB WHICH CONSUMED ALL OF HER ENERGY AND INTEREST...
...PROVED TO BE IMPOSSIBLE WHEN SHE WAS THE CLIENT.
ONE DAY SHE HEARD OF A MAN WHO COULD MAKE MATCHES AS WELL AS SHE COULD.
IF THIS MAN WAS A MATCH FOR HER THEN THE POSSIBILITIES WERE ENDLESS.
SHE TRIED TO CONCENTRATE ON HER WORK, BUT THOUGHTS OF HIM ALWAYS INTRUDED.
FINALLY, SHE FLEW OUT TO MEET THE HANDSOME AND SUCCESSFUL MATCHMAKER...
...SO SHE COULD KILL HIM.
SHE JUST COULDN'T STAND THE COMPETITION.

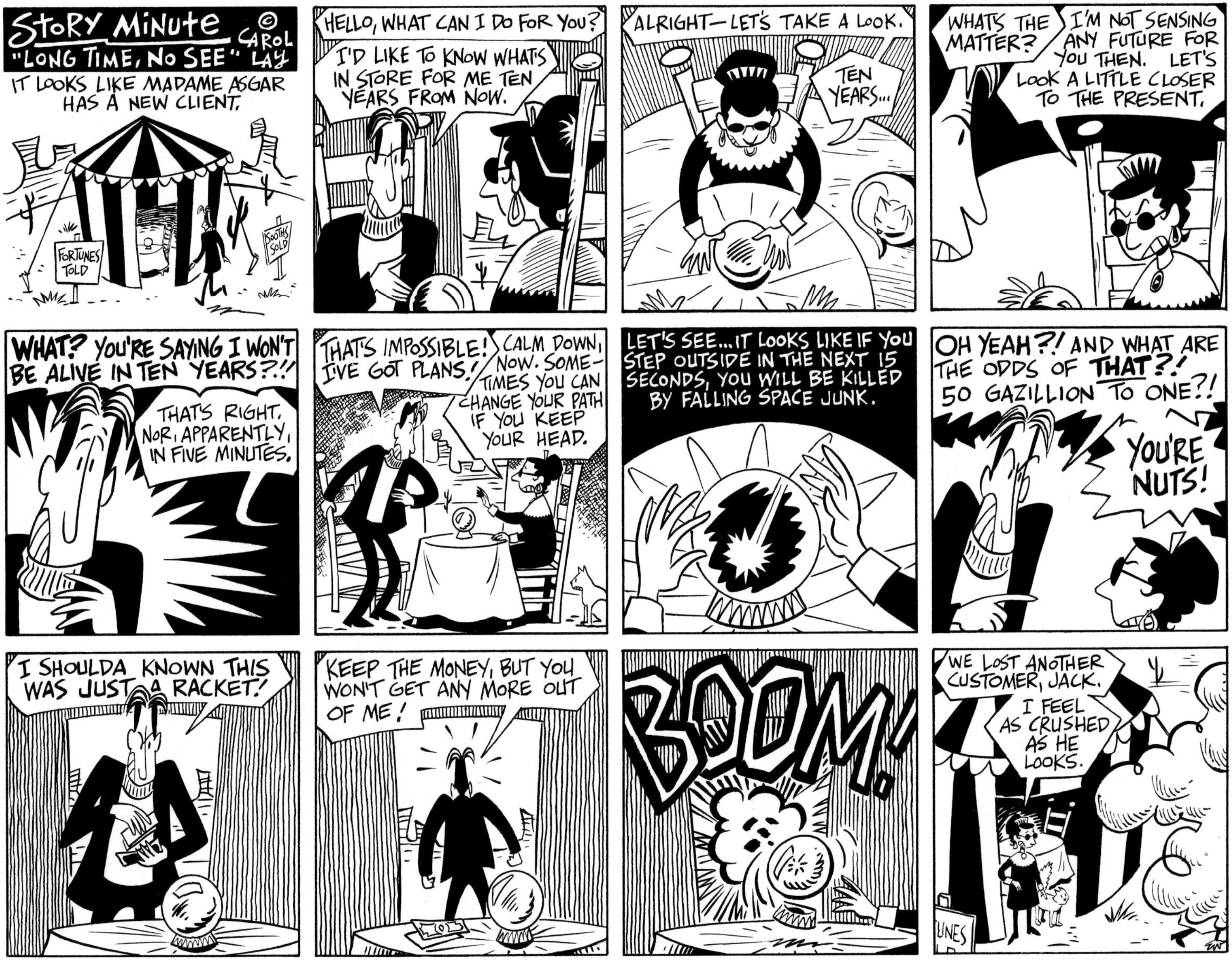
STORY MINUTE
"LONG TIME, NO SEE"
© CAROL LAY
IT LOOKS LIKE MADAME ASGAR HAS A NEW CLIENT.
FORTUNES TOLD
SOOTHS SOLD
HELLO, WHAT CAN I DO FOR YOU?
I'D LIKE TO KNOW WHAT'S IN STORE FOR ME TEN YEARS FROM NOW.
ALRIGHT— LET'S TAKE A LOOK.
TEN YEARS...
WHAT'S THE MATTER?
I'M NOT SENSING ANY FUTURE FOR YOU THEN. LET'S LOOK A LITTLE CLOSER TO THE PRESENT.
WHAT? YOU'RE SAYING I WON'T BE ALIVE IN TEN YEARS?!!
THAT'S RIGHT. NOR, APPARENTLY, IN FIVE MINUTES.
THAT'S IMPOSSIBLE! I'VE GOT PLANS!
CALM DOWN, NOW. SOMETIMES YOU CAN CHANGE YOUR PATH IF YOU KEEP YOUR HEAD.
LET'S SEE... IT LOOKS LIKE IF YOU STEP OUTSIDE IN THE NEXT 15 SECONDS, YOU WILL BE KILLED BY FALLING SPACE JUNK.
OH YEAH?! AND WHAT ARE THE ODDS OF THAT?! 50 GAZILLION TO ONE?!
YOU'RE NUTS!
I SHOULDA KNOWN THIS WAS JUST A RACKET!
KEEP THE MONEY, BUT YOU WON'T GET ANY MORE OUT OF ME!
BOOM!
WE LOST ANOTHER CUSTOMER, JACK.
I FEEL AS CRUSHED AS HE LOOKS.

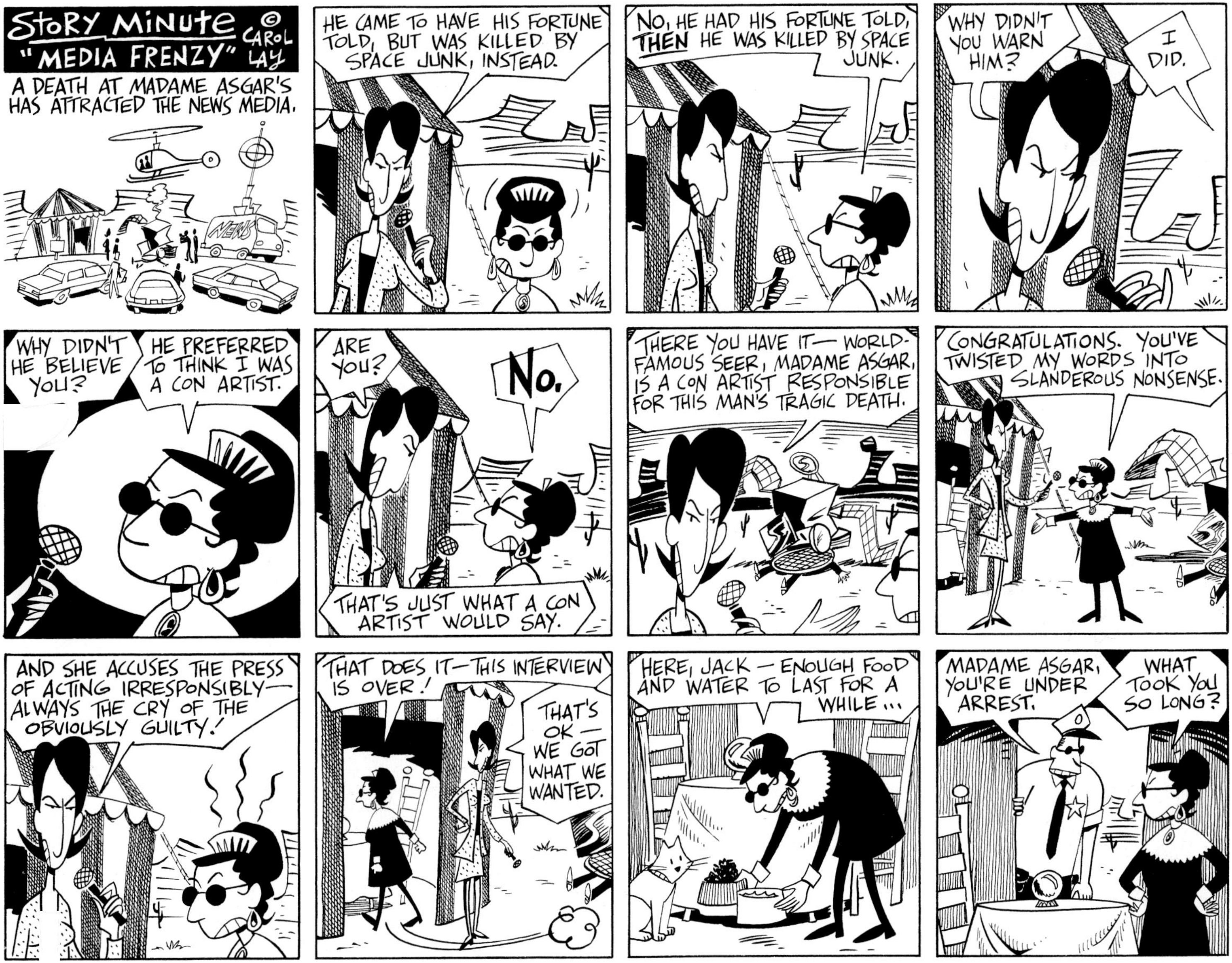
STORY MINUTE
"MEDIA FRENZY"
© CAROL LAY
A DEATH AT MADAME ASGAR'S HAS ATTRACTED THE NEWS MEDIA.
NEWS
HE CAME TO HAVE HIS FORTUNE TOLD, BUT WAS KILLED BY SPACE JUNK, INSTEAD.
NO, HE HAD HIS FORTUNE TOLD, THEN HE WAS KILLED BY SPACE JUNK.
WHY DIDN'T YOU WARN HIM?
I DID.
WHY DIDN'T HE BELIEVE YOU?
HE PREFERRED TO THINK I WAS A CON ARTIST.
ARE YOU?
NO.
THAT'S JUST WHAT A CON ARTIST WOULD SAY.
THERE YOU HAVE IT— WORLD-FAMOUS SEER, MADAME ASGAR, IS A CON ARTIST RESPONSIBLE FOR THIS MAN'S TRAGIC DEATH.
CONGRATULATIONS. YOU'VE TWISTED MY WORDS INTO SLANDEROUS NONSENSE.
AND SHE ACCUSES THE PRESS OF ACTING IRRESPONSIBLY— ALWAYS THE CRY OF THE OBVIOUSLY GUILTY!
THAT DOES IT—THIS INTERVIEW IS OVER!
THAT'S OK— WE GOT WHAT WE WANTED.
HERE, JACK — ENOUGH FOOD AND WATER TO LAST FOR A WHILE...
MADAME ASGAR, YOU'RE UNDER ARREST.
WHAT TOOK YOU SO LONG?

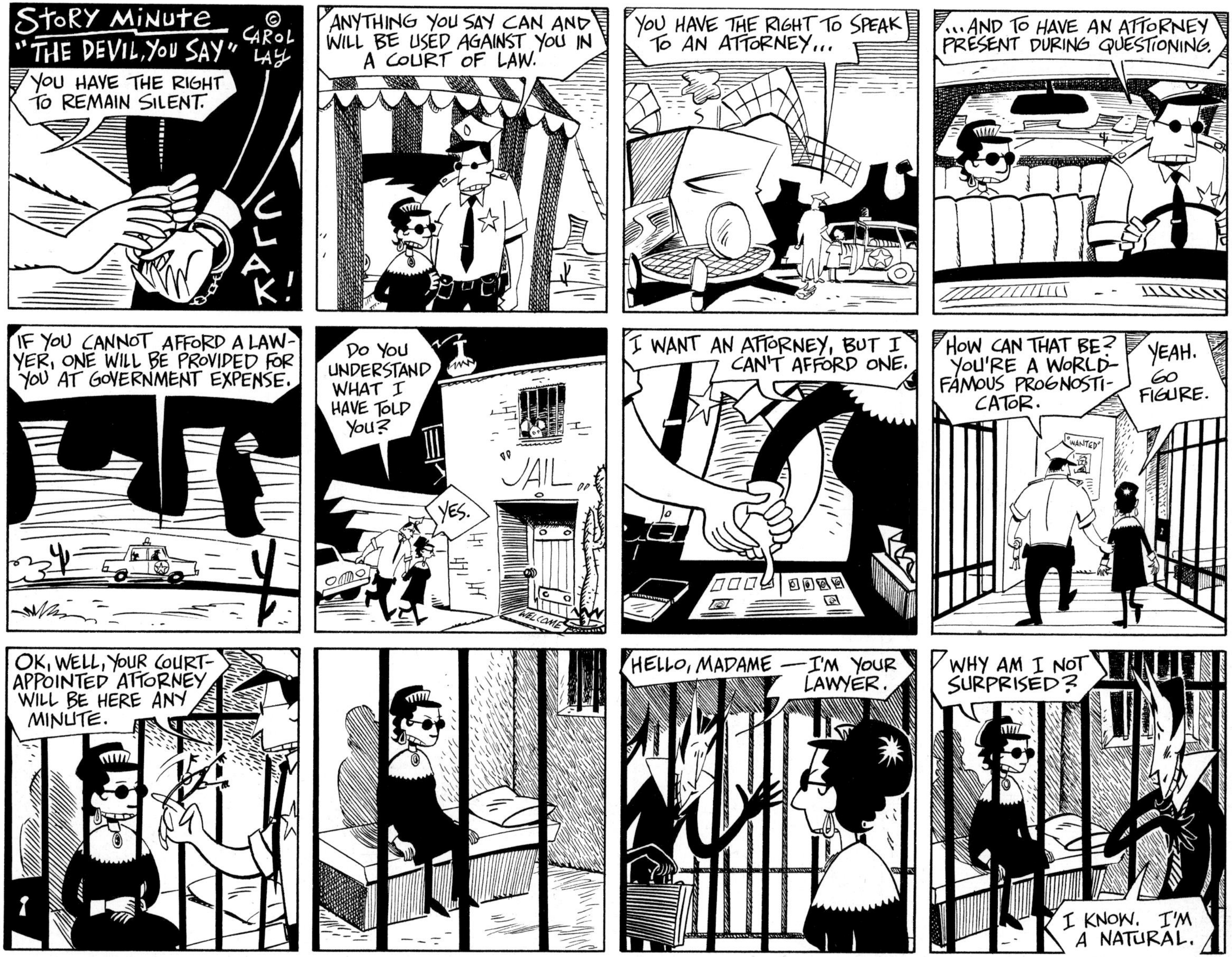
STORY MINUTE
"THE DEVIL, YOU SAY"
© CAROL LAY
YOU HAVE THE RIGHT TO REMAIN SILENT.
CLAK!
ANYTHING YOU SAY CAN AND WILL BE USED AGAINST YOU IN A COURT OF LAW.
YOU HAVE THE RIGHT TO SPEAK TO AN ATTORNEY...
...AND TO HAVE AN ATTORNEY PRESENT DURING QUESTIONING.
IF YOU CANNOT AFFORD A LAWYER, ONE WILL BE PROVIDED FOR YOU AT GOVERNMENT EXPENSE.
DO YOU UNDERSTAND WHAT I HAVE TOLD YOU?
JAIL
YES.
WELCOME
I WANT AN ATTORNEY, BUT I CAN'T AFFORD ONE.
HOW CAN THAT BE? YOU'RE A WORLD-FAMOUS PROGNOSTICATOR.
YEAH. GO FIGURE.
"WANTED"
OK, WELL, YOUR COURT-APPOINTED ATTORNEY WILL BE HERE ANY MINUTE.
HELLO, MADAME — I'M YOUR LAWYER.
WHY AM I NOT SURPRISED?
I KNOW. I'M A NATURAL.

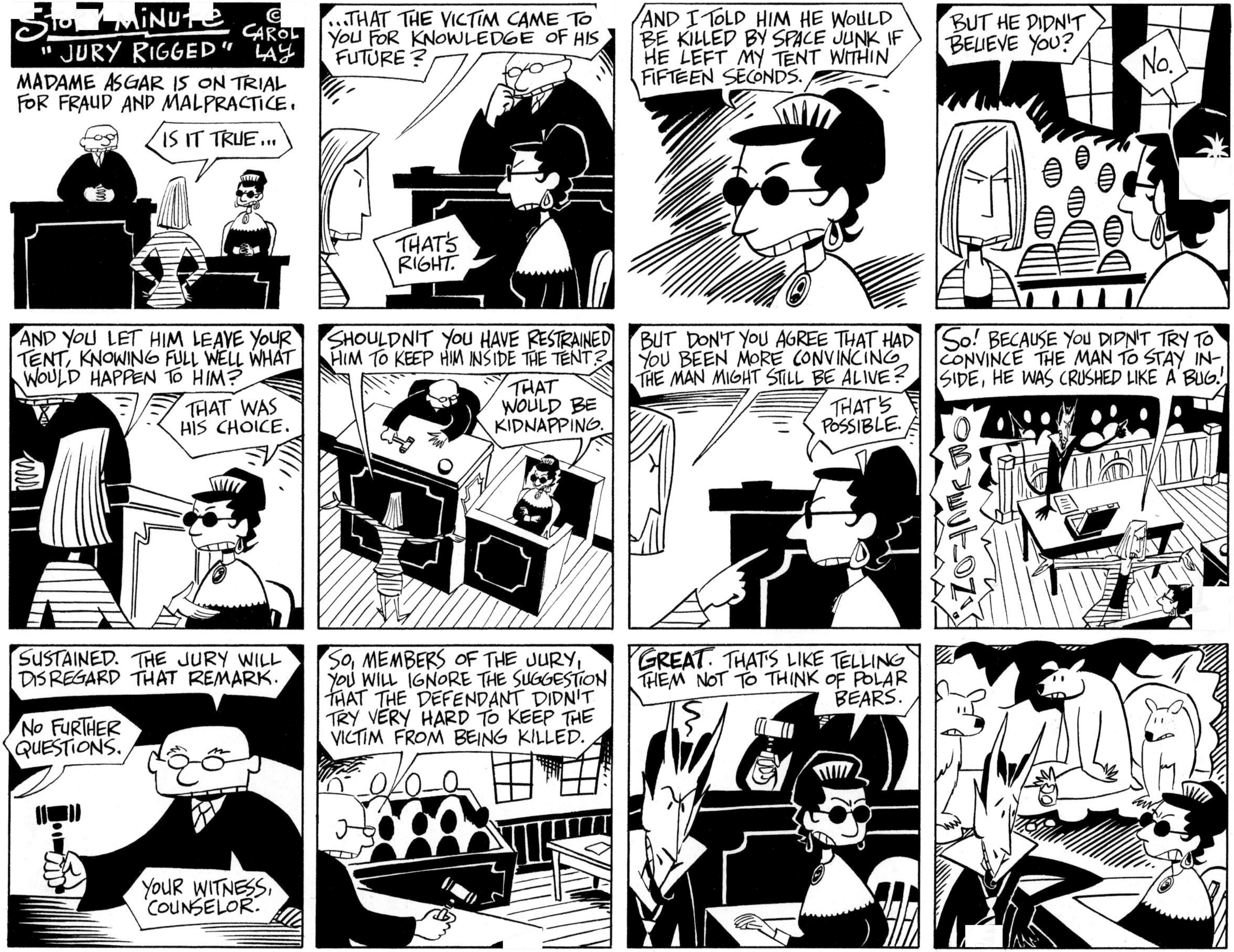
"JURY RIGGED"
© CAROL LAY
MADAME ASGAR IS ON TRIAL FOR FRAUD AND MALPRACTICE.
IS IT TRUE...
...THAT THE VICTIM CAME TO YOU FOR KNOWLEDGE OF HIS FUTURE?
THAT'S RIGHT.
AND I TOLD HIM HE WOULD BE KILLED BY SPACE JUNK IF HE LEFT MY TENT WITHIN FIFTEEN SECONDS.
BUT HE DIDN'T BELIEVE YOU?
NO.
AND YOU LET HIM LEAVE YOUR TENT, KNOWING FULL WELL WHAT WOULD HAPPEN TO HIM?
THAT WAS HIS CHOICE.
SHOULDN'T YOU HAVE RESTRAINED HIM TO KEEP HIM INSIDE THE TENT?
THAT WOULD BE KIDNAPPING.
BUT DON'T YOU AGREE THAT HAD YOU BEEN MORE CONVINCING THE MAN MIGHT STILL BE ALIVE?
THAT'S POSSIBLE.
SO! BECAUSE YOU DIDN'T TRY TO CONVINCE THE MAN TO STAY INSIDE, HE WAS CRUSHED LIKE A BUG!
OBJECTION!
SUSTAINED. THE JURY WILL DISREGARD THAT REMARK.
NO FURTHER QUESTIONS.
YOUR WITNESS, COUNSELOR.
SO, MEMBERS OF THE JURY, YOU WILL IGNORE THE SUGGESTION THAT THE DEFENDANT DIDN'T TRY VERY HARD TO KEEP THE VICTIM FROM BEING KILLED.
GREAT. THAT'S LIKE TELLING THEM NOT TO THINK OF POLAR BEARS.

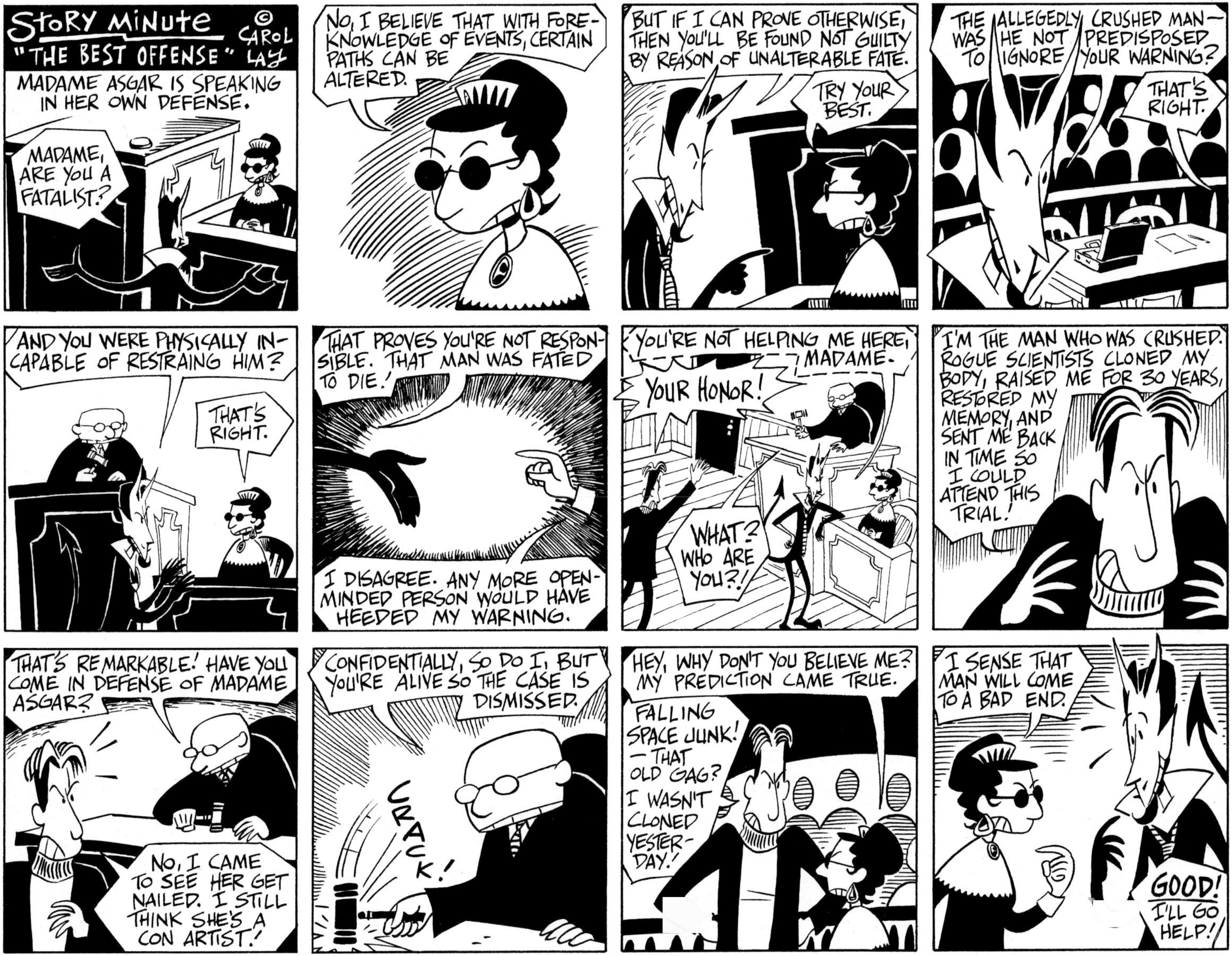

STORY MINUTE
"THE BEST OFFENSE"
© CAROL LAY
MADAME ASGAR IS SPEAKING IN HER OWN DEFENSE.
MADAME, ARE YOU A FATALIST?
NO, I BELIEVE THAT WITH FORE-KNOWLEDGE OF EVENTS, CERTAIN PATHS CAN BE ALTERED.
BUT IF I CAN PROVE OTHERWISE, THEN YOU'LL BE FOUND NOT GUILTY BY REASON OF UNALTERABLE FATE.
TRY YOUR BEST.
THE ALLEGEDLY CRUSHED MAN— WAS HE NOT PREDISPOSED TO IGNORE YOUR WARNING?
THAT'S RIGHT.
AND YOU WERE PHYSICALLY IN-CAPABLE OF RESTRAING HIM?
THAT'S RIGHT.
THAT PROVES YOU'RE NOT RESPON-SIBLE. THAT MAN WAS FATED TO DIE!
I DISAGREE. ANY MORE OPEN-MINDED PERSON WOULD HAVE HEEDED MY WARNING.
YOU'RE NOT HELPING ME HERE, MADAME.
YOUR HONOR!
WHAT? WHO ARE YOU?!
I'M THE MAN WHO WAS CRUSHED. ROGUE SCIENTISTS CLONED MY BODY, RAISED ME FOR 30 YEARS, RESTORED MY MEMORY, AND SENT ME BACK IN TIME SO I COULD ATTEND THIS TRIAL!
THAT'S REMARKABLE! HAVE YOU COME IN DEFENSE OF MADAME ASGAR?
NO, I CAME TO SEE HER GET NAILED. I STILL THINK SHE'S A CON ARTIST!
CONFIDENTIALLY, SO DO I, BUT YOU'RE ALIVE SO THE CASE IS DISMISSED.
CRACK!
HEY, WHY DON'T YOU BELIEVE ME? MY PREDICTION CAME TRUE.
FALLING SPACE JUNK! —THAT OLD GAG? I WASN'T CLONED YESTER-DAY!
I SENSE THAT MAN WILL COME TO A BAD END.
GOOD! I'LL GO HELP!

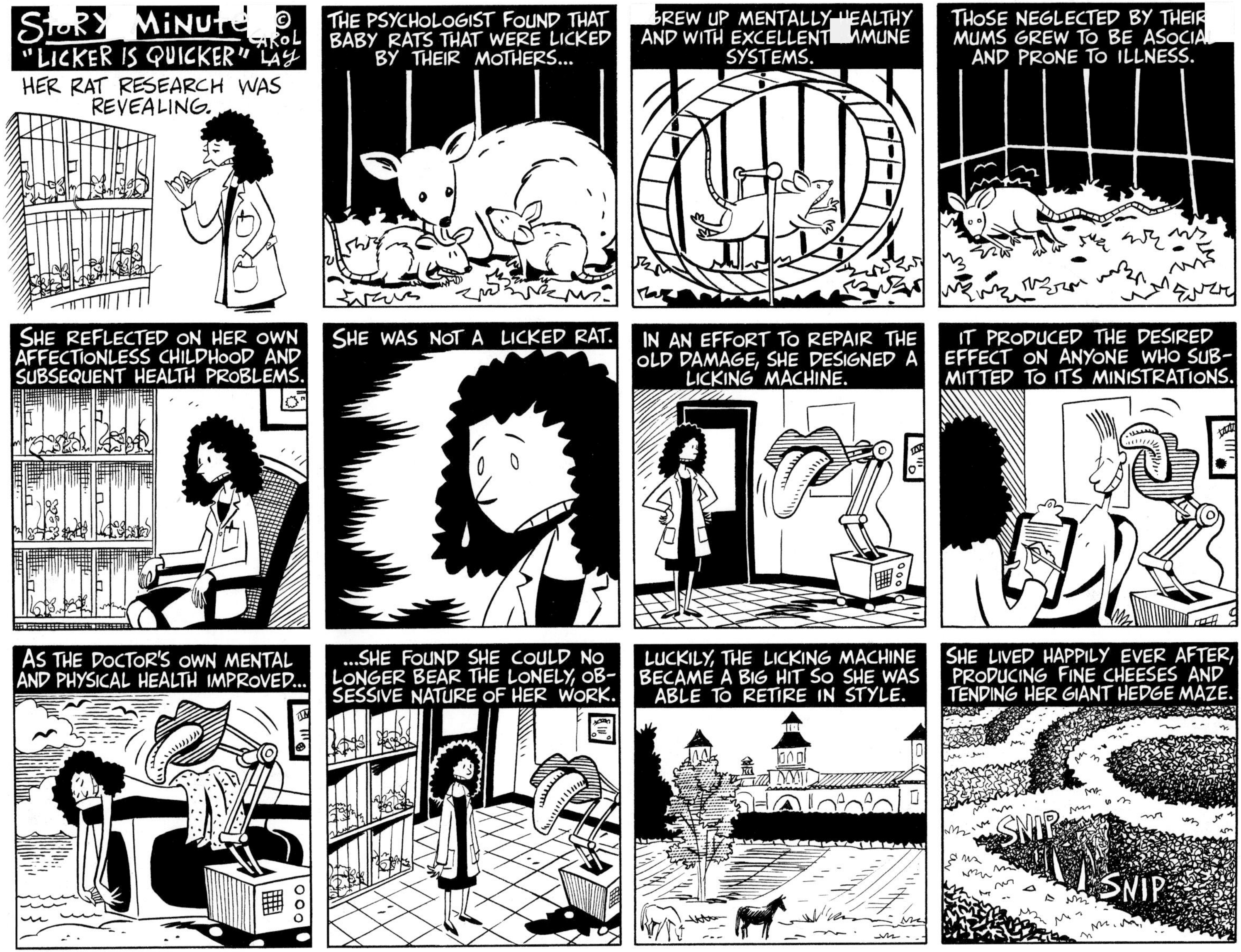

STORY MINUTE © CAROL LAY
"LICKER IS QUICKER"
HER RAT RESEARCH WAS REVEALING.
THE PSYCHOLOGIST FOUND THAT BABY RATS THAT WERE LICKED BY THEIR MOTHERS...
...GREW UP MENTALLY HEALTHY AND WITH EXCELLENT IMMUNE SYSTEMS.
THOSE NEGLECTED BY THEIR MUMS GREW TO BE ASOCIAL AND PRONE TO ILLNESS.
SHE REFLECTED ON HER OWN AFFECTIONLESS CHILDHOOD AND SUBSEQUENT HEALTH PROBLEMS.
SHE WAS NOT A LICKED RAT.
IN AN EFFORT TO REPAIR THE OLD DAMAGE, SHE DESIGNED A LICKING MACHINE.
IT PRODUCED THE DESIRED EFFECT ON ANYONE WHO SUBMITTED TO ITS MINISTRATIONS.
AS THE DOCTOR'S OWN MENTAL AND PHYSICAL HEALTH IMPROVED...
...SHE FOUND SHE COULD NO LONGER BEAR THE LONELY, OBSESSIVE NATURE OF HER WORK.
LUCKILY, THE LICKING MACHINE BECAME A BIG HIT SO SHE WAS ABLE TO RETIRE IN STYLE.
SHE LIVED HAPPILY EVER AFTER, PRODUCING FINE CHEESES AND TENDING HER GIANT HEDGE MAZE.
SNIP
SNIP

 **"TESTING"** CAROL LAY

SHE PAID RAPT ATTENTION TO THOSE IN LINE AHEAD OF HER.

ONE BY ONE THEY WERE BEING QUESTIONED...

...AND ELIMINATED.

WHAT WERE THEY SAYING THAT WAS SO WRONG?

SURE, THE QUESTIONS WERE DIFFICULT...

...BUT THE PENALTY FOR A WRONG ANSWER WAS BARBARIC.

SHE CONTROLLED HER ANXIETY ENOUGH TO PAY ATTENTION TO THE TEST QUESTIONS.

PERHAPS THERE WAS A PATTERN THAT MIGHT HELP WHEN IT CAME TO HER TURN.

THERE WAS. SHE PASSED THE INTELLIGENCE TEST AND, FOR THE MOMENT, KEPT HER LIFE.

BUT NOW CAME PART TWO OF THE TEST.

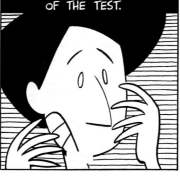

SHE HAD TO COMPLETE THE OBSTACLE COURSE IN LESS THAN A MINUTE.

AND THERE WERE A HELL OF A LOT OF OBSTACLES.

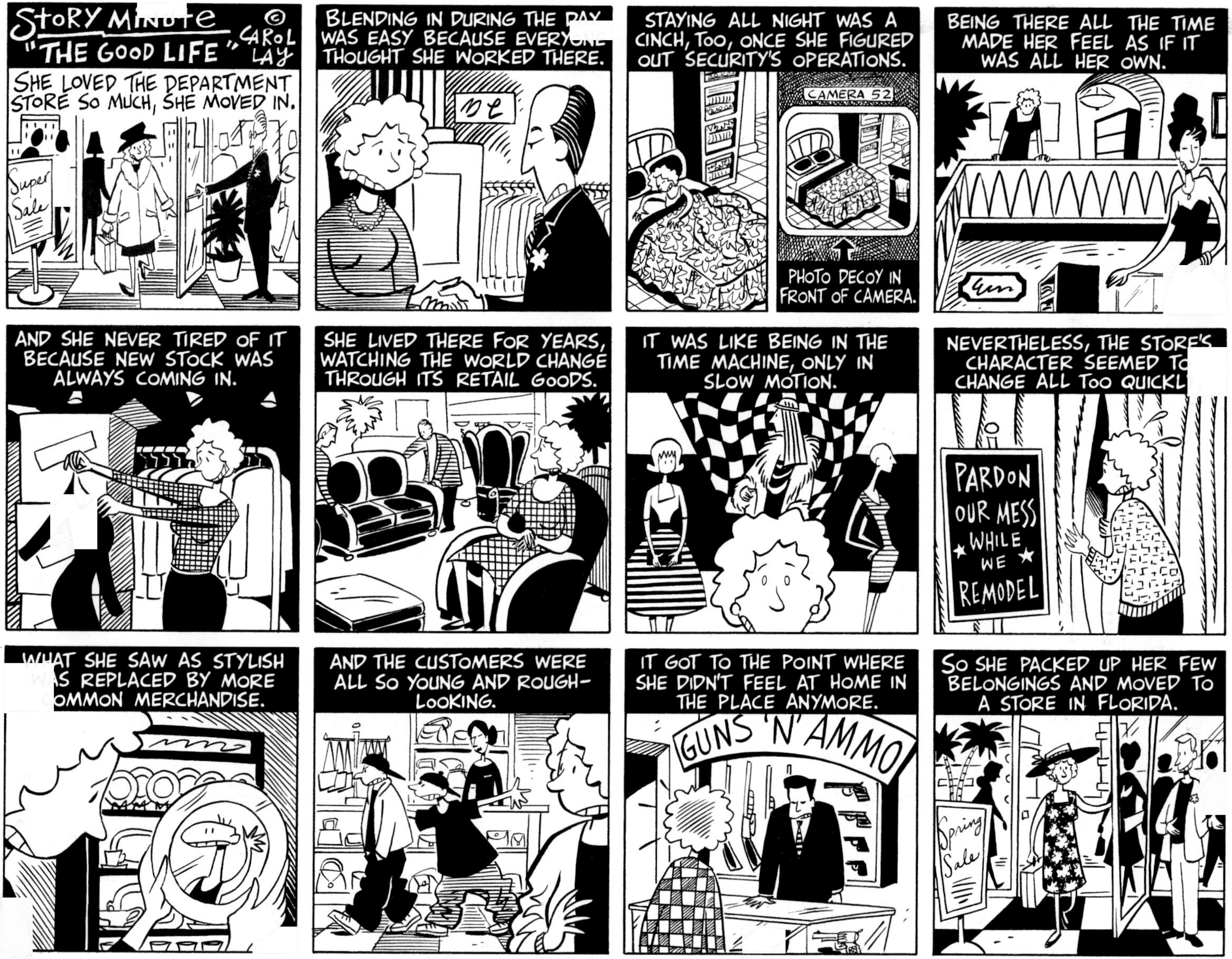
STORY MINUTE
"THE GOOD LIFE"
© CAROL LAY
SHE LOVED THE DEPARTMENT STORE SO MUCH, SHE MOVED IN.
Super Sale
BLENDING IN DURING THE DAY WAS EASY BECAUSE EVERYONE THOUGHT SHE WORKED THERE.
STAYING ALL NIGHT WAS A CINCH, TOO, ONCE SHE FIGURED OUT SECURITY'S OPERATIONS.
CAMERA 52
PHOTO DECOY IN FRONT OF CAMERA.
BEING THERE ALL THE TIME MADE HER FEEL AS IF IT WAS ALL HER OWN.
AND SHE NEVER TIRED OF IT BECAUSE NEW STOCK WAS ALWAYS COMING IN.
SHE LIVED THERE FOR YEARS, WATCHING THE WORLD CHANGE THROUGH ITS RETAIL GOODS.
IT WAS LIKE BEING IN THE TIME MACHINE, ONLY IN SLOW MOTION.
NEVERTHELESS, THE STORE'S CHARACTER SEEMED TO CHANGE ALL TOO QUICKLY.
PARDON OUR MESS WHILE WE REMODEL
WHAT SHE SAW AS STYLISH WAS REPLACED BY MORE COMMON MERCHANDISE.
AND THE CUSTOMERS WERE ALL SO YOUNG AND ROUGH-LOOKING.
IT GOT TO THE POINT WHERE SHE DIDN'T FEEL AT HOME IN THE PLACE ANYMORE.
GUNS 'N' AMMO
SO SHE PACKED UP HER FEW BELONGINGS AND MOVED TO A STORE IN FLORIDA.
Spring Sale

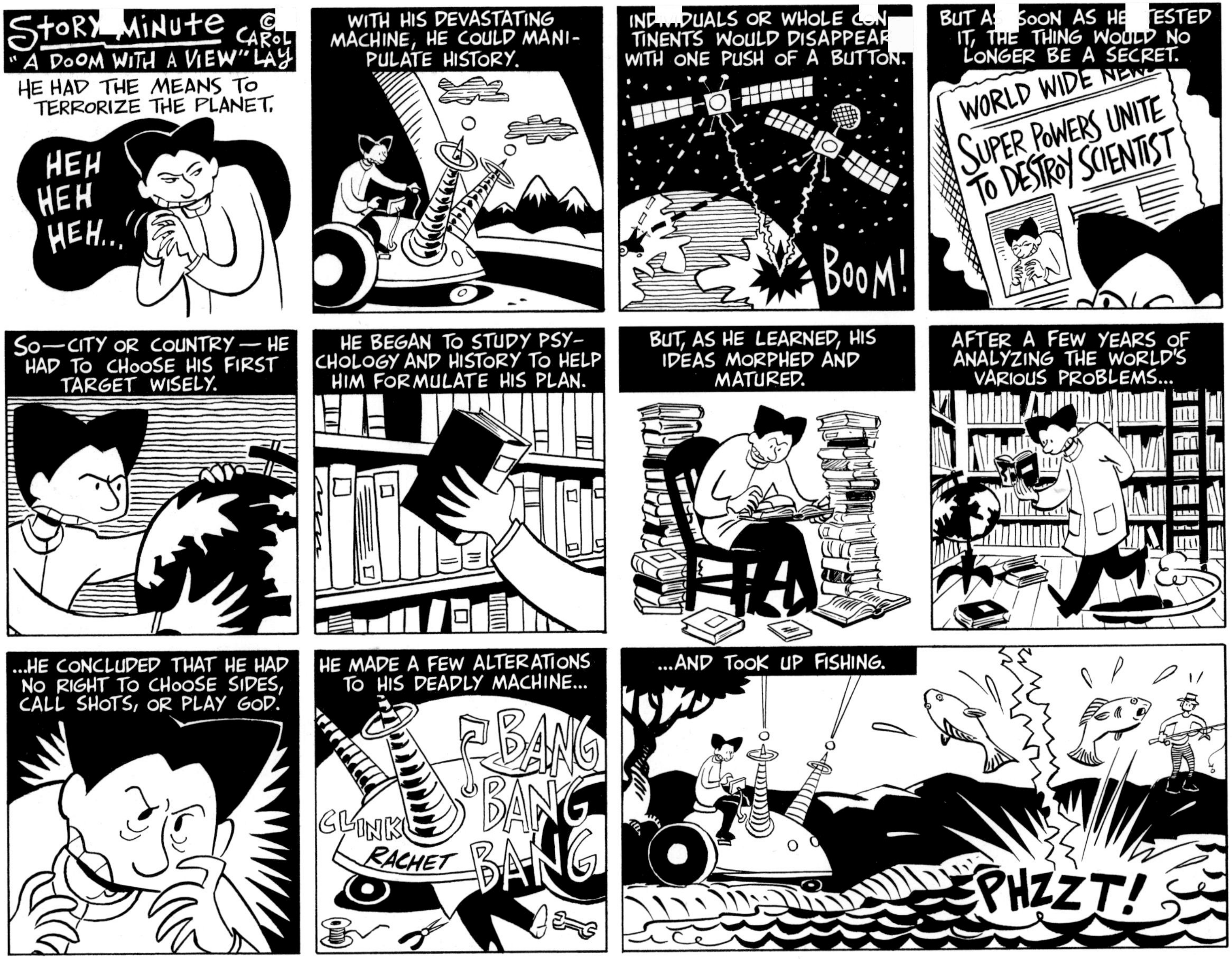
STORY MINUTE
© CAROL LAY
"A DOOM WITH A VIEW"
HE HAD THE MEANS TO TERRORIZE THE PLANET.
HEH HEH HEH...
WITH HIS DEVASTATING MACHINE, HE COULD MANI-PULATE HISTORY.
INDIVIDUALS OR WHOLE CON-TINENTS WOULD DISAPPEAR WITH ONE PUSH OF A BUTTON.
BOOM!
BUT AS SOON AS HE TESTED IT, THE THING WOULD NO LONGER BE A SECRET.
WORLD WIDE NEWS
SUPER POWERS UNITE TO DESTROY SCIENTIST
SO—CITY OR COUNTRY—HE HAD TO CHOOSE HIS FIRST TARGET WISELY.
HE BEGAN TO STUDY PSY-CHOLOGY AND HISTORY TO HELP HIM FORMULATE HIS PLAN.
BUT, AS HE LEARNED, HIS IDEAS MORPHED AND MATURED.
AFTER A FEW YEARS OF ANALYZING THE WORLD'S VARIOUS PROBLEMS...
...HE CONCLUDED THAT HE HAD NO RIGHT TO CHOOSE SIDES, CALL SHOTS, OR PLAY GOD.
HE MADE A FEW ALTERATIONS TO HIS DEADLY MACHINE...
BANG BANG BANG
CLINK
RACHET
...AND TOOK UP FISHING.
PHZZT!

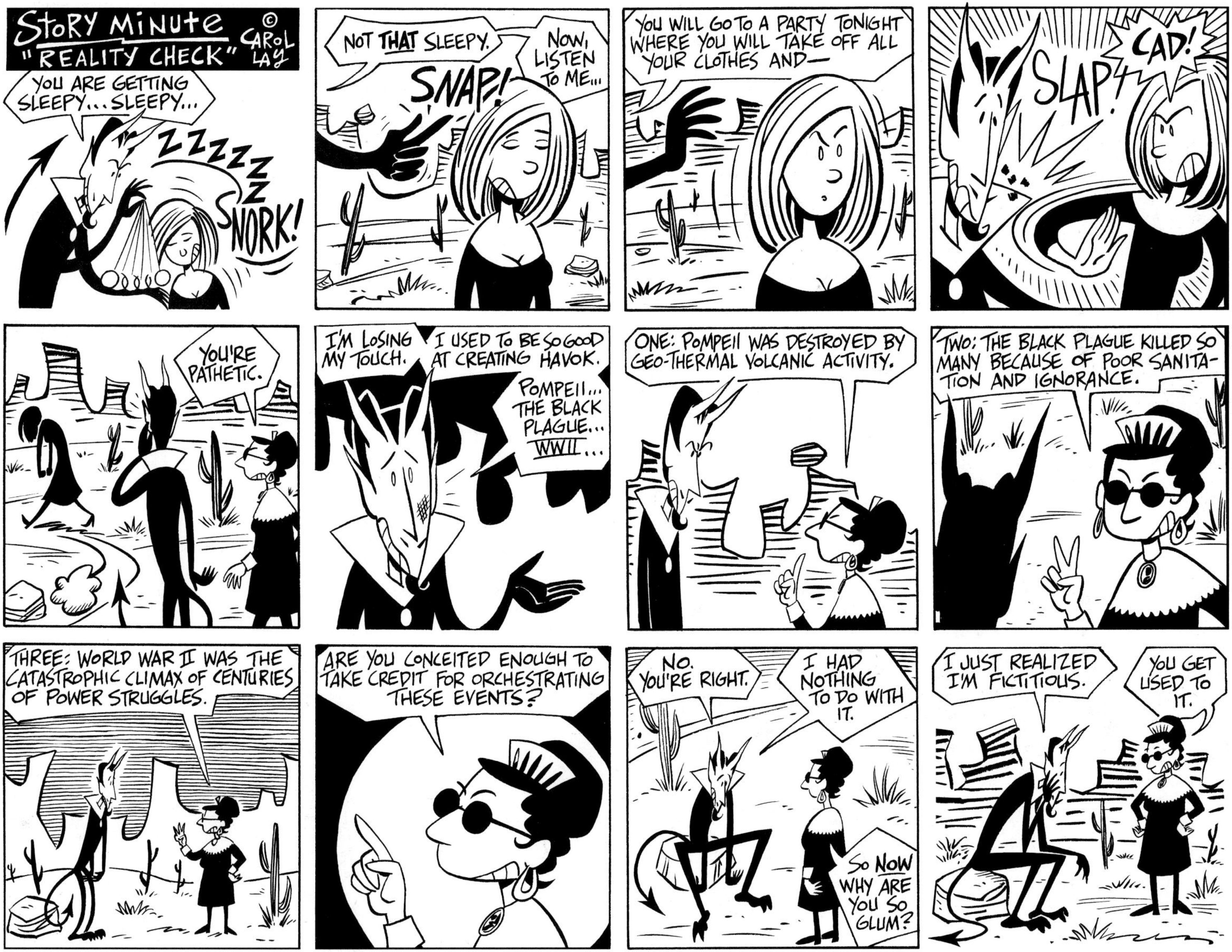
STORY MINUTE
"REALITY CHECK"
© CAROL LAY
YOU ARE GETTING SLEEPY... SLEEPY...
ZZZZZZZ
SNORK!
NOT THAT SLEEPY.
SNAP!
NOW, LISTEN TO ME...
YOU WILL GO TO A PARTY TONIGHT WHERE YOU WILL TAKE OFF ALL YOUR CLOTHES AND—
SLAP!
CAD!
YOU'RE PATHETIC.
I'M LOSING MY TOUCH.
I USED TO BE SO GOOD AT CREATING HAVOK.
POMPEII... THE BLACK PLAGUE... WWII...
ONE: POMPEII WAS DESTROYED BY GEO-THERMAL VOLCANIC ACTIVITY.
TWO: THE BLACK PLAGUE KILLED SO MANY BECAUSE OF POOR SANITATION AND IGNORANCE.
THREE: WORLD WAR II WAS THE CATASTROPHIC CLIMAX OF CENTURIES OF POWER STRUGGLES.
ARE YOU CONCEITED ENOUGH TO TAKE CREDIT FOR ORCHESTRATING THESE EVENTS?
NO. YOU'RE RIGHT.
I HAD NOTHING TO DO WITH IT.
SO NOW WHY ARE YOU SO GLUM?
I JUST REALIZED I'M FICTITIOUS.
YOU GET USED TO IT.

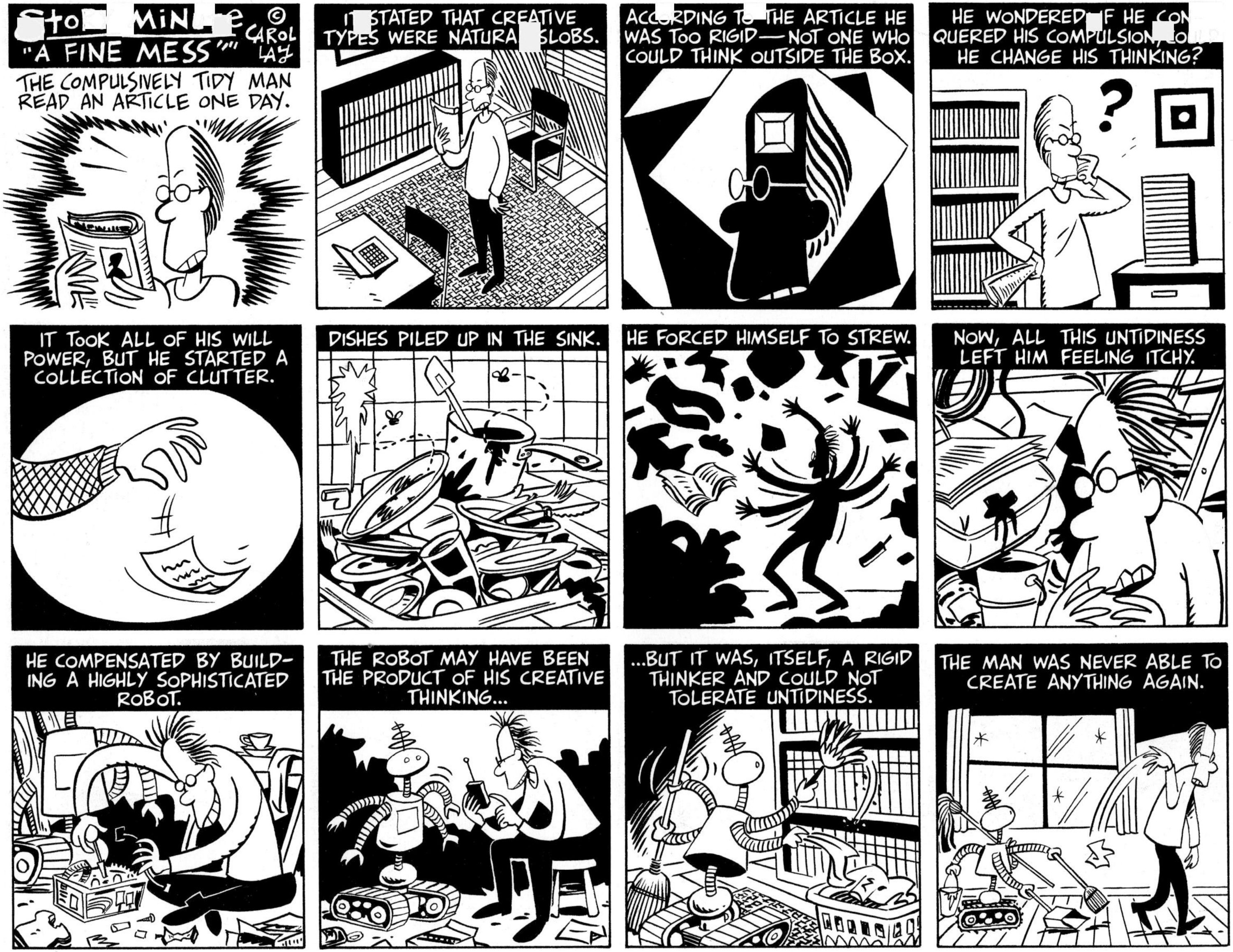
"A FINE MESS"
© CAROL LAY
THE COMPULSIVELY TIDY MAN READ AN ARTICLE ONE DAY.
IT STATED THAT CREATIVE TYPES WERE NATURAL SLOBS.
ACCORDING TO THE ARTICLE HE WAS TOO RIGID — NOT ONE WHO COULD THINK OUTSIDE THE BOX.
HE WONDERED IF HE CONQUERED HIS COMPULSION, COULD HE CHANGE HIS THINKING?
?
IT TOOK ALL OF HIS WILL POWER, BUT HE STARTED A COLLECTION OF CLUTTER.
DISHES PILED UP IN THE SINK.
HE FORCED HIMSELF TO STREW.
NOW, ALL THIS UNTIDINESS LEFT HIM FEELING ITCHY.
HE COMPENSATED BY BUILDING A HIGHLY SOPHISTICATED ROBOT.
THE ROBOT MAY HAVE BEEN THE PRODUCT OF HIS CREATIVE THINKING...
...BUT IT WAS, ITSELF, A RIGID THINKER AND COULD NOT TOLERATE UNTIDINESS.
THE MAN WAS NEVER ABLE TO CREATE ANYTHING AGAIN.

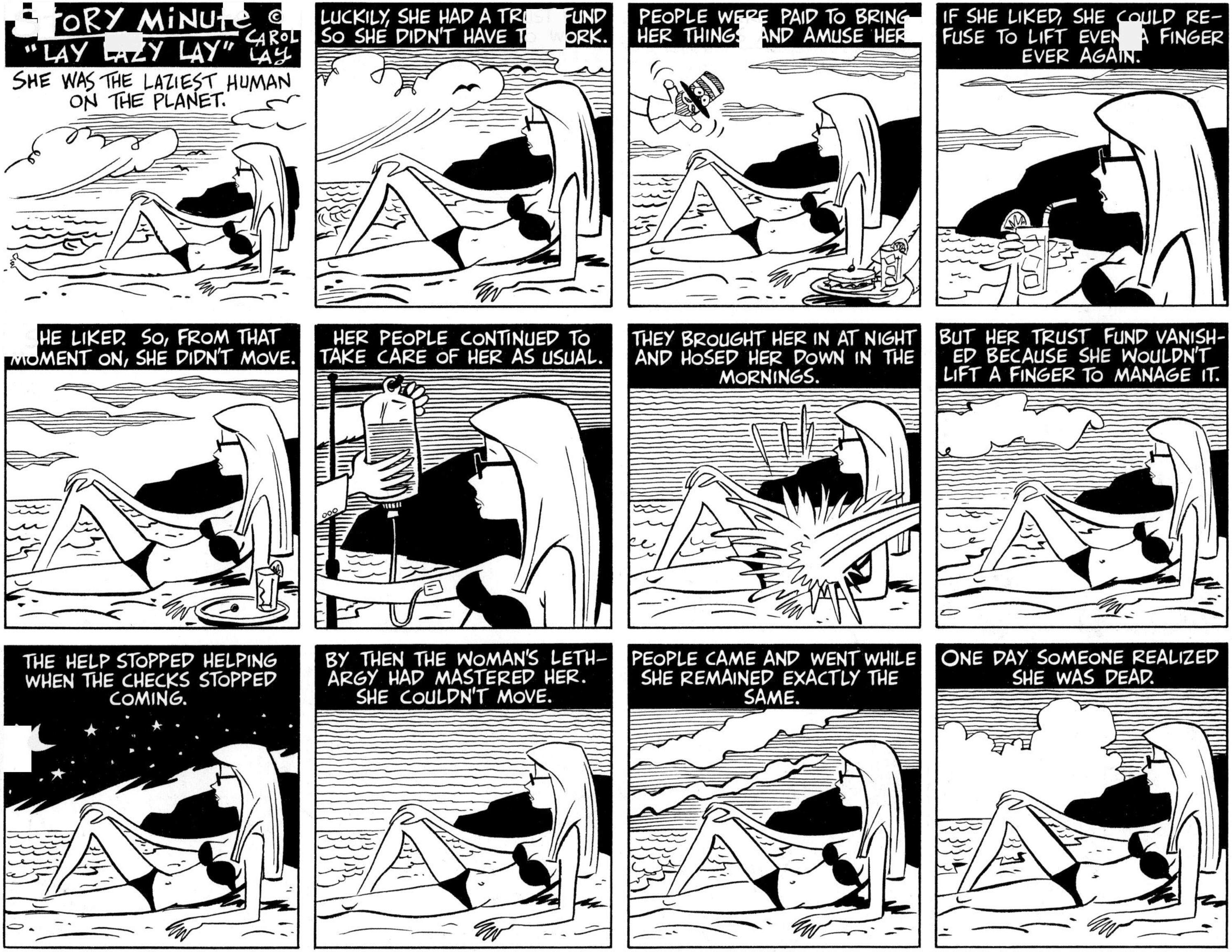
STORY MINUTE © CAROL LAY
"LAY LAZY LAY"
SHE WAS THE LAZIEST HUMAN ON THE PLANET.
LUCKILY, SHE HAD A TRUST FUND SO SHE DIDN'T HAVE TO WORK.
PEOPLE WERE PAID TO BRING HER THINGS AND AMUSE HER.
IF SHE LIKED, SHE COULD REFUSE TO LIFT EVEN A FINGER EVER AGAIN.
SHE LIKED. SO, FROM THAT MOMENT ON, SHE DIDN'T MOVE.
HER PEOPLE CONTINUED TO TAKE CARE OF HER AS USUAL.
THEY BROUGHT HER IN AT NIGHT AND HOSED HER DOWN IN THE MORNINGS.
BUT HER TRUST FUND VANISHED BECAUSE SHE WOULDN'T LIFT A FINGER TO MANAGE IT.
THE HELP STOPPED HELPING WHEN THE CHECKS STOPPED COMING.
BY THEN THE WOMAN'S LETHARGY HAD MASTERED HER. SHE COULDN'T MOVE.
PEOPLE CAME AND WENT WHILE SHE REMAINED EXACTLY THE SAME.
ONE DAY SOMEONE REALIZED SHE WAS DEAD.

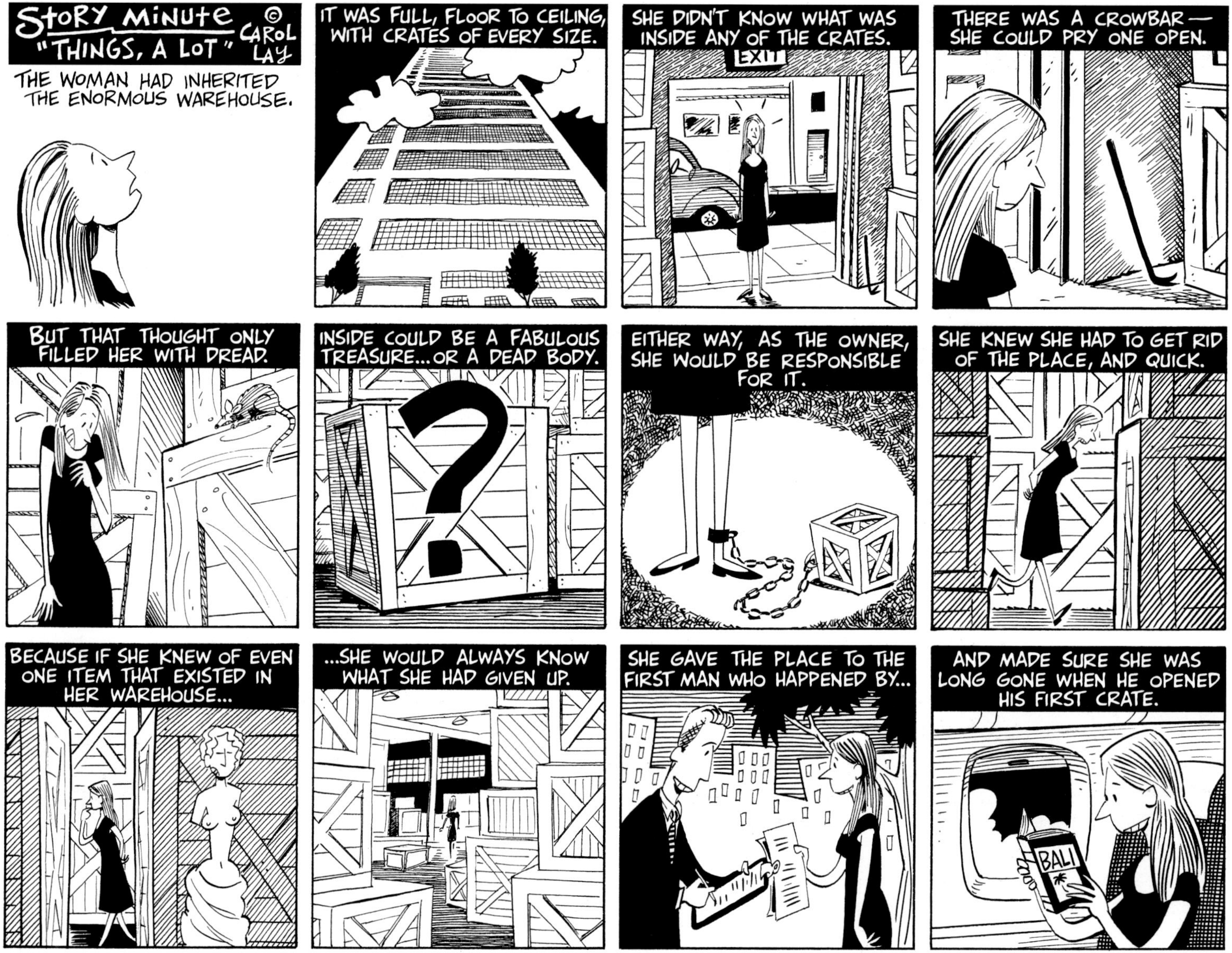
STORY MINUTE
"THINGS, A LOT"
© CAROL LAY
THE WOMAN HAD INHERITED THE ENORMOUS WAREHOUSE.
IT WAS FULL, FLOOR TO CEILING, WITH CRATES OF EVERY SIZE.
SHE DIDN'T KNOW WHAT WAS INSIDE ANY OF THE CRATES.
EXIT
THERE WAS A CROWBAR— SHE COULD PRY ONE OPEN.
BUT THAT THOUGHT ONLY FILLED HER WITH DREAD.
INSIDE COULD BE A FABULOUS TREASURE...OR A DEAD BODY.
EITHER WAY, AS THE OWNER, SHE WOULD BE RESPONSIBLE FOR IT.
SHE KNEW SHE HAD TO GET RID OF THE PLACE, AND QUICK.
BECAUSE IF SHE KNEW OF EVEN ONE ITEM THAT EXISTED IN HER WAREHOUSE...
...SHE WOULD ALWAYS KNOW WHAT SHE HAD GIVEN UP.
SHE GAVE THE PLACE TO THE FIRST MAN WHO HAPPENED BY...
AND MADE SURE SHE WAS LONG GONE WHEN HE OPENED HIS FIRST CRATE.
BALI

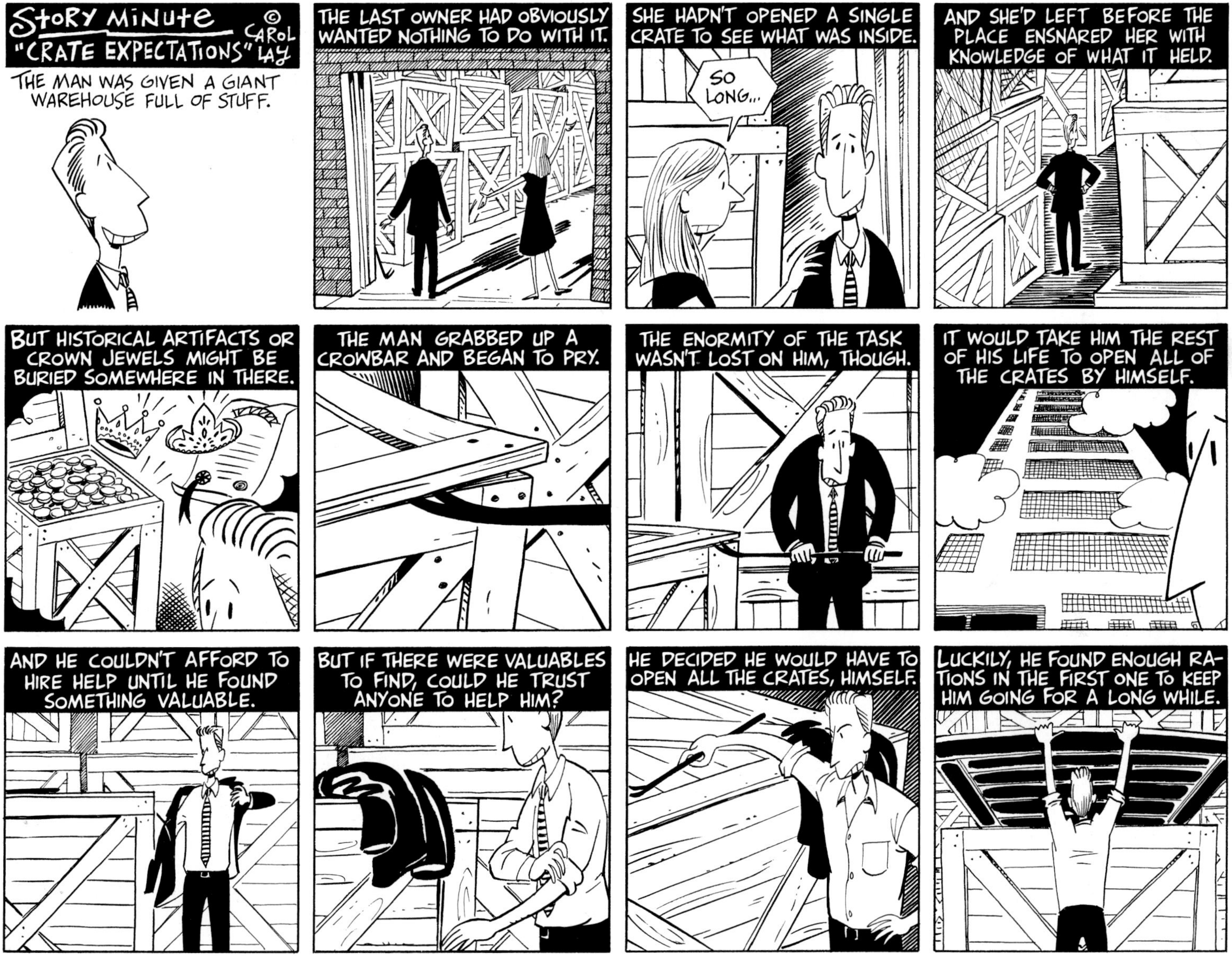

STORY MINUTE
"CRATE EXPECTATIONS"
© CAROL LAY
THE MAN WAS GIVEN A GIANT WAREHOUSE FULL OF STUFF.
THE LAST OWNER HAD OBVIOUSLY WANTED NOTHING TO DO WITH IT.
SHE HADN'T OPENED A SINGLE CRATE TO SEE WHAT WAS INSIDE.
SO LONG...
AND SHE'D LEFT BEFORE THE PLACE ENSNARED HER WITH KNOWLEDGE OF WHAT IT HELD.
BUT HISTORICAL ARTIFACTS OR CROWN JEWELS MIGHT BE BURIED SOMEWHERE IN THERE.
THE MAN GRABBED UP A CROWBAR AND BEGAN TO PRY.
THE ENORMITY OF THE TASK WASN'T LOST ON HIM, THOUGH.
IT WOULD TAKE HIM THE REST OF HIS LIFE TO OPEN ALL OF THE CRATES BY HIMSELF.
AND HE COULDN'T AFFORD TO HIRE HELP UNTIL HE FOUND SOMETHING VALUABLE.
BUT IF THERE WERE VALUABLES TO FIND, COULD HE TRUST ANYONE TO HELP HIM?
HE DECIDED HE WOULD HAVE TO OPEN ALL THE CRATES, HIMSELF.
LUCKILY, HE FOUND ENOUGH RATIONS IN THE FIRST ONE TO KEEP HIM GOING FOR A LONG WHILE.

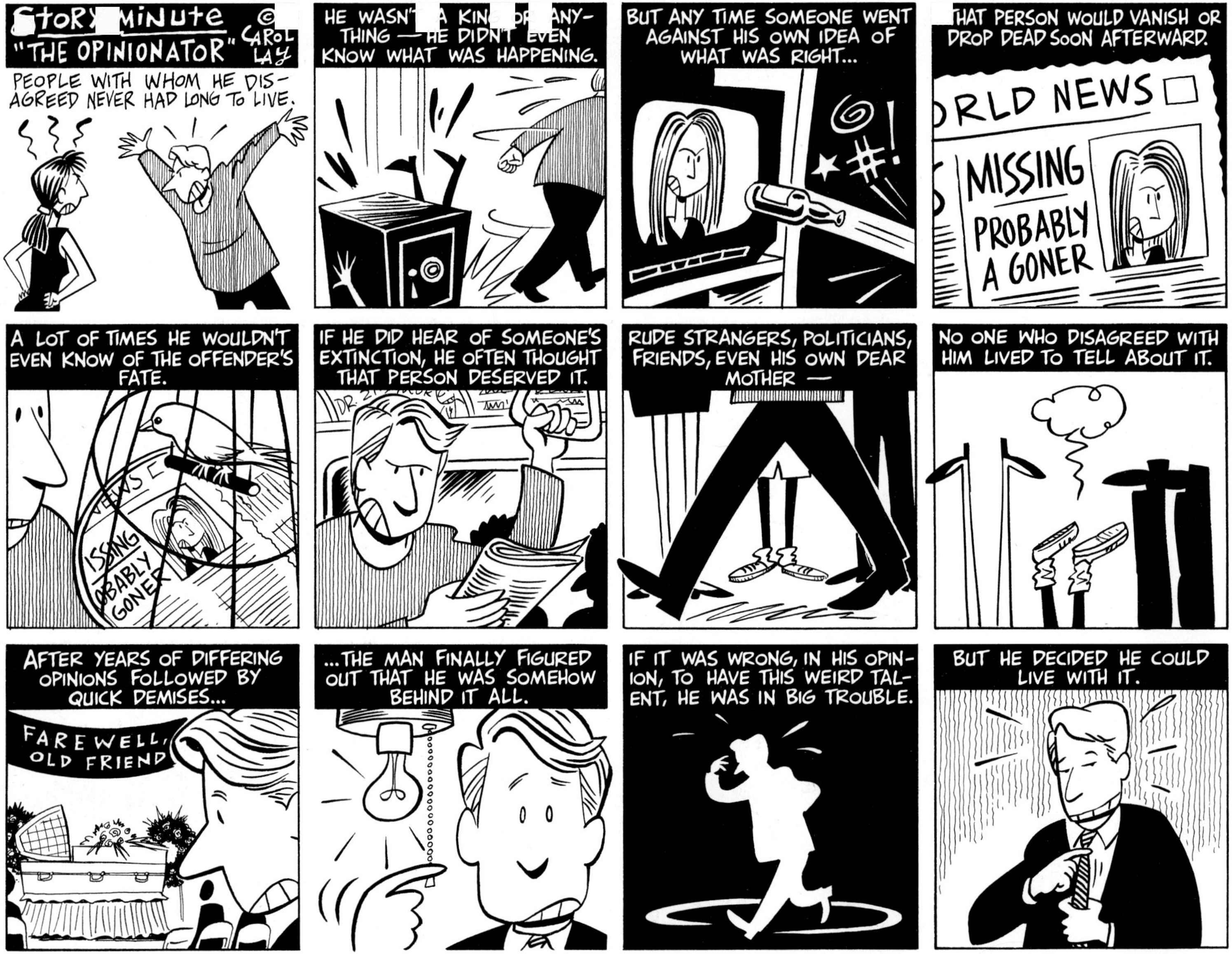
STORY MINUTE
"THE OPINIONATOR"
© CAROL LAY
PEOPLE WITH WHOM HE DIS-AGREED NEVER HAD LONG TO LIVE.
HE WASN'T A KING OR ANY-THING — HE DIDN'T EVEN KNOW WHAT WAS HAPPENING.
BUT ANY TIME SOMEONE WENT AGAINST HIS OWN IDEA OF WHAT WAS RIGHT...
THAT PERSON WOULD VANISH OR DROP DEAD SOON AFTERWARD.
ORLD NEWS
MISSING
PROBABLY A GONER
A LOT OF TIMES HE WOULDN'T EVEN KNOW OF THE OFFENDER'S FATE.
ISSING
OBABLY GONER
IF HE DID HEAR OF SOMEONE'S EXTINCTION, HE OFTEN THOUGHT THAT PERSON DESERVED IT.
RUDE STRANGERS, POLITICIANS, FRIENDS, EVEN HIS OWN DEAR MOTHER —
NO ONE WHO DISAGREED WITH HIM LIVED TO TELL ABOUT IT.
AFTER YEARS OF DIFFERING OPINIONS FOLLOWED BY QUICK DEMISES...
FAREWELL, OLD FRIEND
...THE MAN FINALLY FIGURED OUT THAT HE WAS SOMEHOW BEHIND IT ALL.
IF IT WAS WRONG, IN HIS OPIN-ION, TO HAVE THIS WEIRD TAL-ENT, HE WAS IN BIG TROUBLE.
BUT HE DECIDED HE COULD LIVE WITH IT.

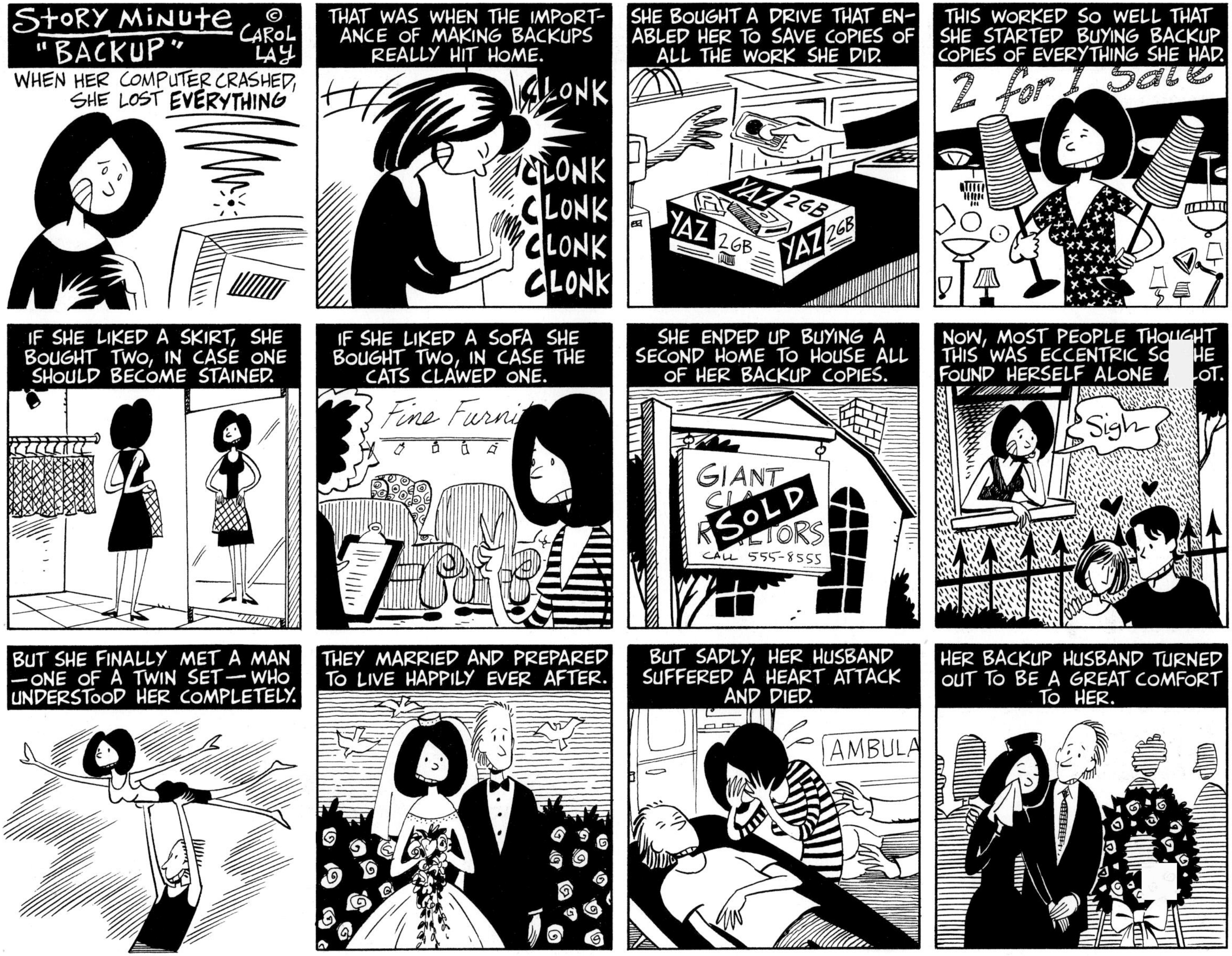

STORY MINUTE
"BACKUP"
© CAROL LAY
WHEN HER COMPUTER CRASHED, SHE LOST EVERYTHING
THAT WAS WHEN THE IMPORTANCE OF MAKING BACKUPS REALLY HIT HOME.
CLONK
CLONK
CLONK
CLONK
CLONK
SHE BOUGHT A DRIVE THAT ENABLED HER TO SAVE COPIES OF ALL THE WORK SHE DID.
YAZ 2GB
YAZ 2GB
YAZ 2GB
THIS WORKED SO WELL THAT SHE STARTED BUYING BACKUP COPIES OF EVERYTHING SHE HAD.
2 for 1 Sale
IF SHE LIKED A SKIRT, SHE BOUGHT TWO, IN CASE ONE SHOULD BECOME STAINED.
IF SHE LIKED A SOFA SHE BOUGHT TWO, IN CASE THE CATS CLAWED ONE.
Fine Furnit
SHE ENDED UP BUYING A SECOND HOME TO HOUSE ALL OF HER BACKUP COPIES.
GIANT
SOLD
LTORS
CALL 555-8555
NOW, MOST PEOPLE THOUGHT THIS WAS ECCENTRIC SO HE FOUND HERSELF ALONE LOT.
Sigh
BUT SHE FINALLY MET A MAN —ONE OF A TWIN SET— WHO UNDERSTOOD HER COMPLETELY.
THEY MARRIED AND PREPARED TO LIVE HAPPILY EVER AFTER.
BUT SADLY, HER HUSBAND SUFFERED A HEART ATTACK AND DIED.
AMBULA
HER BACKUP HUSBAND TURNED OUT TO BE A GREAT COMFORT TO HER.

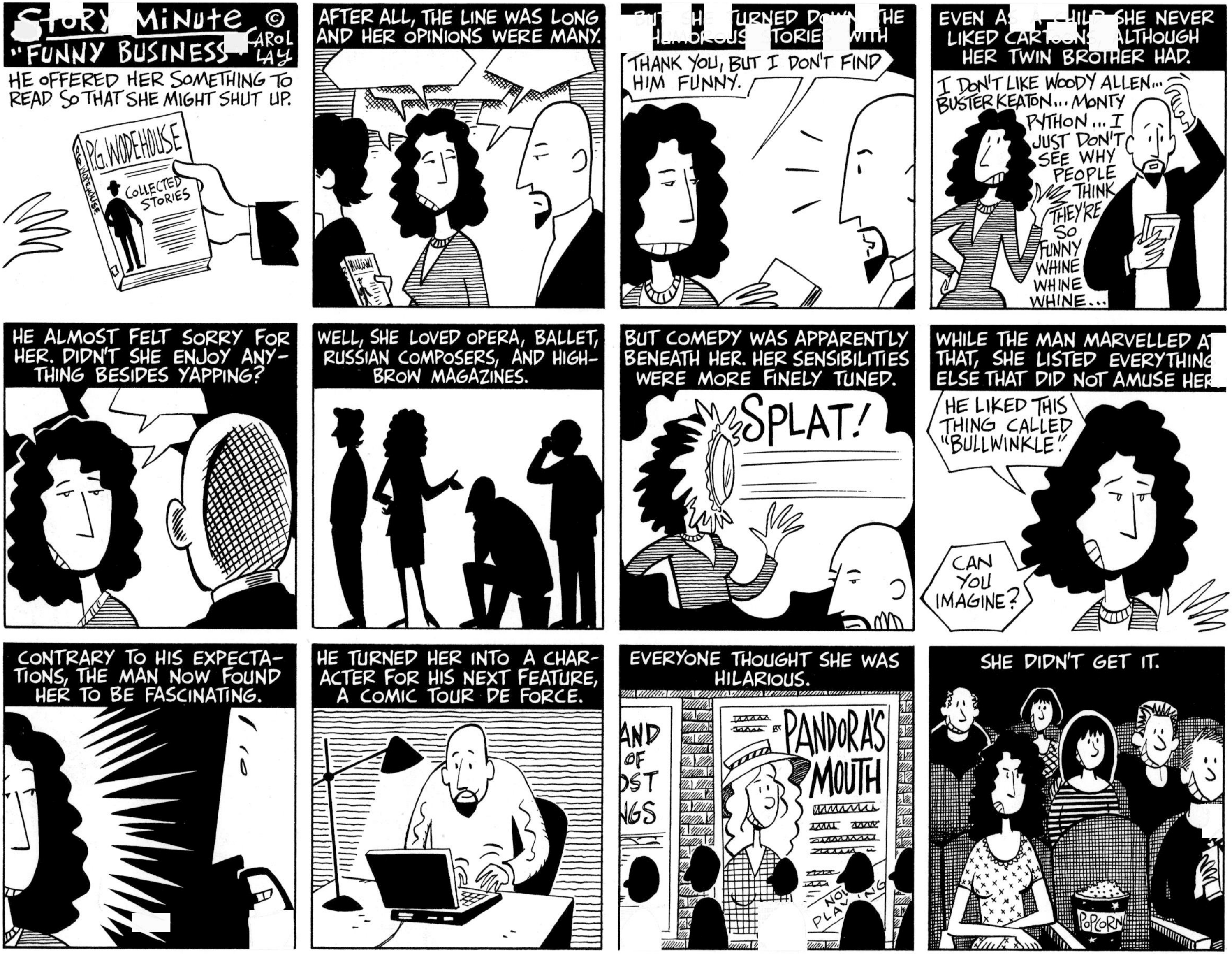
STORY MINUTE © CAROL LAY
"FUNNY BUSINESS"
HE OFFERED HER SOMETHING TO READ SO THAT SHE MIGHT SHUT UP.
P.G. WODEHOUSE
COLLECTED STORIES
AFTER ALL, THE LINE WAS LONG AND HER OPINIONS WERE MANY.
BUT SHE TURNED DOWN THE HUMOROUS STORIES WITH
THANK YOU, BUT I DON'T FIND HIM FUNNY.
EVEN AS A CHILD SHE NEVER LIKED CARTOONS, ALTHOUGH HER TWIN BROTHER HAD.
I DON'T LIKE WOODY ALLEN... BUSTER KEATON... MONTY PYTHON... I JUST DON'T SEE WHY PEOPLE THINK THEY'RE SO FUNNY WHINE WHINE WHINE...
HE ALMOST FELT SORRY FOR HER. DIDN'T SHE ENJOY ANYTHING BESIDES YAPPING?
WELL, SHE LOVED OPERA, BALLET, RUSSIAN COMPOSERS, AND HIGH-BROW MAGAZINES.
BUT COMEDY WAS APPARENTLY BENEATH HER. HER SENSIBILITIES WERE MORE FINELY TUNED.
SPLAT!
WHILE THE MAN MARVELLED AT THAT, SHE LISTED EVERYTHING ELSE THAT DID NOT AMUSE HER.
HE LIKED THIS THING CALLED "BULLWINKLE."
CAN YOU IMAGINE?
CONTRARY TO HIS EXPECTATIONS, THE MAN NOW FOUND HER TO BE FASCINATING.
HE TURNED HER INTO A CHARACTER FOR HIS NEXT FEATURE, A COMIC TOUR DE FORCE.
EVERYONE THOUGHT SHE WAS HILARIOUS.
PANDORA'S MOUTH
NOW PLAYING
SHE DIDN'T GET IT.
POPCORN

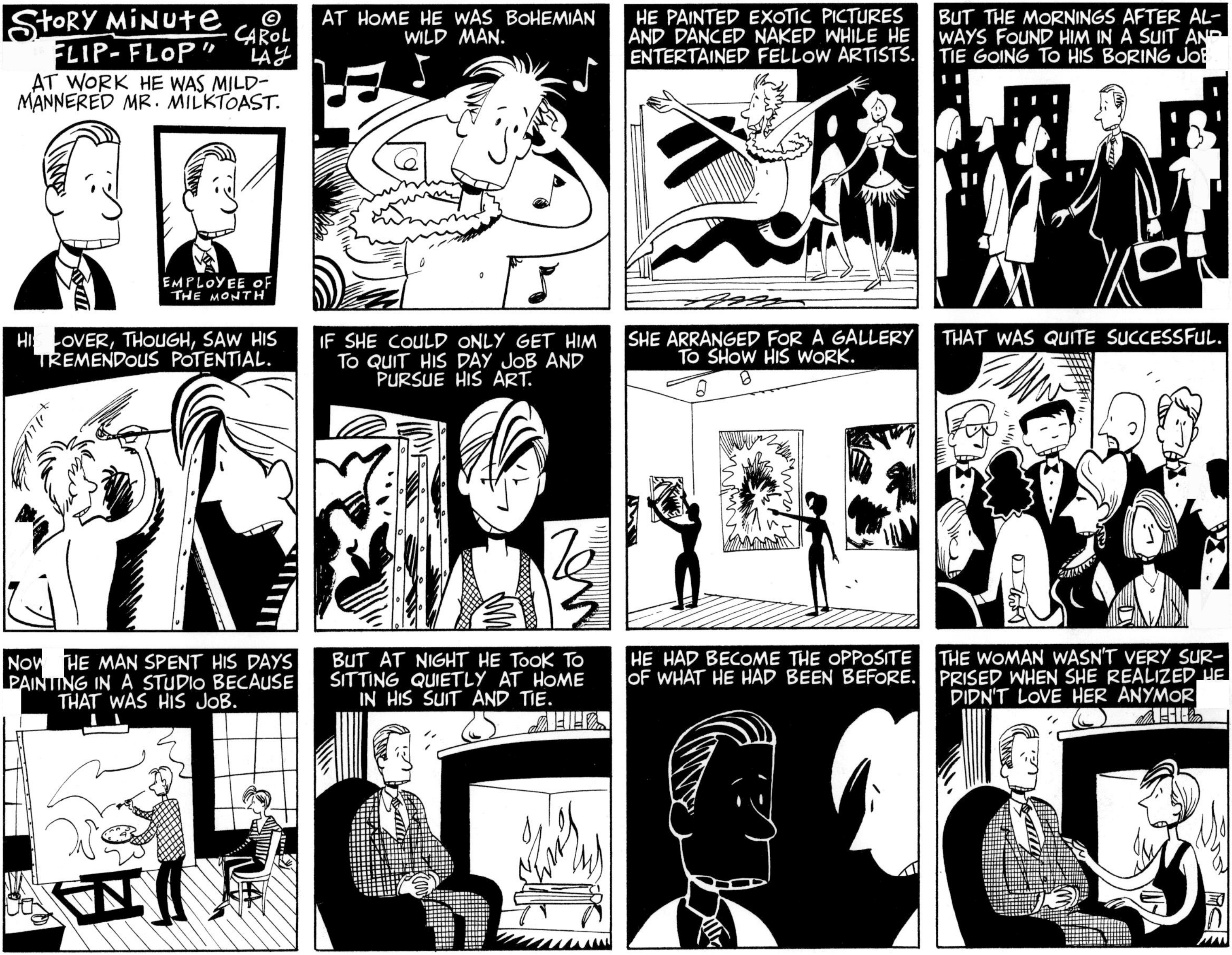
STORY MINUTE
"FLIP-FLOP"
© CAROL LAY
AT WORK HE WAS MILD-MANNERED MR. MILKTOAST.
EMPLOYEE OF THE MONTH
AT HOME HE WAS BOHEMIAN WILD MAN.
HE PAINTED EXOTIC PICTURES AND DANCED NAKED WHILE HE ENTERTAINED FELLOW ARTISTS.
BUT THE MORNINGS AFTER ALWAYS FOUND HIM IN A SUIT AND TIE GOING TO HIS BORING JOB.
HIS LOVER, THOUGH, SAW HIS TREMENDOUS POTENTIAL.
IF SHE COULD ONLY GET HIM TO QUIT HIS DAY JOB AND PURSUE HIS ART.
SHE ARRANGED FOR A GALLERY TO SHOW HIS WORK.
THAT WAS QUITE SUCCESSFUL.
NOW THE MAN SPENT HIS DAYS PAINTING IN A STUDIO BECAUSE THAT WAS HIS JOB.
BUT AT NIGHT HE TOOK TO SITTING QUIETLY AT HOME IN HIS SUIT AND TIE.
HE HAD BECOME THE OPPOSITE OF WHAT HE HAD BEEN BEFORE.
THE WOMAN WASN'T VERY SURPRISED WHEN SHE REALIZED HE DIDN'T LOVE HER ANYMOR

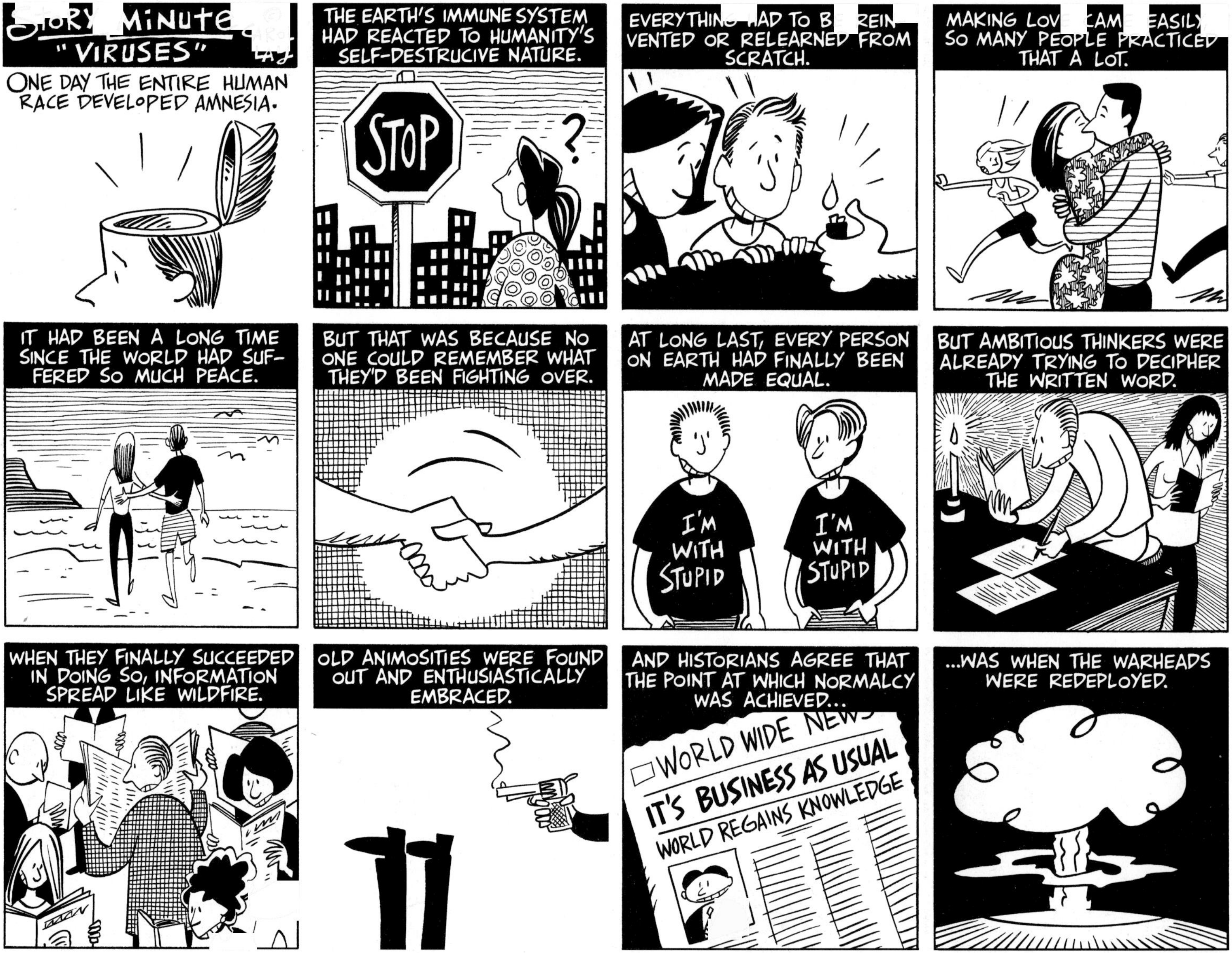
MINUTE
"VIRUSES"
ONE DAY THE ENTIRE HUMAN RACE DEVELOPED AMNESIA.
THE EARTH'S IMMUNE SYSTEM HAD REACTED TO HUMANITY'S SELF-DESTRUCIVE NATURE.
STOP
?
EVERYTHIN AD TO B REIN-VENTED OR RELEARNED FROM SCRATCH.
MAKING LOV CAM EASILY. SO MANY PEOPLE PRACTICED THAT A LOT.
IT HAD BEEN A LONG TIME SINCE THE WORLD HAD SUF-FERED SO MUCH PEACE.
BUT THAT WAS BECAUSE NO ONE COULD REMEMBER WHAT THEY'D BEEN FIGHTING OVER.
AT LONG LAST, EVERY PERSON ON EARTH HAD FINALLY BEEN MADE EQUAL.
I'M WITH STUPID
I'M WITH STUPID
BUT AMBITIOUS THINKERS WERE ALREADY TRYING TO DECIPHER THE WRITTEN WORD.
WHEN THEY FINALLY SUCCEEDED IN DOING SO, INFORMATION SPREAD LIKE WILDFIRE.
OLD ANIMOSITIES WERE FOUND OUT AND ENTHUSIASTICALLY EMBRACED.
AND HISTORIANS AGREE THAT THE POINT AT WHICH NORMALCY WAS ACHIEVED...
WORLD WIDE
IT'S BUSINESS AS USUAL
WORLD REGAINS KNOWLEDGE
...WAS WHEN THE WARHEADS WERE REDEPLOYED.

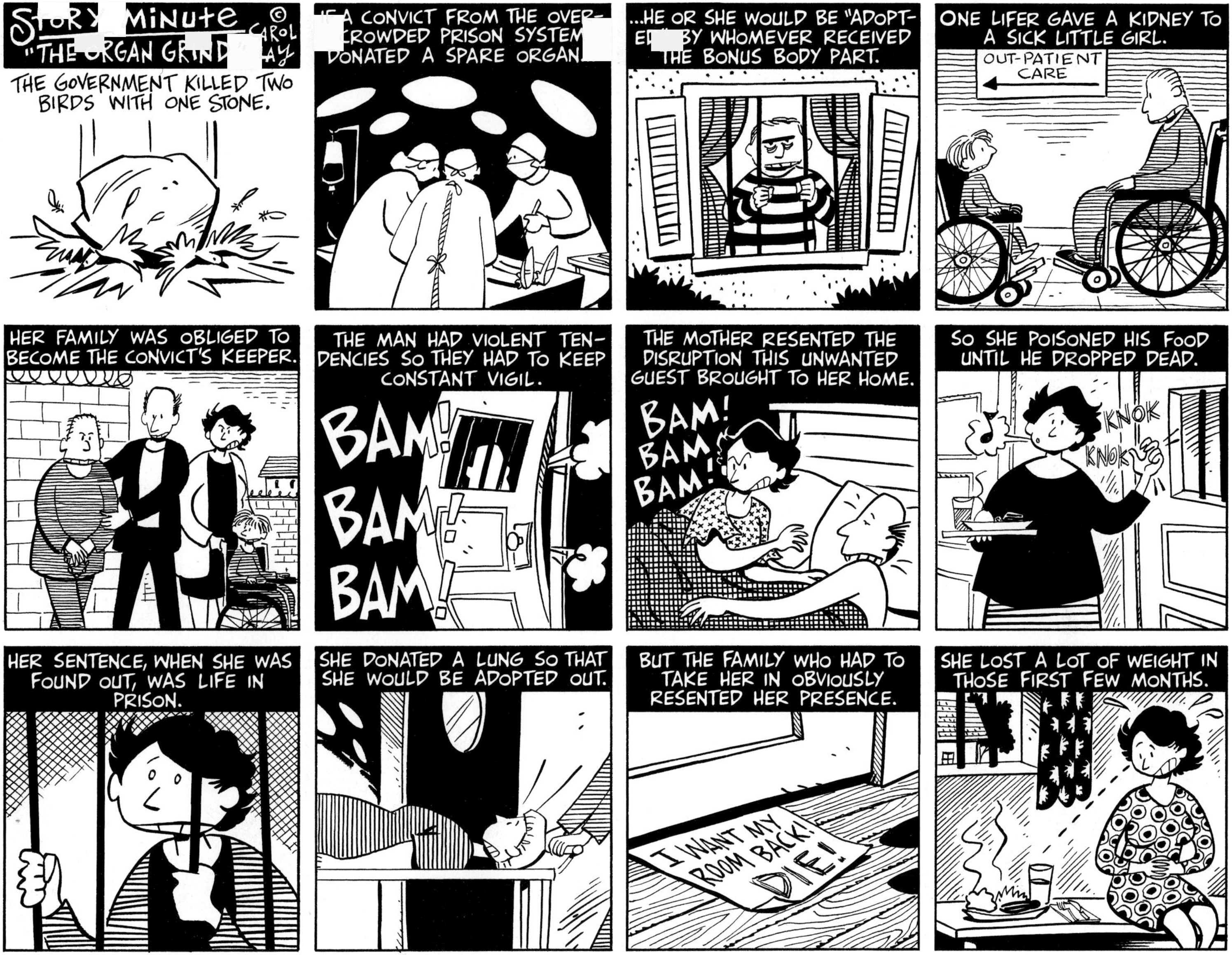

STORY MINUTE ©
"THE ORGAN GRIND
CAROL LAY
THE GOVERNMENT KILLED TWO BIRDS WITH ONE STONE.
A CONVICT FROM THE OVER-CROWDED PRISON SYSTEM DONATED A SPARE ORGAN
...HE OR SHE WOULD BE "ADOPT-ED" BY WHOMEVER RECEIVED THE BONUS BODY PART.
ONE LIFER GAVE A KIDNEY TO A SICK LITTLE GIRL.
OUT-PATIENT CARE
HER FAMILY WAS OBLIGED TO BECOME THE CONVICT'S KEEPER.
THE MAN HAD VIOLENT TEN-DENCIES SO THEY HAD TO KEEP CONSTANT VIGIL.
BAM! BAM! BAM!
THE MOTHER RESENTED THE DISRUPTION THIS UNWANTED GUEST BROUGHT TO HER HOME.
BAM! BAM! BAM!
SO SHE POISONED HIS FOOD UNTIL HE DROPPED DEAD.
KNOK KNOK
HER SENTENCE, WHEN SHE WAS FOUND OUT, WAS LIFE IN PRISON.
SHE DONATED A LUNG SO THAT SHE WOULD BE ADOPTED OUT.
BUT THE FAMILY WHO HAD TO TAKE HER IN OBVIOUSLY RESENTED HER PRESENCE.
I WANT MY ROOM BACK! DIE!
SHE LOST A LOT OF WEIGHT IN THOSE FIRST FEW MONTHS.

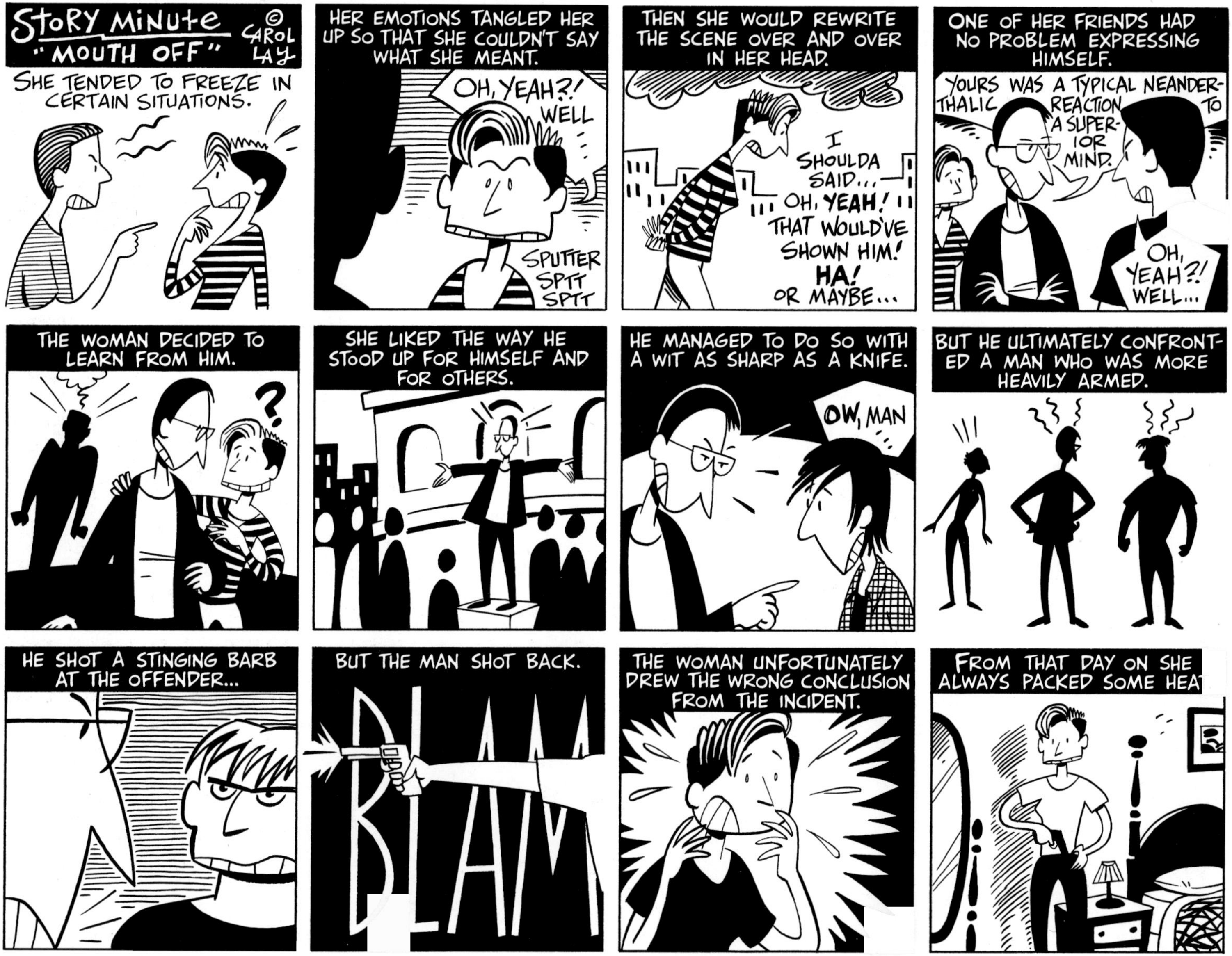

STORY MINUTE "MOUTH OFF"
© CAROL LAY
SHE TENDED TO FREEZE IN CERTAIN SITUATIONS.
HER EMOTIONS TANGLED HER UP SO THAT SHE COULDN'T SAY WHAT SHE MEANT.
OH, YEAH?! WELL
SPUTTER SPTT SPTT
THEN SHE WOULD REWRITE THE SCENE OVER AND OVER IN HER HEAD.
I SHOULDA SAID... OH, YEAH! THAT WOULD'VE SHOWN HIM! HA! OR MAYBE...
ONE OF HER FRIENDS HAD NO PROBLEM EXPRESSING HIMSELF.
YOURS WAS A TYPICAL NEANDERTHALIC REACTION TO A SUPERIOR MIND.
OH, YEAH?! WELL...
THE WOMAN DECIDED TO LEARN FROM HIM.
?
SHE LIKED THE WAY HE STOOD UP FOR HIMSELF AND FOR OTHERS.
HE MANAGED TO DO SO WITH A WIT AS SHARP AS A KNIFE.
OW, MAN
BUT HE ULTIMATELY CONFRONTED A MAN WHO WAS MORE HEAVILY ARMED.
HE SHOT A STINGING BARB AT THE OFFENDER...
BUT THE MAN SHOT BACK.
BLAM
THE WOMAN UNFORTUNATELY DREW THE WRONG CONCLUSION FROM THE INCIDENT.
FROM THAT DAY ON SHE ALWAYS PACKED SOME HEAT

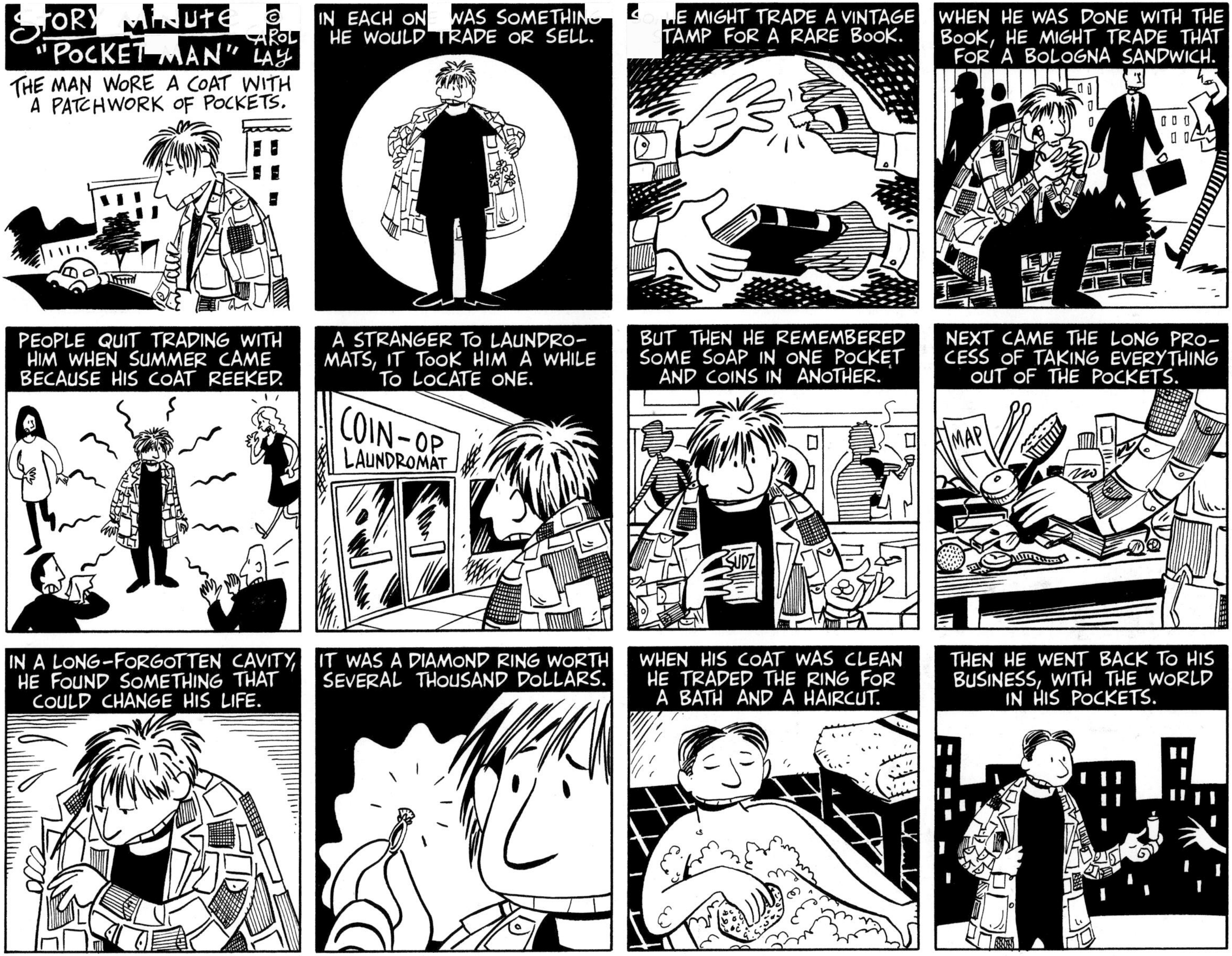
STORY MINUTE
©CAROL LAY
"POCKET MAN"
THE MAN WORE A COAT WITH A PATCHWORK OF POCKETS.
IN EACH ONE WAS SOMETHING HE WOULD TRADE OR SELL.
HE MIGHT TRADE A VINTAGE STAMP FOR A RARE BOOK.
WHEN HE WAS DONE WITH THE BOOK, HE MIGHT TRADE THAT FOR A BOLOGNA SANDWICH.
PEOPLE QUIT TRADING WITH HIM WHEN SUMMER CAME BECAUSE HIS COAT REEKED.
A STRANGER TO LAUNDROMATS, IT TOOK HIM A WHILE TO LOCATE ONE.
COIN-OP LAUNDROMAT
BUT THEN HE REMEMBERED SOME SOAP IN ONE POCKET AND COINS IN ANOTHER.
SUDZ
NEXT CAME THE LONG PROCESS OF TAKING EVERYTHING OUT OF THE POCKETS.
MAP
IN A LONG-FORGOTTEN CAVITY, HE FOUND SOMETHING THAT COULD CHANGE HIS LIFE.
IT WAS A DIAMOND RING WORTH SEVERAL THOUSAND DOLLARS.
WHEN HIS COAT WAS CLEAN HE TRADED THE RING FOR A BATH AND A HAIRCUT.
THEN HE WENT BACK TO HIS BUSINESS, WITH THE WORLD IN HIS POCKETS.

Story Minute
"JUDGMENT DAYS"
© CAROL LAY

Panel 1: HE WAS CONSTANTLY COMMENTING ON WOMEN'S LOOKS.

YOU'RE WAY TOO HEAVY IN THE UDDERS.

Panel 2: EVEN BEAUTIFUL WOMEN WERE HARD-PRESSED TO MEET HIS IDEALS.

SHE'LL HAVE A BIG BUTT WHEN SHE GETS OLD.

Panel 3: SO HE MARRIED ONE WHO CAME FROM STOCK THAT NEVER GREW FAT.

Panel 4: SHE SHARED HIS PREJUDICE AGAINST IMPERFECT PEOPLE...

HER ANKLES ARE THICK AS LAMP POSTS.

Panel 5: ...AND, TOGETHER, THEY RUINED THEIR CHILDREN.

DO YOU THINK HER NOSE IS TOO BIG?

Panel 6: THEIR SON GREW UP TO MEASURE PEOPLE THE SAME WAY HIS PARENTS DID.

YOU'RE AS FLAT AS A PANCAKE.

Panel 7: THEIR DAUGHTER WANTED TO LIVE UP TO ALL THEIR IDEALS...

Panel 8: BUT THOSE WERE BEYOND HER REACH.

Panel 9: AND, AS HARSH AS HER FAMILY WAS AT NOTING HER SHORTCOMINGS...

Panel 10: ...SHE HAD LEARNED FROM THEM ALL, AND EXCELLED AT IT, HERSELF.

Panel 11: SHE COULD SEE ONLY ONE WAY TO MAKE THEM ALL BE HAPPY WITH HER...

Panel 12: AND THAT WAS TO GIVE THEM PLENTY TO TALK ABOUT.

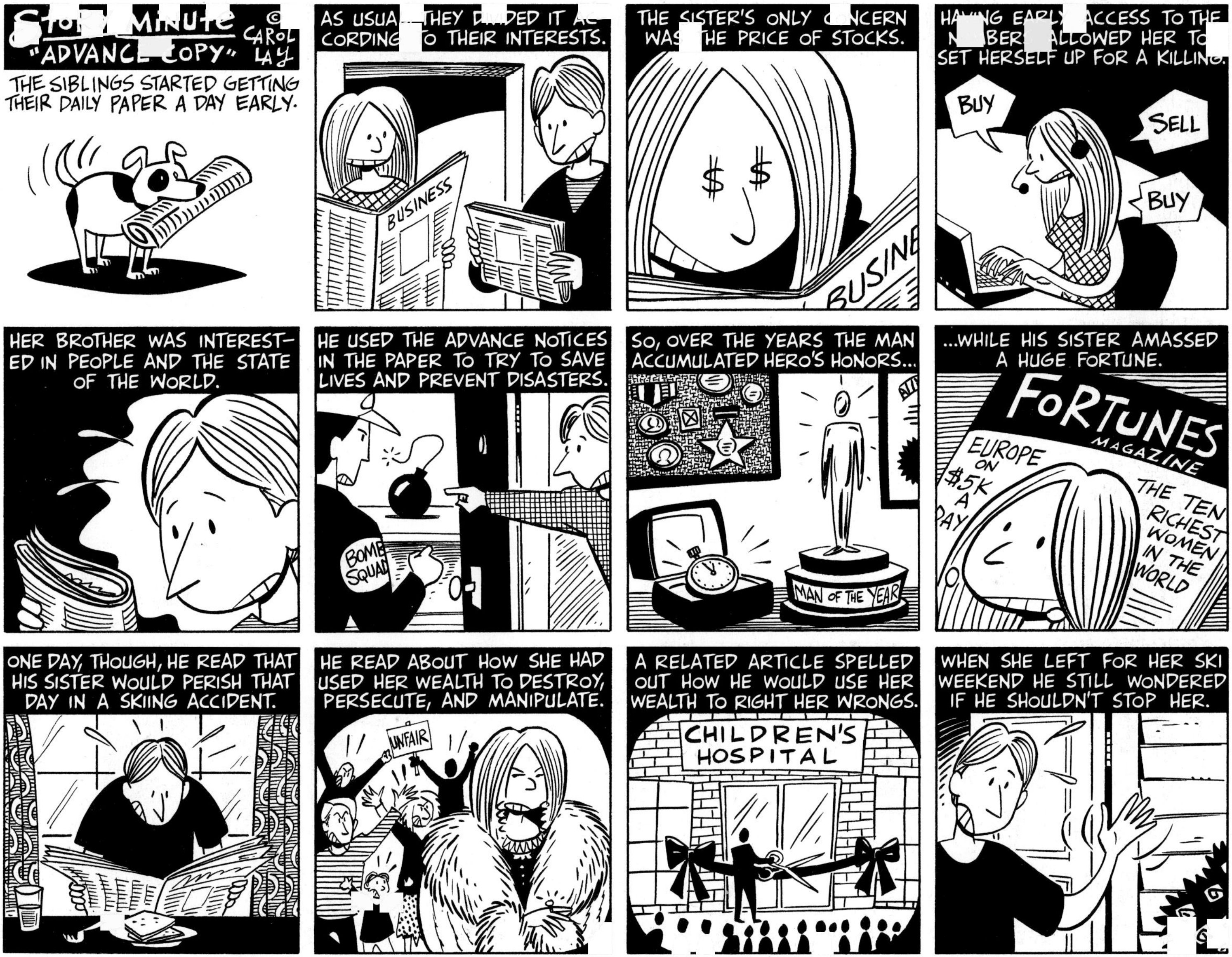

STORY MINUTE
"ADVANCE COPY"
© CAROL LAY
THE SIBLINGS STARTED GETTING THEIR DAILY PAPER A DAY EARLY.
AS USUAL, THEY DIVIDED IT ACCORDING TO THEIR INTERESTS.
BUSINESS
THE SISTER'S ONLY CONCERN WAS THE PRICE OF STOCKS.
$ $
BUSINE
HAVING EARLY ACCESS TO THE NUMBERS ALLOWED HER TO SET HERSELF UP FOR A KILLING.
BUY
SELL
BUY
HER BROTHER WAS INTERESTED IN PEOPLE AND THE STATE OF THE WORLD.
HE USED THE ADVANCE NOTICES IN THE PAPER TO TRY TO SAVE LIVES AND PREVENT DISASTERS.
BOMB SQUAD
SO, OVER THE YEARS THE MAN ACCUMULATED HERO'S HONORS...
MAN OF THE YEAR
...WHILE HIS SISTER AMASSED A HUGE FORTUNE.
FORTUNES MAGAZINE
EUROPE ON $5K A DAY
THE TEN RICHEST WOMEN IN THE WORLD
ONE DAY, THOUGH, HE READ THAT HIS SISTER WOULD PERISH THAT DAY IN A SKIING ACCIDENT.
HE READ ABOUT HOW SHE HAD USED HER WEALTH TO DESTROY, PERSECUTE, AND MANIPULATE.
UNFAIR
A RELATED ARTICLE SPELLED OUT HOW HE WOULD USE HER WEALTH TO RIGHT HER WRONGS.
CHILDREN'S HOSPITAL
WHEN SHE LEFT FOR HER SKI WEEKEND HE STILL WONDERED IF HE SHOULDN'T STOP HER.

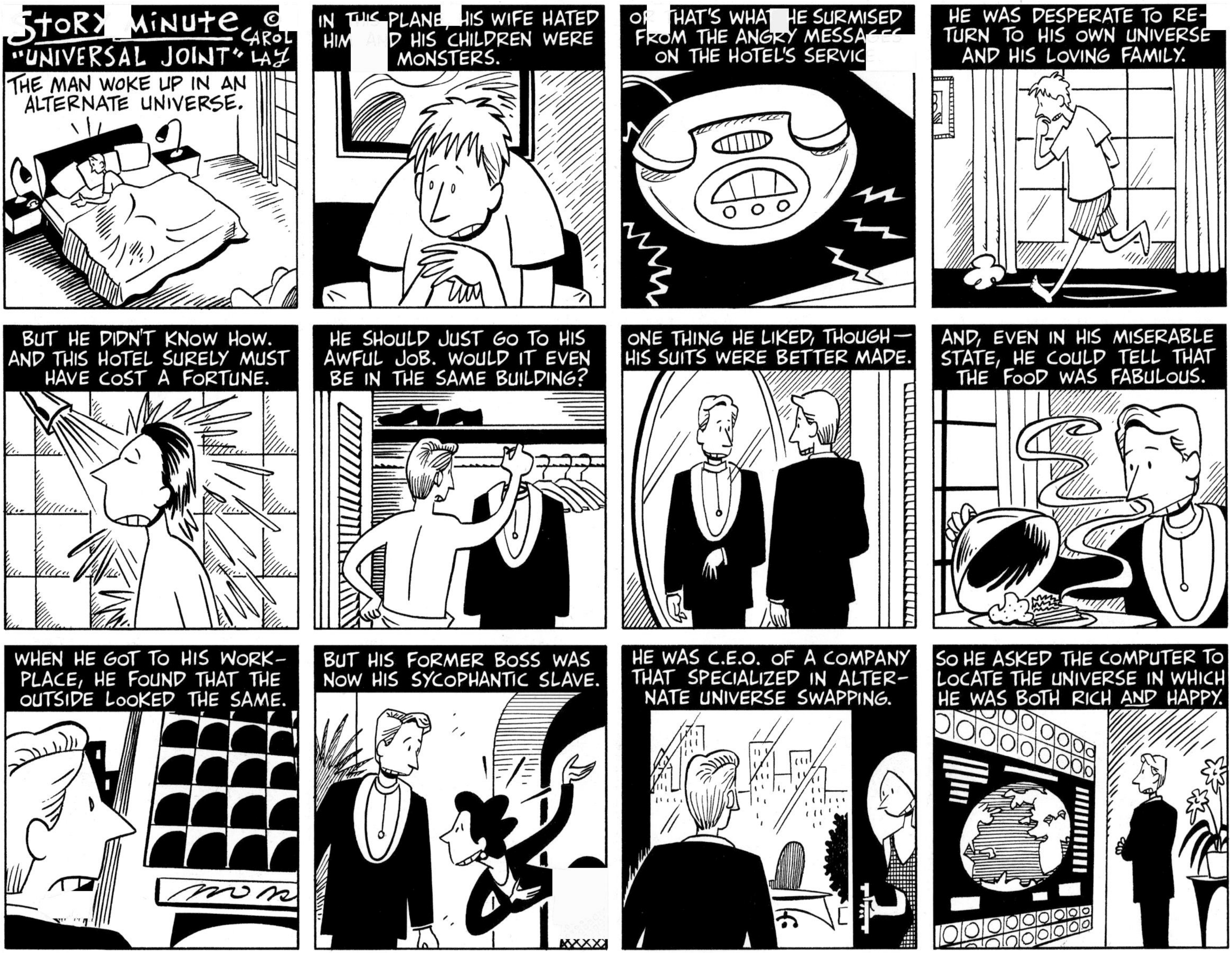

StorY Minute
©CAROL LAY
"UNIVERSAL JOINT"
THE MAN WOKE UP IN AN ALTERNATE UNIVERSE.
IN THIS PLANE, HIS WIFE HATED HIM AND HIS CHILDREN WERE MONSTERS.
OR THAT'S WHAT HE SURMISED FROM THE ANGRY MESSAGES ON THE HOTEL'S SERVIC
HE WAS DESPERATE TO RETURN TO HIS OWN UNIVERSE AND HIS LOVING FAMILY.
BUT HE DIDN'T KNOW HOW. AND THIS HOTEL SURELY MUST HAVE COST A FORTUNE.
HE SHOULD JUST GO TO HIS AWFUL JOB. WOULD IT EVEN BE IN THE SAME BUILDING?
ONE THING HE LIKED, THOUGH— HIS SUITS WERE BETTER MADE.
AND, EVEN IN HIS MISERABLE STATE, HE COULD TELL THAT THE FOOD WAS FABULOUS.
WHEN HE GOT TO HIS WORKPLACE, HE FOUND THAT THE OUTSIDE LOOKED THE SAME.
BUT HIS FORMER BOSS WAS NOW HIS SYCOPHANTIC SLAVE.
HE WAS C.E.O. OF A COMPANY THAT SPECIALIZED IN ALTERNATE UNIVERSE SWAPPING.
SO HE ASKED THE COMPUTER TO LOCATE THE UNIVERSE IN WHICH HE WAS BOTH RICH AND HAPPY.

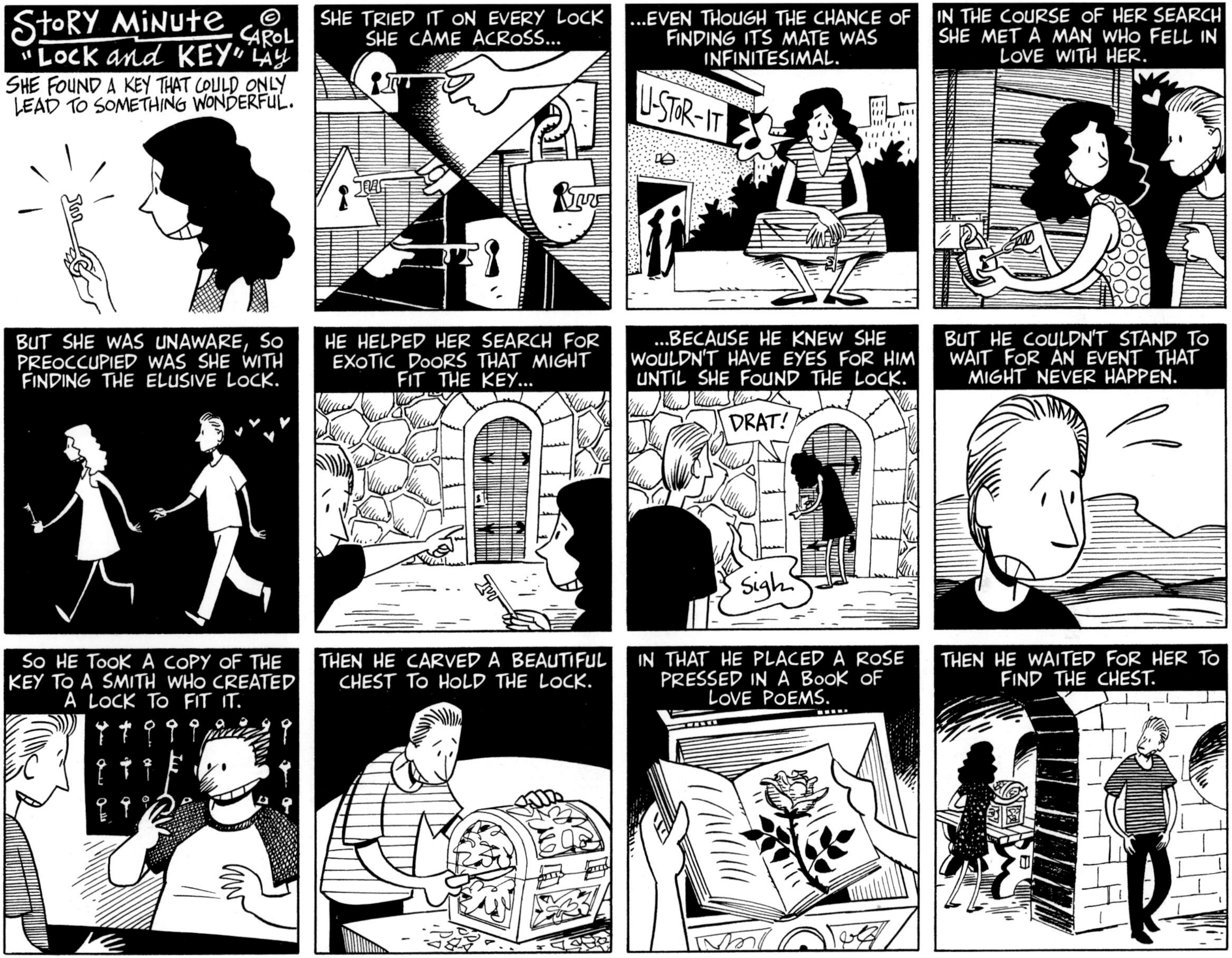
STORY MINUTE "LOCK and KEY" © CAROL LAY
SHE FOUND A KEY THAT COULD ONLY LEAD TO SOMETHING WONDERFUL.
SHE TRIED IT ON EVERY LOCK SHE CAME ACROSS...
...EVEN THOUGH THE CHANCE OF FINDING ITS MATE WAS INFINITESIMAL.
U-STOR-IT
IN THE COURSE OF HER SEARCH SHE MET A MAN WHO FELL IN LOVE WITH HER.
BUT SHE WAS UNAWARE, SO PREOCCUPIED WAS SHE WITH FINDING THE ELUSIVE LOCK.
HE HELPED HER SEARCH FOR EXOTIC DOORS THAT MIGHT FIT THE KEY...
...BECAUSE HE KNEW SHE WOULDN'T HAVE EYES FOR HIM UNTIL SHE FOUND THE LOCK.
DRAT!
Sigh.
BUT HE COULDN'T STAND TO WAIT FOR AN EVENT THAT MIGHT NEVER HAPPEN.
SO HE TOOK A COPY OF THE KEY TO A SMITH WHO CREATED A LOCK TO FIT IT.
THEN HE CARVED A BEAUTIFUL CHEST TO HOLD THE LOCK.
IN THAT HE PLACED A ROSE PRESSED IN A BOOK OF LOVE POEMS.
THEN HE WAITED FOR HER TO FIND THE CHEST.

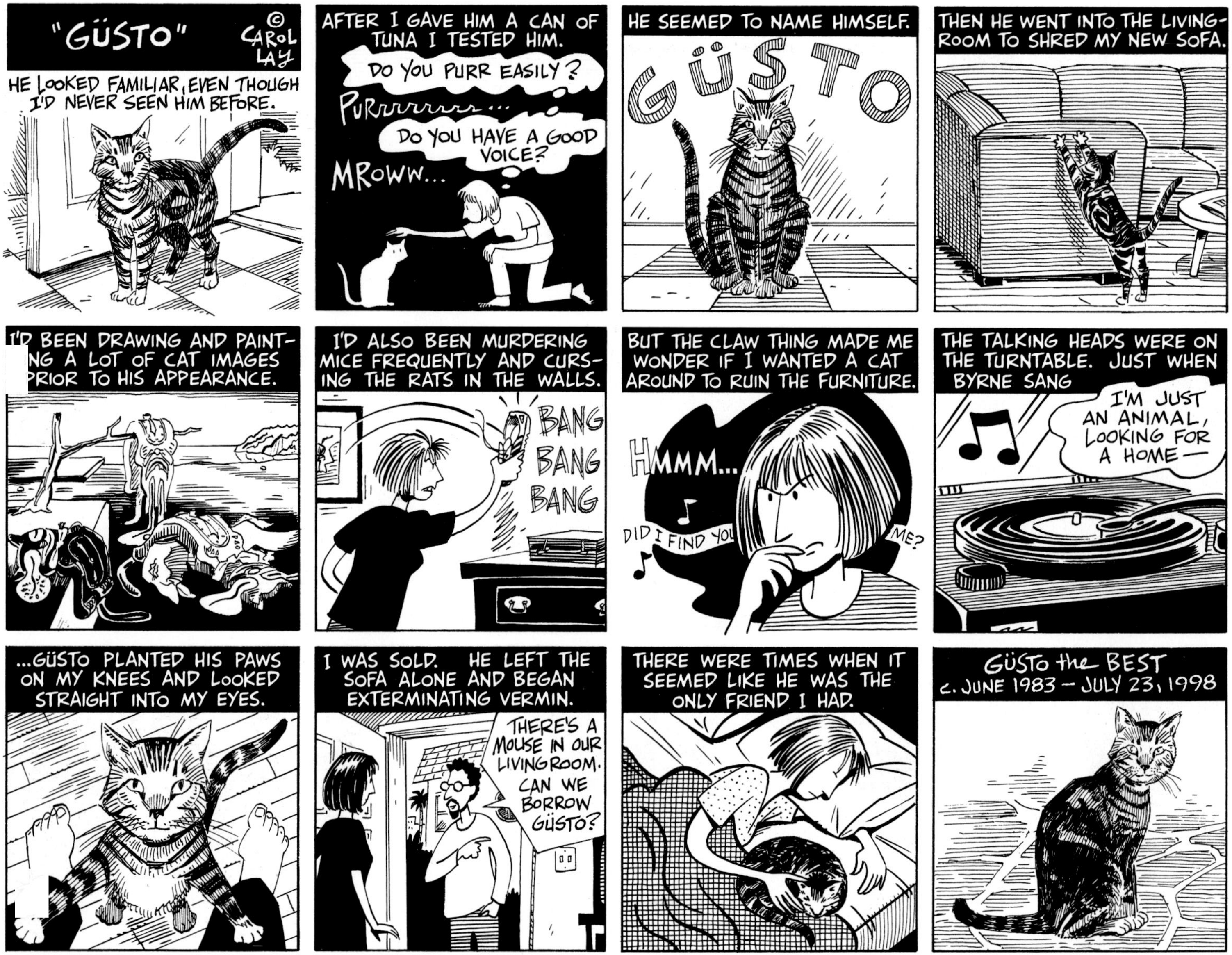
"GÜSTO"
© CAROL LAY
HE LOOKED FAMILIAR, EVEN THOUGH I'D NEVER SEEN HIM BEFORE.
AFTER I GAVE HIM A CAN OF TUNA I TESTED HIM.
DO YOU PURR EASILY?
PURRRRRRRR...
DO YOU HAVE A GOOD VOICE?
MROWW...
HE SEEMED TO NAME HIMSELF.
GÜSTO
THEN HE WENT INTO THE LIVING-ROOM TO SHRED MY NEW SOFA.
I'D BEEN DRAWING AND PAINT-
NG A LOT OF CAT IMAGES
PRIOR TO HIS APPEARANCE.
I'D ALSO BEEN MURDERING MICE FREQUENTLY AND CURSING THE RATS IN THE WALLS.
BANG BANG BANG
BUT THE CLAW THING MADE ME WONDER IF I WANTED A CAT AROUND TO RUIN THE FURNITURE.
HMMM...
DID I FIND YOU
ME?
THE TALKING HEADS WERE ON THE TURNTABLE. JUST WHEN BYRNE SANG
I'M JUST AN ANIMAL, LOOKING FOR A HOME—
...GÜSTO PLANTED HIS PAWS ON MY KNEES AND LOOKED STRAIGHT INTO MY EYES.
I WAS SOLD. HE LEFT THE SOFA ALONE AND BEGAN EXTERMINATING VERMIN.
THERE'S A MOUSE IN OUR LIVING ROOM. CAN WE BORROW GÜSTO?
THERE WERE TIMES WHEN IT SEEMED LIKE HE WAS THE ONLY FRIEND I HAD.
GÜSTO the BEST
c. JUNE 1983 — JULY 23, 1998

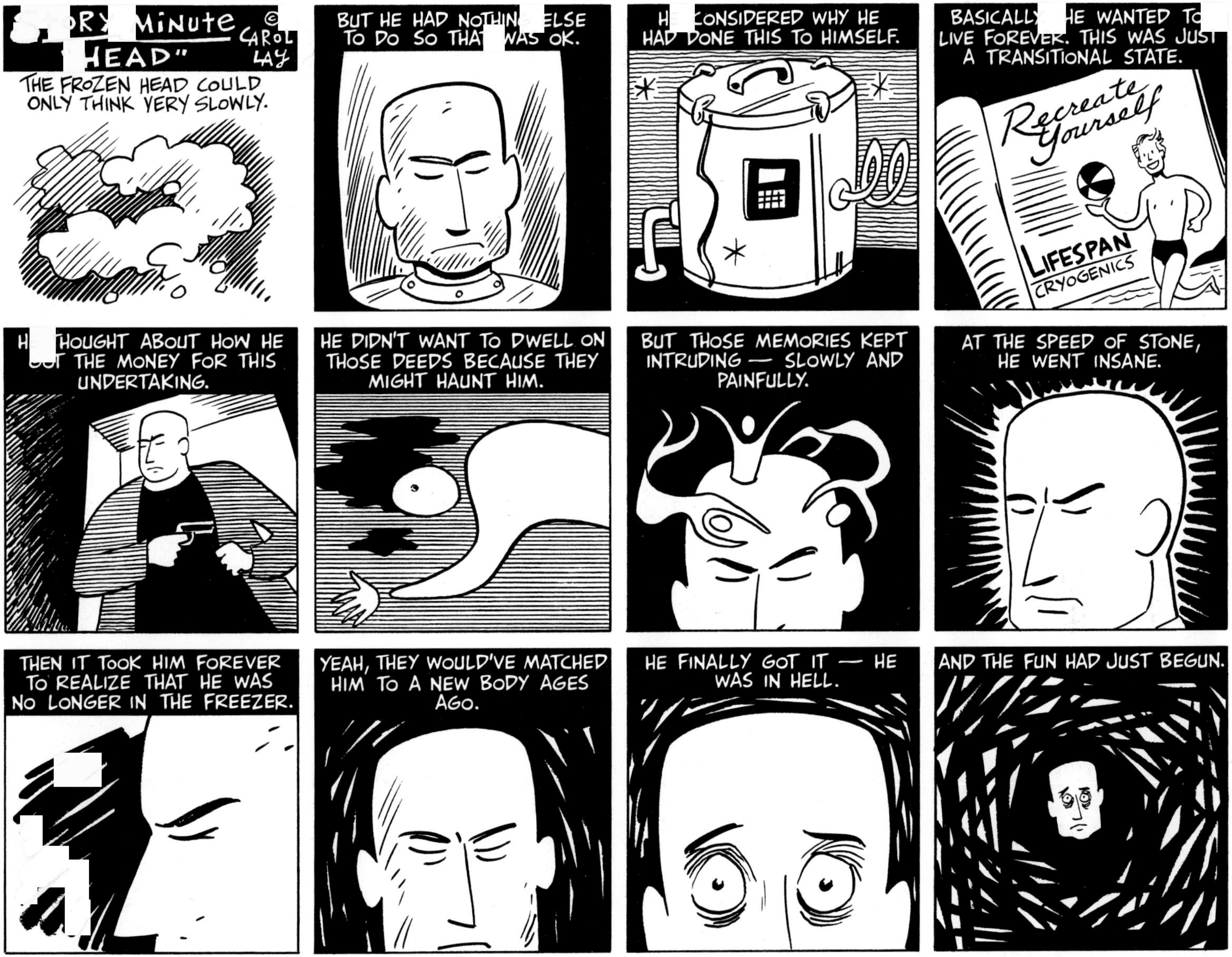
ORY Minute
"HEAD"
© CAROL LAY
THE FROZEN HEAD COULD ONLY THINK VERY SLOWLY.
BUT HE HAD NOTHING ELSE TO DO SO THAT WAS OK.
HE CONSIDERED WHY HE HAD DONE THIS TO HIMSELF.
BASICALLY, HE WANTED TO LIVE FOREVER. THIS WAS JUST A TRANSITIONAL STATE.
Recreate Yourself
LIFESPAN CRYOGENICS
HE THOUGHT ABOUT HOW HE GOT THE MONEY FOR THIS UNDERTAKING.
HE DIDN'T WANT TO DWELL ON THOSE DEEDS BECAUSE THEY MIGHT HAUNT HIM.
BUT THOSE MEMORIES KEPT INTRUDING — SLOWLY AND PAINFULLY.
AT THE SPEED OF STONE, HE WENT INSANE.
THEN IT TOOK HIM FOREVER TO REALIZE THAT HE WAS NO LONGER IN THE FREEZER.
YEAH, THEY WOULD'VE MATCHED HIM TO A NEW BODY AGES AGO.
HE FINALLY GOT IT — HE WAS IN HELL.
AND THE FUN HAD JUST BEGUN.

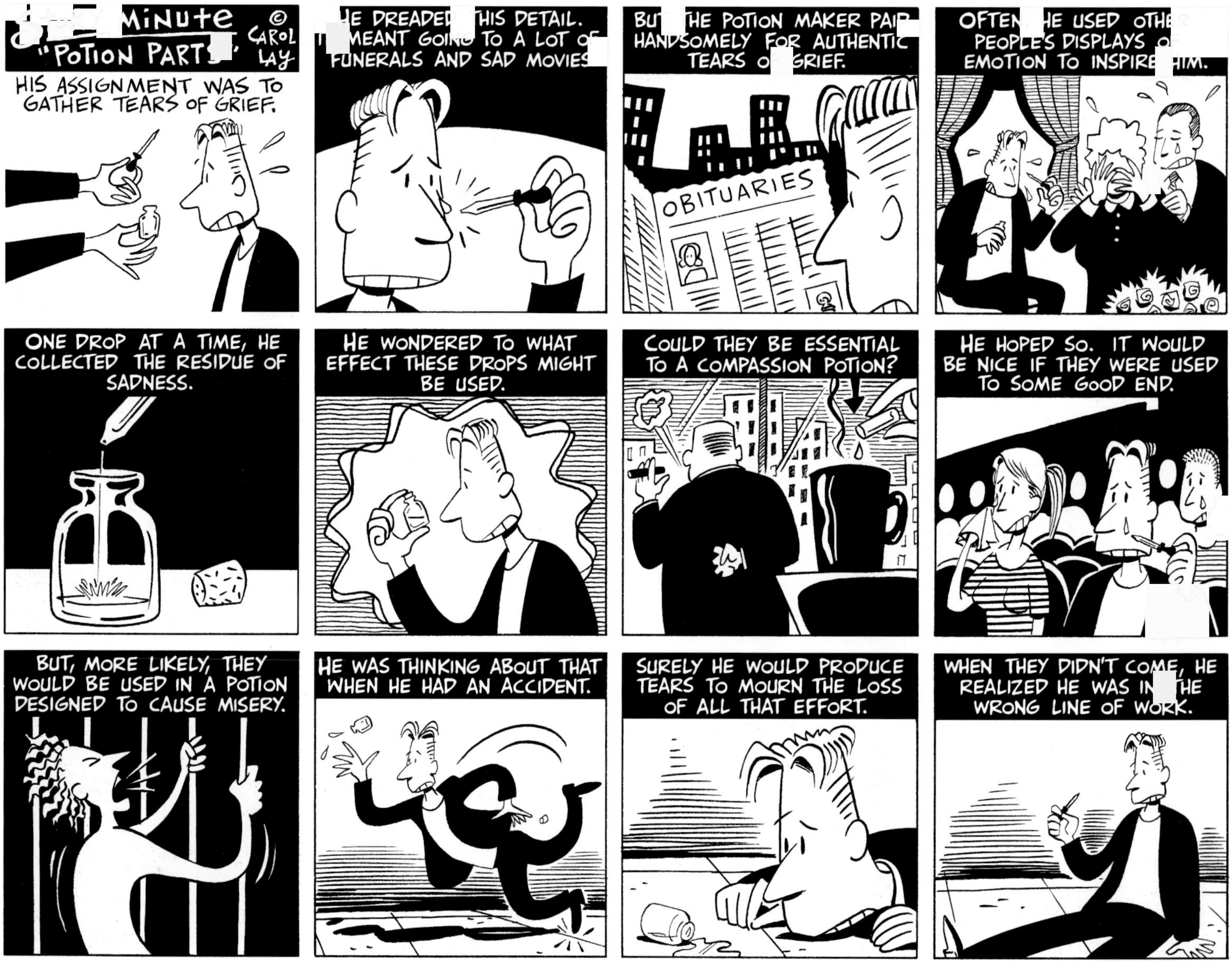
MINUTE
"POTION PART
© CAROL LAY
HIS ASSIGNMENT WAS TO GATHER TEARS OF GRIEF.
E DREADE HIS DETAIL. MEANT GOING TO A LOT OF FUNERALS AND SAD MOVIES
BU HE POTION MAKER PAI HANDSOMELY FOR AUTHENTIC TEARS O GRIEF.
OBITUARIES
OFTEN HE USED OTHE PEOPLE'S DISPLAYS O EMOTION TO INSPIRE HIM.
ONE DROP AT A TIME, HE COLLECTED THE RESIDUE OF SADNESS.
HE WONDERED TO WHAT EFFECT THESE DROPS MIGHT BE USED.
COULD THEY BE ESSENTIAL TO A COMPASSION POTION?
HE HOPED SO. IT WOULD BE NICE IF THEY WERE USED TO SOME GOOD END.
BUT, MORE LIKELY, THEY WOULD BE USED IN A POTION DESIGNED TO CAUSE MISERY.
HE WAS THINKING ABOUT THAT WHEN HE HAD AN ACCIDENT.
SURELY HE WOULD PRODUCE TEARS TO MOURN THE LOSS OF ALL THAT EFFORT.
WHEN THEY DIDN'T COME, HE REALIZED HE WAS IN HE WRONG LINE OF WO K.

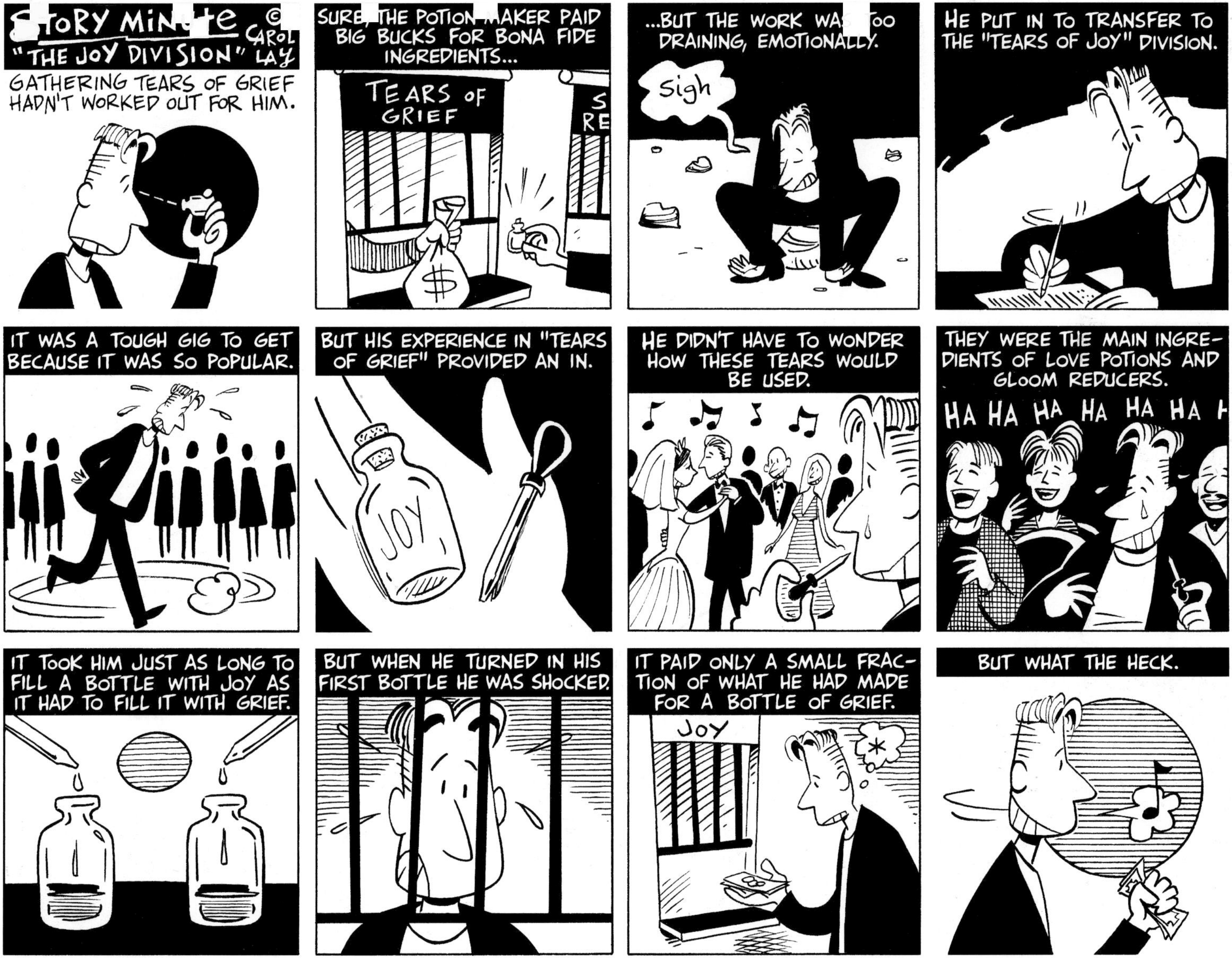
STORY MINUTE © CAROL LAY
"THE JOY DIVISION"
GATHERING TEARS OF GRIEF HADN'T WORKED OUT FOR HIM.
SURE, THE POTION MAKER PAID BIG BUCKS FOR BONA FIDE INGREDIENTS...
TEARS OF GRIEF
...BUT THE WORK WAS TOO DRAINING, EMOTIONALLY.
Sigh
HE PUT IN TO TRANSFER TO THE "TEARS OF JOY" DIVISION.
IT WAS A TOUGH GIG TO GET BECAUSE IT WAS SO POPULAR.
BUT HIS EXPERIENCE IN "TEARS OF GRIEF" PROVIDED AN IN.
JOY
HE DIDN'T HAVE TO WONDER HOW THESE TEARS WOULD BE USED.
THEY WERE THE MAIN INGREDIENTS OF LOVE POTIONS AND GLOOM REDUCERS.
HA HA HA HA HA HA
IT TOOK HIM JUST AS LONG TO FILL A BOTTLE WITH JOY AS IT HAD TO FILL IT WITH GRIEF.
BUT WHEN HE TURNED IN HIS FIRST BOTTLE HE WAS SHOCKED.
IT PAID ONLY A SMALL FRACTION OF WHAT HE HAD MADE FOR A BOTTLE OF GRIEF.
JOY
BUT WHAT THE HECK.

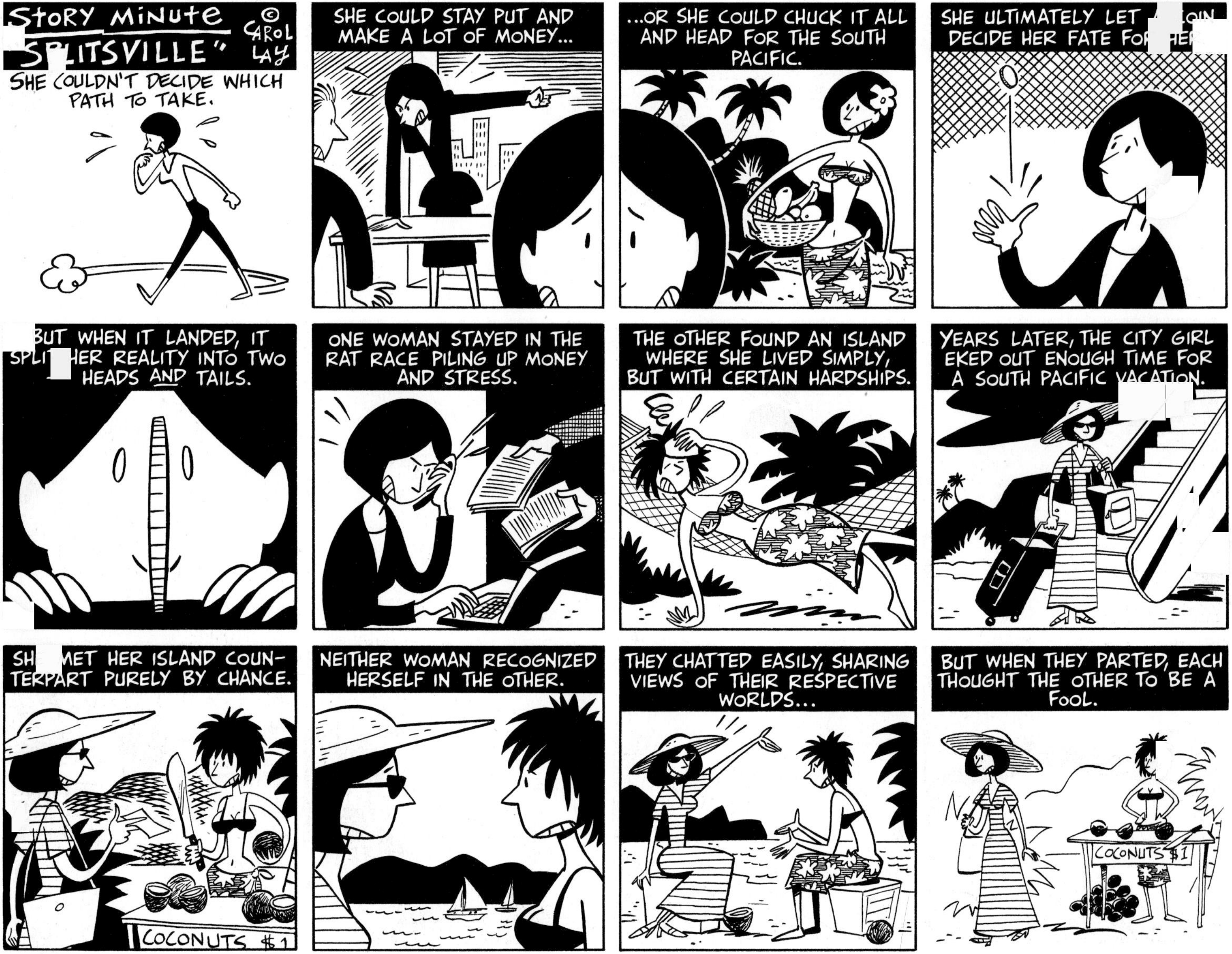
STORY MINUTE
"SPLITSVILLE"
© CAROL LAY
SHE COULDN'T DECIDE WHICH PATH TO TAKE.
SHE COULD STAY PUT AND MAKE A LOT OF MONEY...
...OR SHE COULD CHUCK IT ALL AND HEAD FOR THE SOUTH PACIFIC.
SHE ULTIMATELY LET A COIN DECIDE HER FATE FOR HER.
BUT WHEN IT LANDED, IT SPLIT HER REALITY INTO TWO HEADS AND TAILS.
ONE WOMAN STAYED IN THE RAT RACE PILING UP MONEY AND STRESS.
THE OTHER FOUND AN ISLAND WHERE SHE LIVED SIMPLY, BUT WITH CERTAIN HARDSHIPS.
YEARS LATER, THE CITY GIRL EKED OUT ENOUGH TIME FOR A SOUTH PACIFIC VACATION.
SHE MET HER ISLAND COUNTERPART PURELY BY CHANCE.
COCONUTS $1
NEITHER WOMAN RECOGNIZED HERSELF IN THE OTHER.
THEY CHATTED EASILY, SHARING VIEWS OF THEIR RESPECTIVE WORLDS...
BUT WHEN THEY PARTED, EACH THOUGHT THE OTHER TO BE A FOOL.
COCONUTS $1

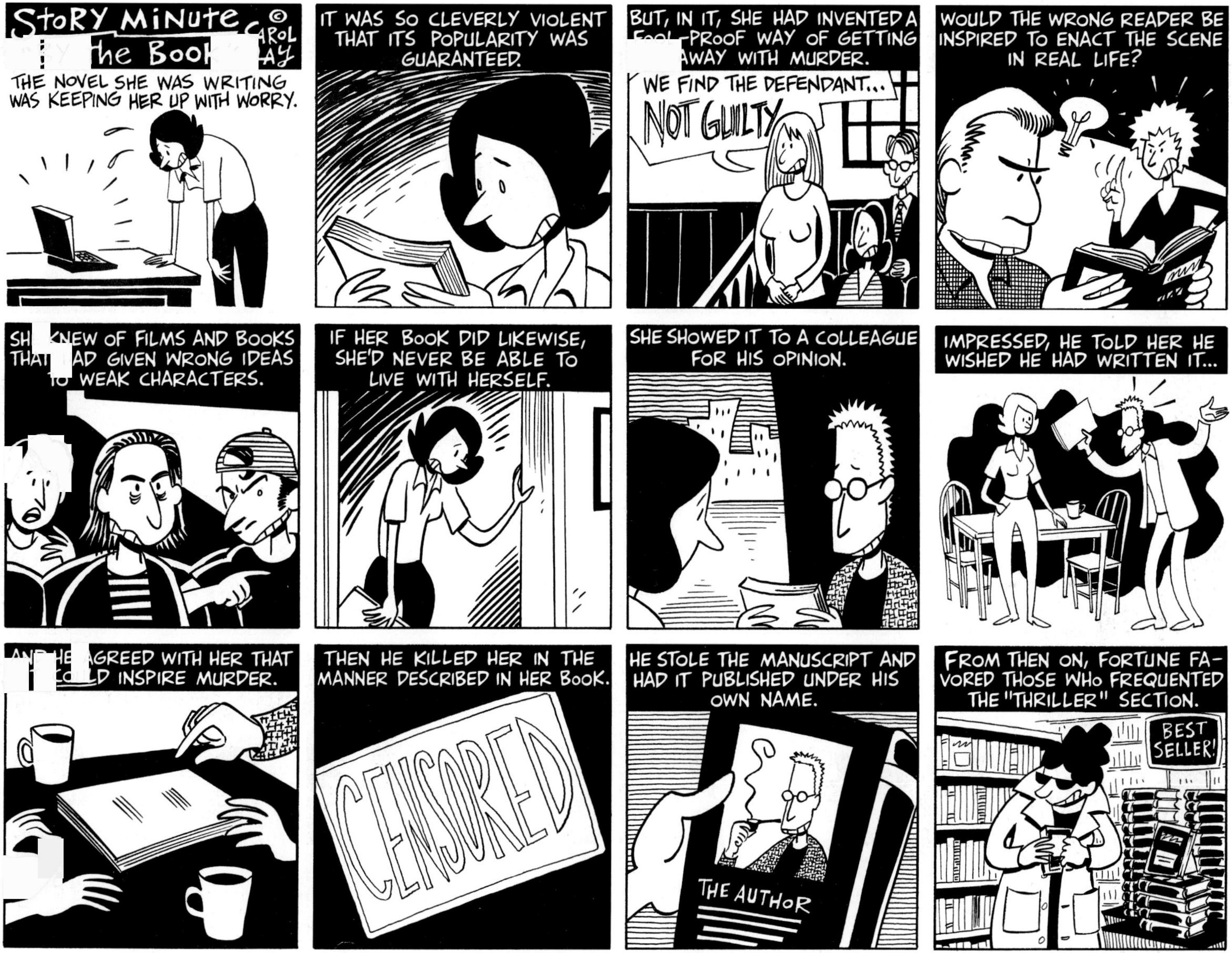
STORY MINUTE
the Book
© CAROL LAY
THE NOVEL SHE WAS WRITING WAS KEEPING HER UP WITH WORRY.
IT WAS SO CLEVERLY VIOLENT THAT ITS POPULARITY WAS GUARANTEED.
BUT, IN IT, SHE HAD INVENTED A …PROOF WAY OF GETTING AWAY WITH MURDER.
WE FIND THE DEFENDANT...
NOT GUILTY
WOULD THE WRONG READER BE INSPIRED TO ENACT THE SCENE IN REAL LIFE?
SH… KNEW OF FILMS AND BOOKS THA… AD GIVEN WRONG IDEAS …O WEAK CHARACTERS.
IF HER BOOK DID LIKEWISE, SHE'D NEVER BE ABLE TO LIVE WITH HERSELF.
SHE SHOWED IT TO A COLLEAGUE FOR HIS OPINION.
IMPRESSED, HE TOLD HER HE WISHED HE HAD WRITTEN IT...
…HE AGREED WITH HER THAT …OULD INSPIRE MURDER.
THEN HE KILLED HER IN THE MANNER DESCRIBED IN HER BOOK.
CENSORED
HE STOLE THE MANUSCRIPT AND HAD IT PUBLISHED UNDER HIS OWN NAME.
THE AUTHOR
FROM THEN ON, FORTUNE FAVORED THOSE WHO FREQUENTED THE "THRILLER" SECTION.
BEST SELLER!

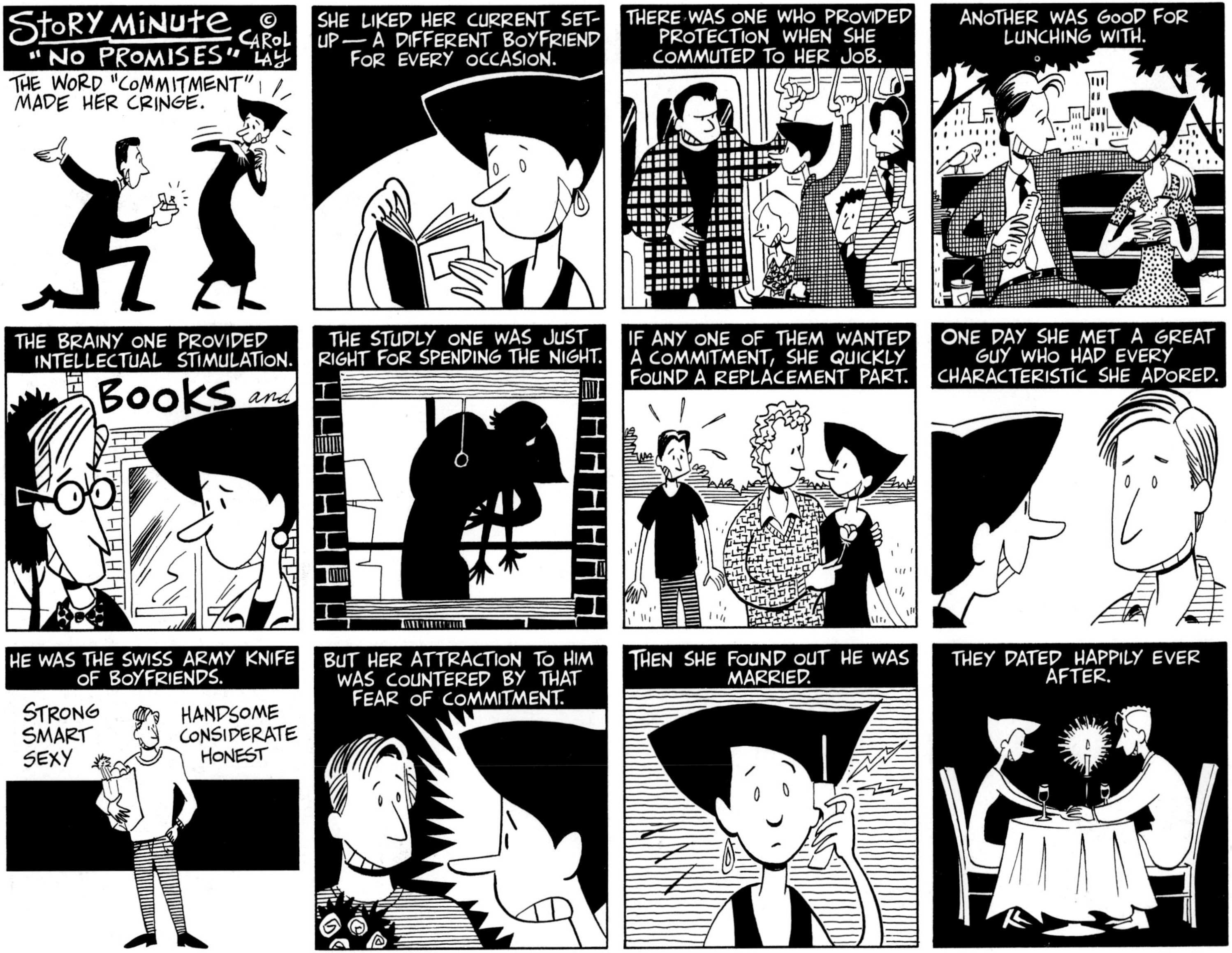

STORY MINUTE
"NO PROMISES"
© CAROL LAY
THE WORD "COMMITMENT" MADE HER CRINGE.
SHE LIKED HER CURRENT SET-UP — A DIFFERENT BOYFRIEND FOR EVERY OCCASION.
THERE WAS ONE WHO PROVIDED PROTECTION WHEN SHE COMMUTED TO HER JOB.
ANOTHER WAS GOOD FOR LUNCHING WITH.
THE BRAINY ONE PROVIDED INTELLECTUAL STIMULATION.
BOOKS and
THE STUDLY ONE WAS JUST RIGHT FOR SPENDING THE NIGHT.
IF ANY ONE OF THEM WANTED A COMMITMENT, SHE QUICKLY FOUND A REPLACEMENT PART.
ONE DAY SHE MET A GREAT GUY WHO HAD EVERY CHARACTERISTIC SHE ADORED.
HE WAS THE SWISS ARMY KNIFE OF BOYFRIENDS.
STRONG
SMART
SEXY
HANDSOME
CONSIDERATE
HONEST
BUT HER ATTRACTION TO HIM WAS COUNTERED BY THAT FEAR OF COMMITMENT.
THEN SHE FOUND OUT HE WAS MARRIED.
THEY DATED HAPPILY EVER AFTER.

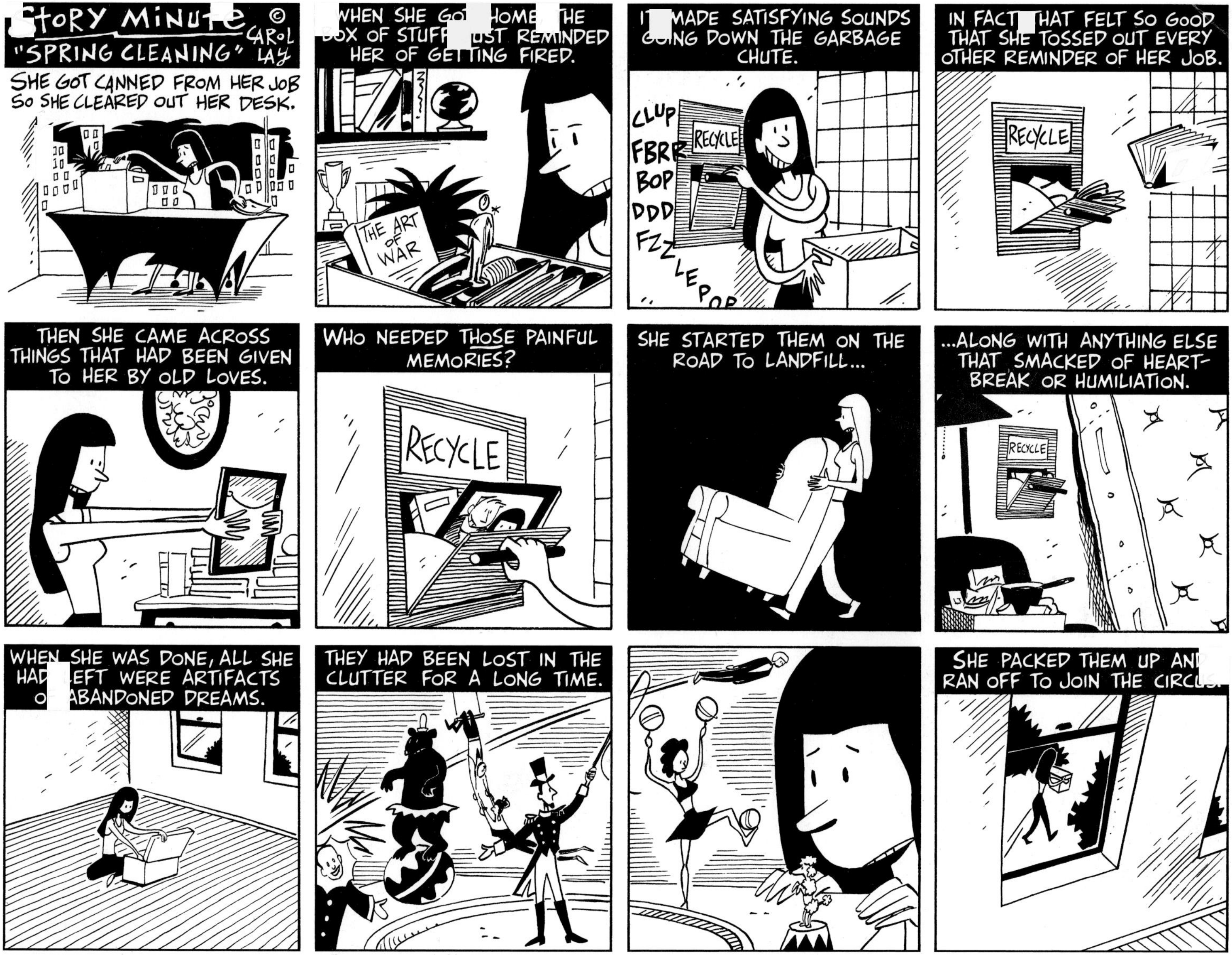
STORY MINUTE © CAROL LAY
"SPRING CLEANING"
SHE GOT CANNED FROM HER JOB SO SHE CLEARED OUT HER DESK.
WHEN SHE GOT HOME, THE BOX OF STUFF JUST REMINDED HER OF GETTING FIRED.
THE ART OF WAR
IT MADE SATISFYING SOUNDS GOING DOWN THE GARBAGE CHUTE.
RECYCLE
CLUP
FBRR
BOP
DDD
FZZLEPOP
IN FACT, THAT FELT SO GOOD THAT SHE TOSSED OUT EVERY OTHER REMINDER OF HER JOB.
RECYCLE
THEN SHE CAME ACROSS THINGS THAT HAD BEEN GIVEN TO HER BY OLD LOVES.
WHO NEEDED THOSE PAINFUL MEMORIES?
RECYCLE
SHE STARTED THEM ON THE ROAD TO LANDFILL...
...ALONG WITH ANYTHING ELSE THAT SMACKED OF HEART-BREAK OR HUMILIATION.
RECYCLE
WHEN SHE WAS DONE, ALL SHE HAD LEFT WERE ARTIFACTS OF ABANDONED DREAMS.
THEY HAD BEEN LOST IN THE CLUTTER FOR A LONG TIME.
SHE PACKED THEM UP AND RAN OFF TO JOIN THE CIRCUS.

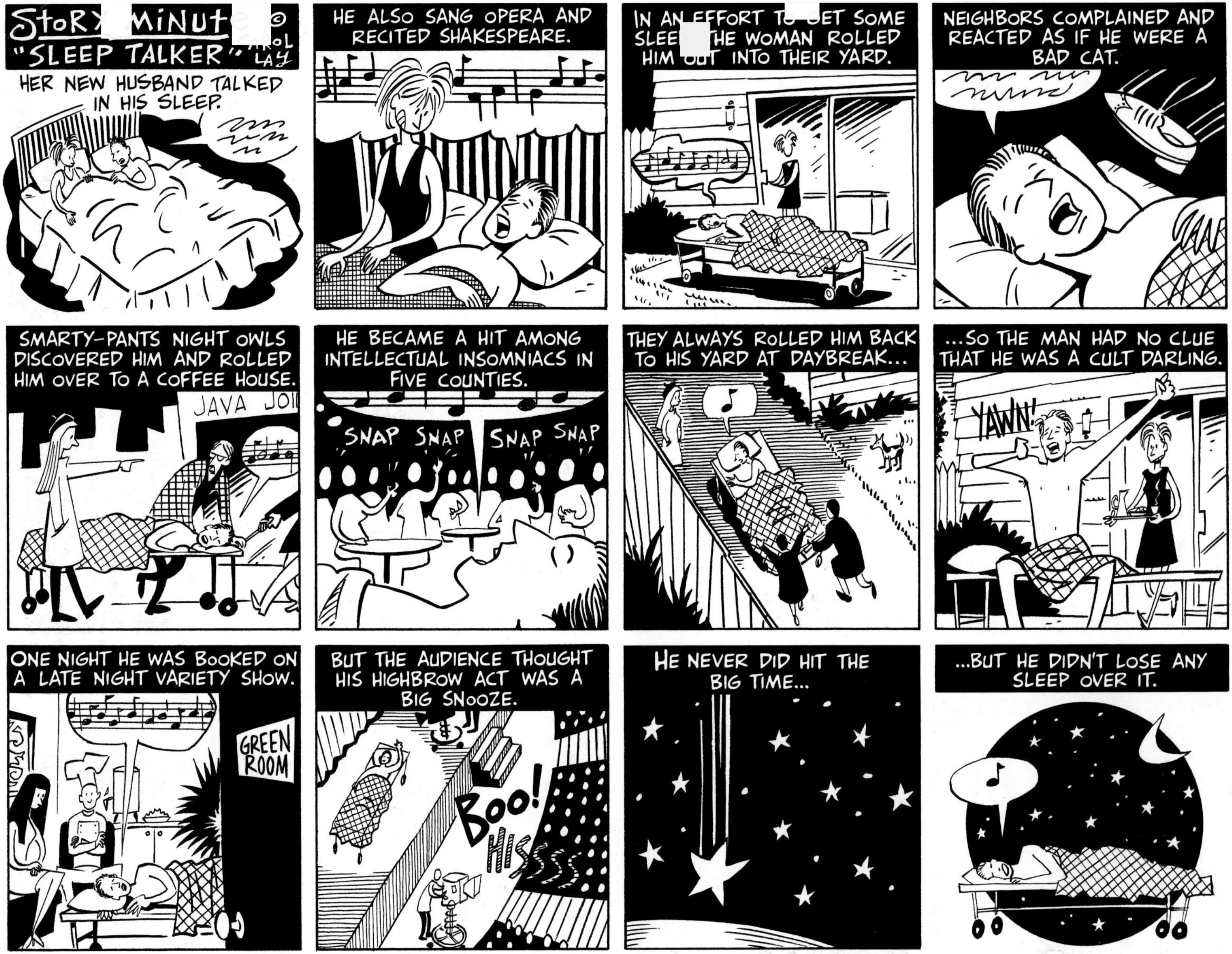

StoRY MiNUT…
"SLEEP TALKER" © …ROL LAY
HER NEW HUSBAND TALKED IN HIS SLEEP.
HE ALSO SANG OPERA AND RECITED SHAKESPEARE.
IN AN …FFORT TO …ET SOME SLEE… THE WOMAN ROLLED HIM OUT INTO THEIR YARD.
NEIGHBORS COMPLAINED AND REACTED AS IF HE WERE A BAD CAT.
SMARTY-PANTS NIGHT OWLS DISCOVERED HIM AND ROLLED HIM OVER TO A COFFEE HOUSE.
JAVA JO
HE BECAME A HIT AMONG INTELLECTUAL INSOMNIACS IN FIVE COUNTIES.
SNAP SNAP SNAP SNAP
THEY ALWAYS ROLLED HIM BACK TO HIS YARD AT DAYBREAK...
...SO THE MAN HAD NO CLUE THAT HE WAS A CULT DARLING.
YAWN!
ONE NIGHT HE WAS BOOKED ON A LATE NIGHT VARIETY SHOW.
GREEN ROOM
BUT THE AUDIENCE THOUGHT HIS HIGHBROW ACT WAS A BIG SNOOZE.
BOO!
HISSS
HE NEVER DID HIT THE BIG TIME...
...BUT HE DIDN'T LOSE ANY SLEEP OVER IT.

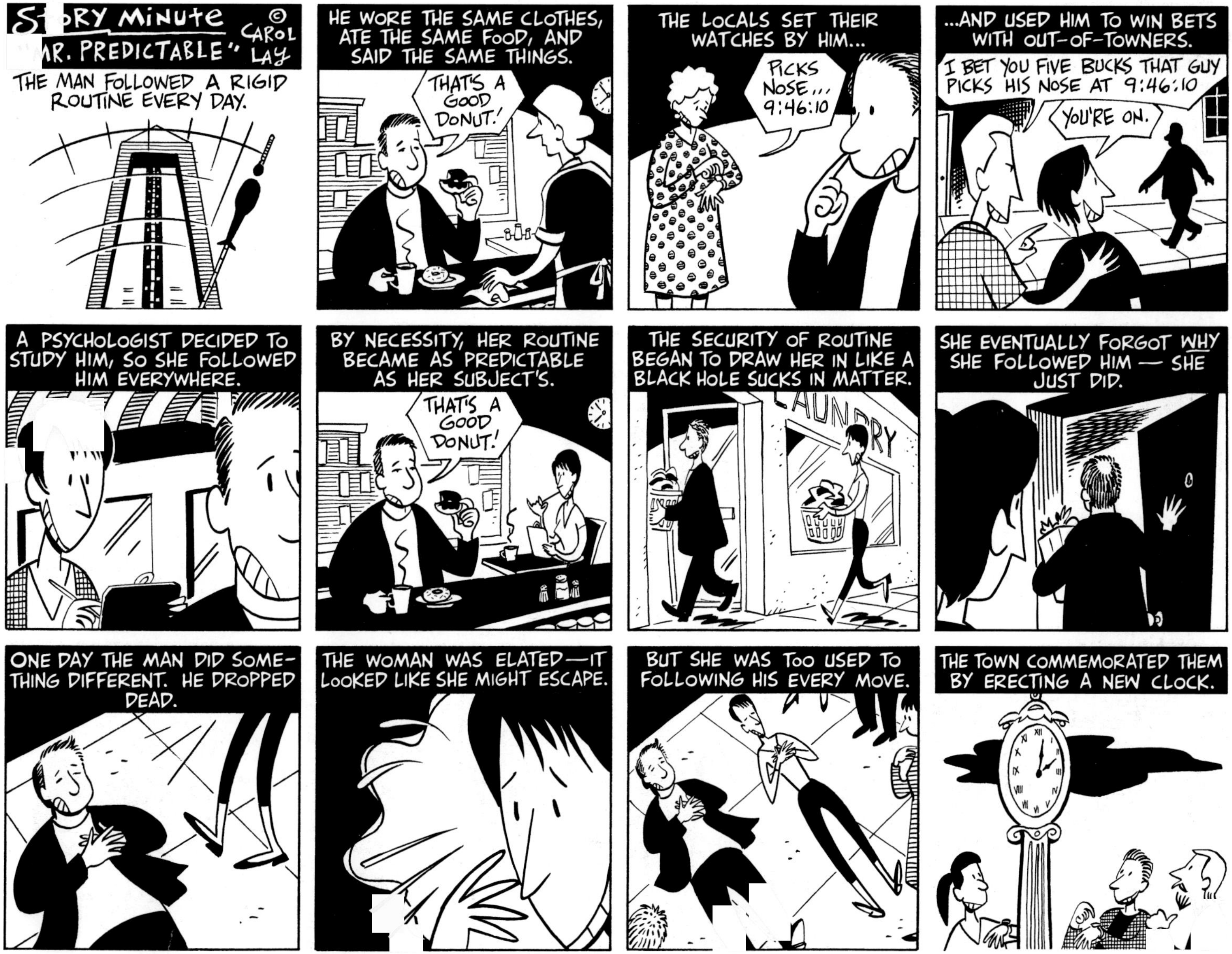
ORY MINUTE
R. PREDICTABLE
© CAROL LAY
THE MAN FOLLOWED A RIGID ROUTINE EVERY DAY.
HE WORE THE SAME CLOTHES, ATE THE SAME FOOD, AND SAID THE SAME THINGS.
THAT'S A GOOD DONUT!
THE LOCALS SET THEIR WATCHES BY HIM...
PICKS NOSE... 9:46:10
...AND USED HIM TO WIN BETS WITH OUT-OF-TOWNERS.
I BET YOU FIVE BUCKS THAT GUY PICKS HIS NOSE AT 9:46:10
YOU'RE ON.
A PSYCHOLOGIST DECIDED TO STUDY HIM, SO SHE FOLLOWED HIM EVERYWHERE.
BY NECESSITY, HER ROUTINE BECAME AS PREDICTABLE AS HER SUBJECT'S.
THAT'S A GOOD DONUT!
THE SECURITY OF ROUTINE BEGAN TO DRAW HER IN LIKE A BLACK HOLE SUCKS IN MATTER.
LAUNDRY
SHE EVENTUALLY FORGOT WHY SHE FOLLOWED HIM — SHE JUST DID.
ONE DAY THE MAN DID SOMETHING DIFFERENT. HE DROPPED DEAD.
THE WOMAN WAS ELATED—IT LOOKED LIKE SHE MIGHT ESCAPE.
BUT SHE WAS TOO USED TO FOLLOWING HIS EVERY MOVE.
THE TOWN COMMEMORATED THEM BY ERECTING A NEW CLOCK.

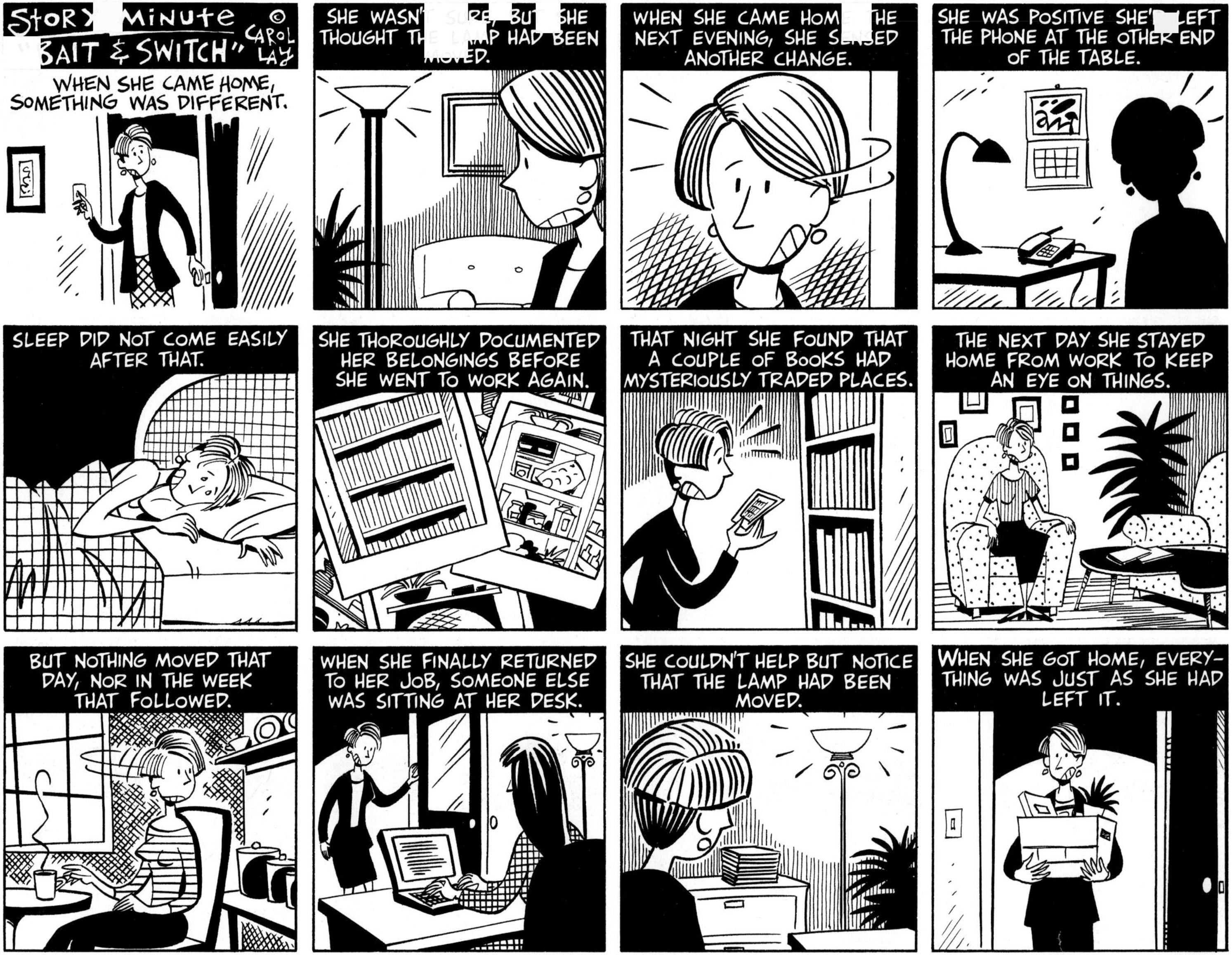
STORY MINUTE © CAROL LAY
"BAIT & SWITCH"
WHEN SHE CAME HOME, SOMETHING WAS DIFFERENT.
SHE WASN'T SURE, BUT SHE THOUGHT THE LAMP HAD BEEN MOVED.
WHEN SHE CAME HOME THE NEXT EVENING, SHE SENSED ANOTHER CHANGE.
SHE WAS POSITIVE SHE'D LEFT THE PHONE AT THE OTHER END OF THE TABLE.
SLEEP DID NOT COME EASILY AFTER THAT.
SHE THOROUGHLY DOCUMENTED HER BELONGINGS BEFORE SHE WENT TO WORK AGAIN.
THAT NIGHT SHE FOUND THAT A COUPLE OF BOOKS HAD MYSTERIOUSLY TRADED PLACES.
THE NEXT DAY SHE STAYED HOME FROM WORK TO KEEP AN EYE ON THINGS.
BUT NOTHING MOVED THAT DAY, NOR IN THE WEEK THAT FOLLOWED.
WHEN SHE FINALLY RETURNED TO HER JOB, SOMEONE ELSE WAS SITTING AT HER DESK.
SHE COULDN'T HELP BUT NOTICE THAT THE LAMP HAD BEEN MOVED.
WHEN SHE GOT HOME, EVERY-THING WAS JUST AS SHE HAD LEFT IT.

STORY MINUTE ©
"KIDNAPPERS, INC." CAROL LAY

THE WOMAN COULDN'T GET HER HARRIED HUSBAND TO TAKE TIME OFF.

SO SHE STAGED A BOGUS KIDNAPPING AND MET HIM IN THE TROPICS FOR SOME R&R.

AFTER A WHILE SHE PAID HIS "RANSOM" AND HE RETURNED TO WORK, REFRESHED.

SHE COULD SEE HOW OTHER MIDDLE MANAGERS MIGHT BENEFIT FROM FORCED ESCAPES.

SO SHE STARTED ARRANGING CLANDESTINE KIDNAPPING PACKAGES FOR A FANCY PRICE.

THIS WAS A FEDERAL OFFENSE SO SHE HAD TO BE VERY SELECTIVE.

HER "GUESTS" KEPT QUIET IN EXCHANGE FOR KEEPING THEIR JOBS.

NON-DISCLOSURE AGREEMENT

ONE TIME AN F.B.I. AGENT GOT TOO CLOSE TO FINDING HER OUT.

HE WAS KIDNAPPED TO FIJI WHERE HE SPENT A DELIGHTFUL FEW WEEKS.

THE BUREAU WOULDN'T PAY HIS RANSOM, THOUGH — GOVERNMENT POLICY.

RANSOM
DO NOT PAY

DISTURBED BY HIS EMPLOYER'S LACK OF LOYALTY, THE AGENT JOINED KIDNAPPERS, INC...

HIGH FIVE

...AND USED HIS EXPERIENCE TO HELP HIS ABDUCTRESS COVER HER TRACKS.

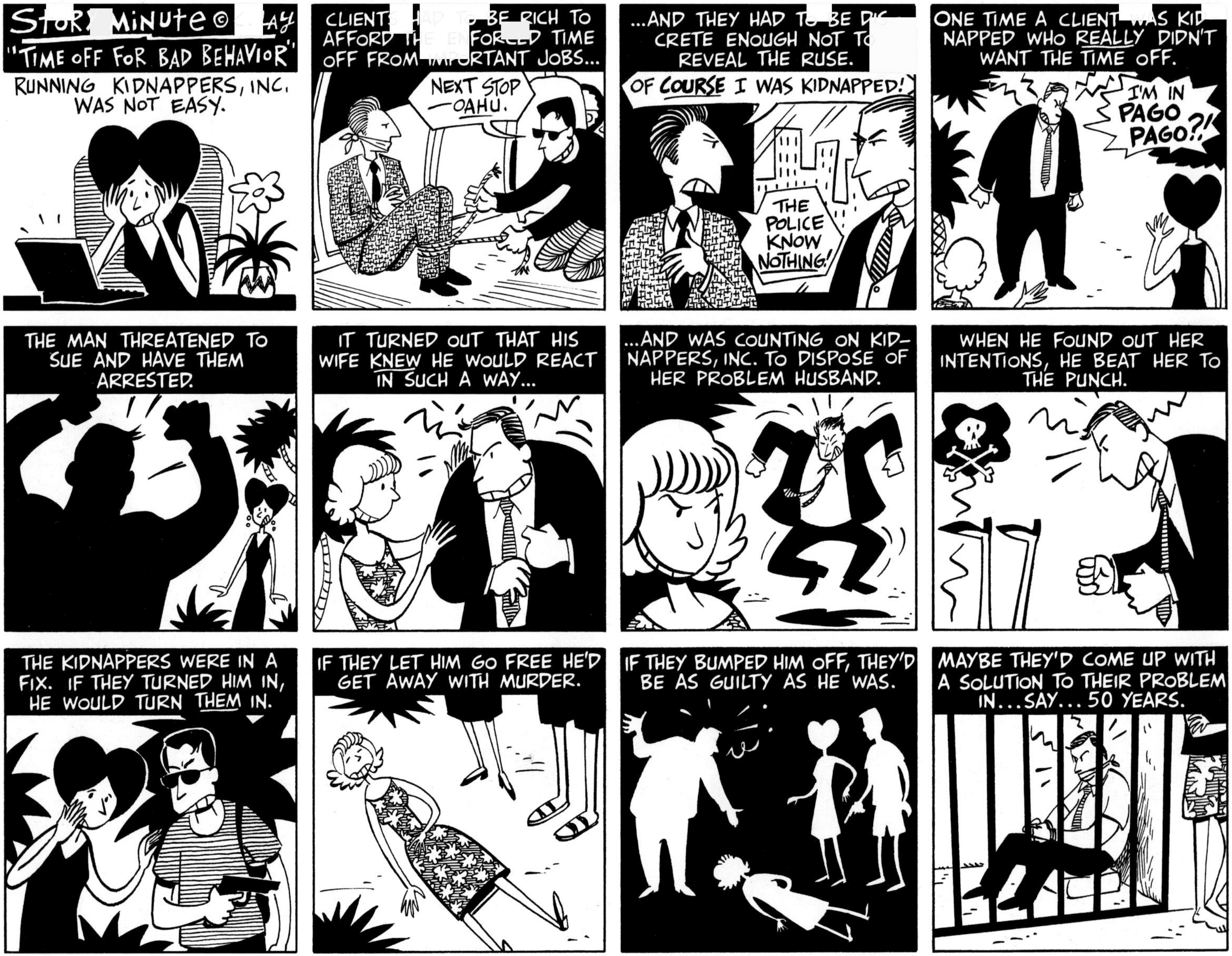

STORY MINUTE © K. LAY
"TIME OFF FOR BAD BEHAVIOR"
RUNNING KIDNAPPERS, INC. WAS NOT EASY.
CLIENTS HAD TO BE RICH TO AFFORD THE ENFORCED TIME OFF FROM IMPORTANT JOBS...
NEXT STOP —OAHU.
...AND THEY HAD TO BE DIS-CRETE ENOUGH NOT TO REVEAL THE RUSE.
OF COURSE I WAS KIDNAPPED!
THE POLICE KNOW NOTHING!
ONE TIME A CLIENT WAS KID-NAPPED WHO REALLY DIDN'T WANT THE TIME OFF.
I'M IN PAGO PAGO?!
THE MAN THREATENED TO SUE AND HAVE THEM ARRESTED.
IT TURNED OUT THAT HIS WIFE KNEW HE WOULD REACT IN SUCH A WAY...
...AND WAS COUNTING ON KID-NAPPERS, INC. TO DISPOSE OF HER PROBLEM HUSBAND.
WHEN HE FOUND OUT HER INTENTIONS, HE BEAT HER TO THE PUNCH.
THE KIDNAPPERS WERE IN A FIX. IF THEY TURNED HIM IN, HE WOULD TURN THEM IN.
IF THEY LET HIM GO FREE HE'D GET AWAY WITH MURDER.
IF THEY BUMPED HIM OFF, THEY'D BE AS GUILTY AS HE WAS.
MAYBE THEY'D COME UP WITH A SOLUTION TO THEIR PROBLEM IN...SAY...50 YEARS.

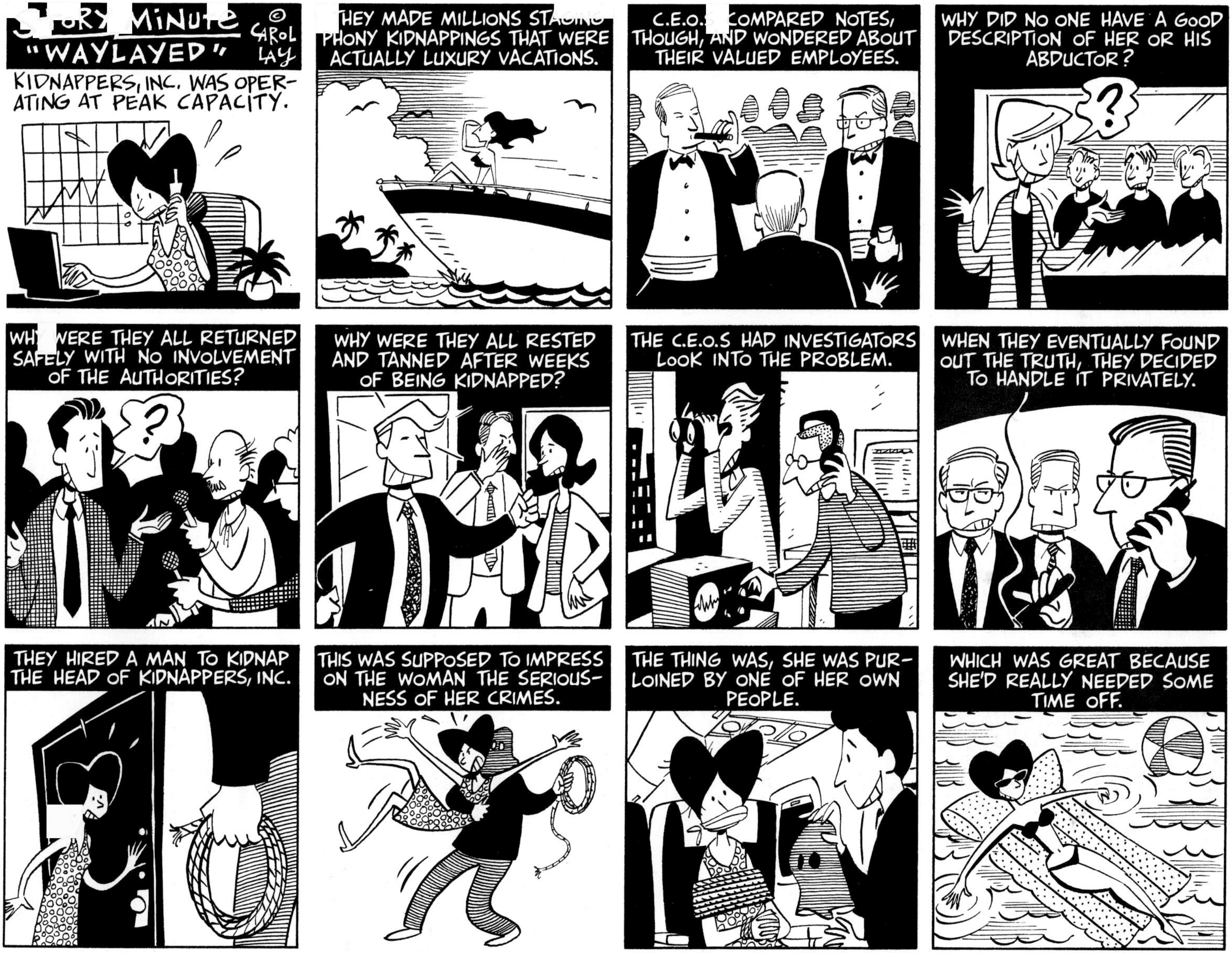
STORY MINUTE
"WAYLAYED"
© CAROL LAY
KIDNAPPERS, INC. WAS OPERATING AT PEAK CAPACITY.
THEY MADE MILLIONS STAGING PHONY KIDNAPPINGS THAT WERE ACTUALLY LUXURY VACATIONS.
C.E.O.S COMPARED NOTES, THOUGH, AND WONDERED ABOUT THEIR VALUED EMPLOYEES.
WHY DID NO ONE HAVE A GOOD DESCRIPTION OF HER OR HIS ABDUCTOR?
?
WHY WERE THEY ALL RETURNED SAFELY WITH NO INVOLVEMENT OF THE AUTHORITIES?
?
WHY WERE THEY ALL RESTED AND TANNED AFTER WEEKS OF BEING KIDNAPPED?
THE C.E.O.S HAD INVESTIGATORS LOOK INTO THE PROBLEM.
WHEN THEY EVENTUALLY FOUND OUT THE TRUTH, THEY DECIDED TO HANDLE IT PRIVATELY.
THEY HIRED A MAN TO KIDNAP THE HEAD OF KIDNAPPERS, INC.
THIS WAS SUPPOSED TO IMPRESS ON THE WOMAN THE SERIOUSNESS OF HER CRIMES.
THE THING WAS, SHE WAS PURLOINED BY ONE OF HER OWN PEOPLE.
WHICH WAS GREAT BECAUSE SHE'D REALLY NEEDED SOME TIME OFF.

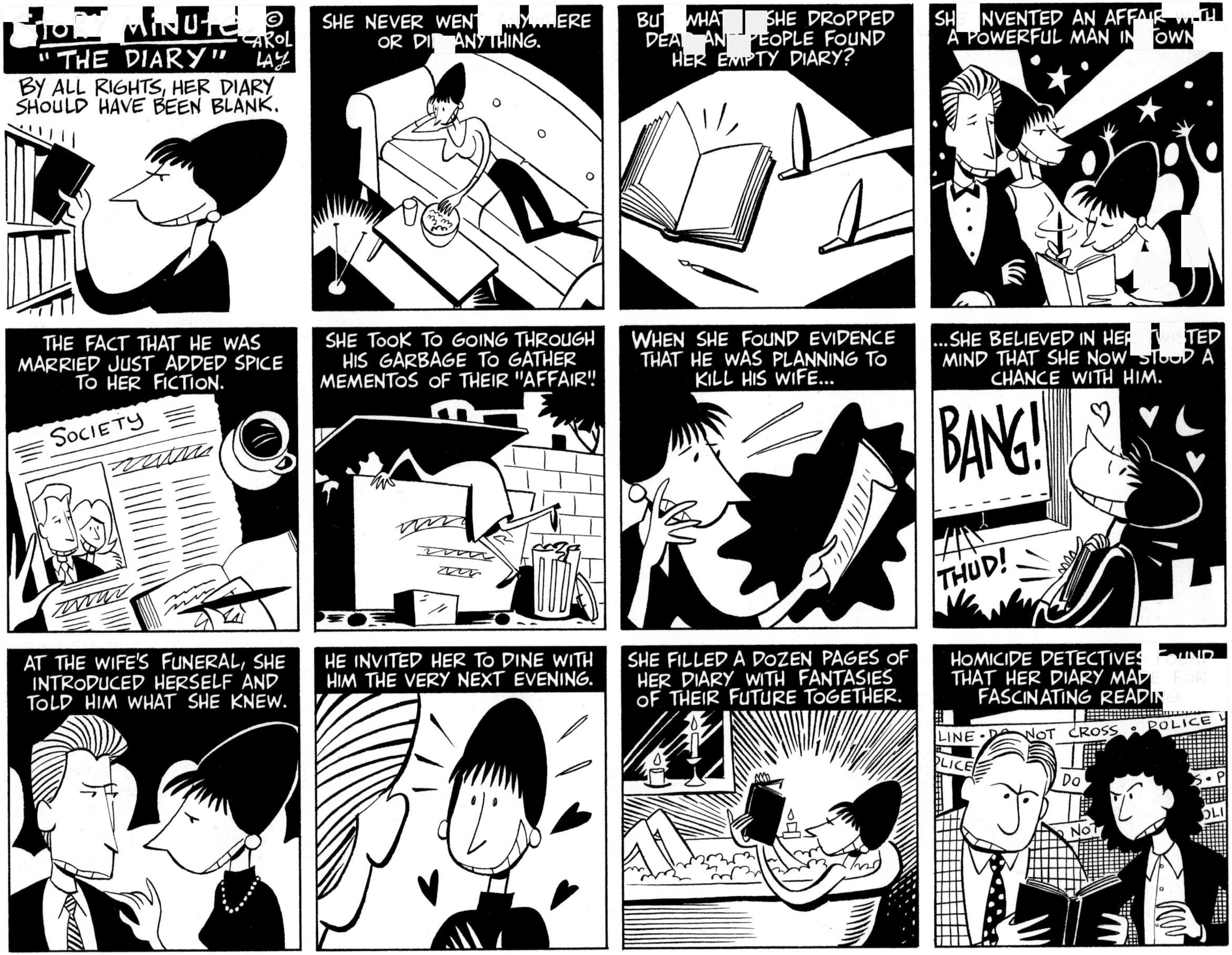

MINUTE
© CAROL LAY
"THE DIARY"
BY ALL RIGHTS, HER DIARY SHOULD HAVE BEEN BLANK.
SHE NEVER WENT ANYWHERE OR DID ANYTHING.
BUT WHAT IF SHE DROPPED DEAD AND PEOPLE FOUND HER EMPTY DIARY?
SHE INVENTED AN AFFAIR WITH A POWERFUL MAN IN TOWN.
THE FACT THAT HE WAS MARRIED JUST ADDED SPICE TO HER FICTION.
SOCIETY
SHE TOOK TO GOING THROUGH HIS GARBAGE TO GATHER MEMENTOS OF THEIR "AFFAIR"!
WHEN SHE FOUND EVIDENCE THAT HE WAS PLANNING TO KILL HIS WIFE...
...SHE BELIEVED IN HER TWISTED MIND THAT SHE NOW STOOD A CHANCE WITH HIM.
BANG!
THUD!
AT THE WIFE'S FUNERAL, SHE INTRODUCED HERSELF AND TOLD HIM WHAT SHE KNEW.
HE INVITED HER TO DINE WITH HIM THE VERY NEXT EVENING.
SHE FILLED A DOZEN PAGES OF HER DIARY WITH FANTASIES OF THEIR FUTURE TOGETHER.
HOMICIDE DETECTIVES FOUND THAT HER DIARY MADE FOR FASCINATING READING.
LINE • DO NOT CROSS • POLICE

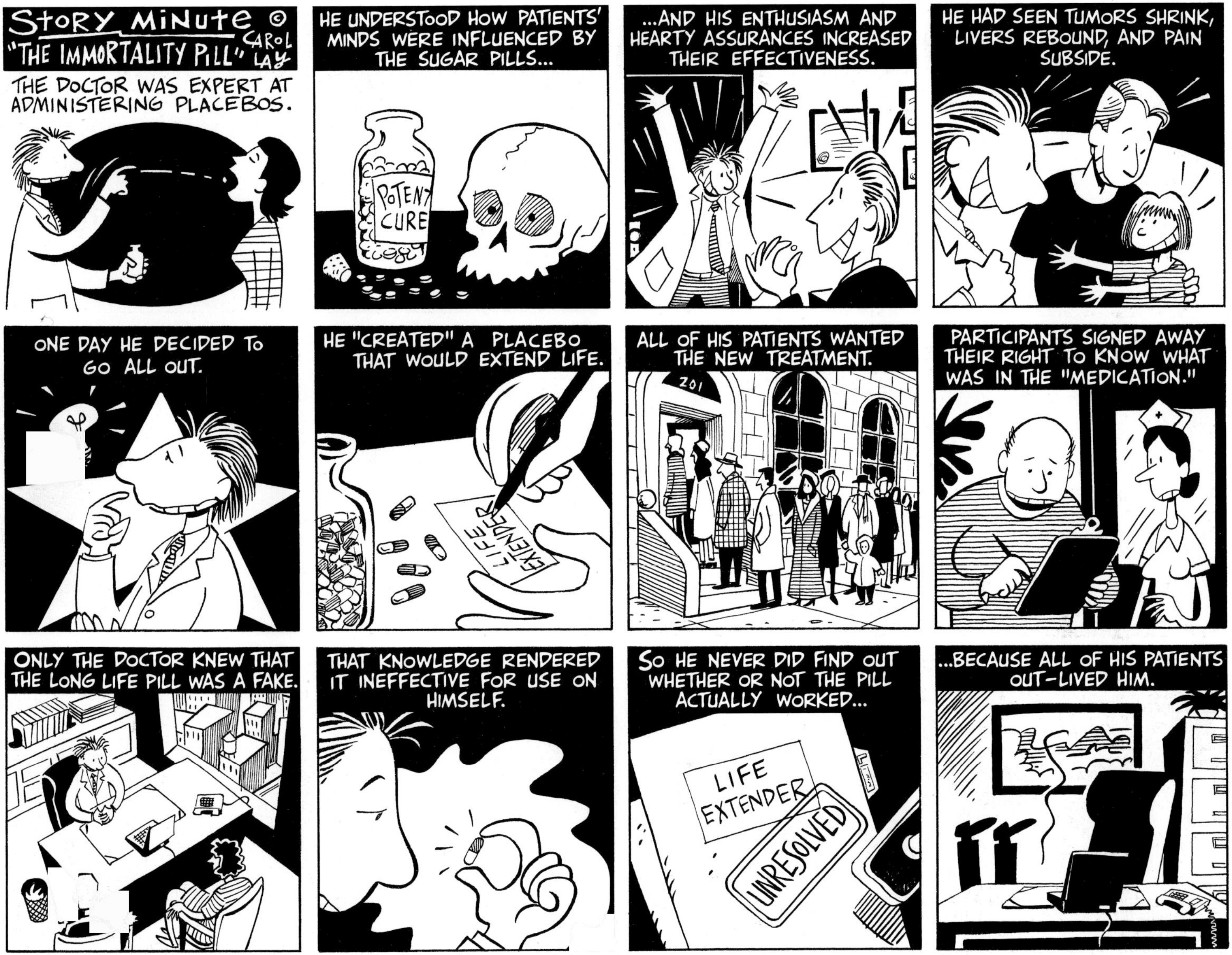
STORY MINUTE © CAROL LAY
"THE IMMORTALITY PILL"
THE DOCTOR WAS EXPERT AT ADMINISTERING PLACEBOS.
HE UNDERSTOOD HOW PATIENTS' MINDS WERE INFLUENCED BY THE SUGAR PILLS...
POTENT CURE
...AND HIS ENTHUSIASM AND HEARTY ASSURANCES INCREASED THEIR EFFECTIVENESS.
HE HAD SEEN TUMORS SHRINK, LIVERS REBOUND, AND PAIN SUBSIDE.
ONE DAY HE DECIDED TO GO ALL OUT.
HE "CREATED" A PLACEBO THAT WOULD EXTEND LIFE.
LIFE EXTENDER
ALL OF HIS PATIENTS WANTED THE NEW TREATMENT.
201
PARTICIPANTS SIGNED AWAY THEIR RIGHT TO KNOW WHAT WAS IN THE "MEDICATION."
ONLY THE DOCTOR KNEW THAT THE LONG LIFE PILL WAS A FAKE.
THAT KNOWLEDGE RENDERED IT INEFFECTIVE FOR USE ON HIMSELF.
SO HE NEVER DID FIND OUT WHETHER OR NOT THE PILL ACTUALLY WORKED...
LIFE EXTENDER
UNRESOLVED
...BECAUSE ALL OF HIS PATIENTS OUT-LIVED HIM.

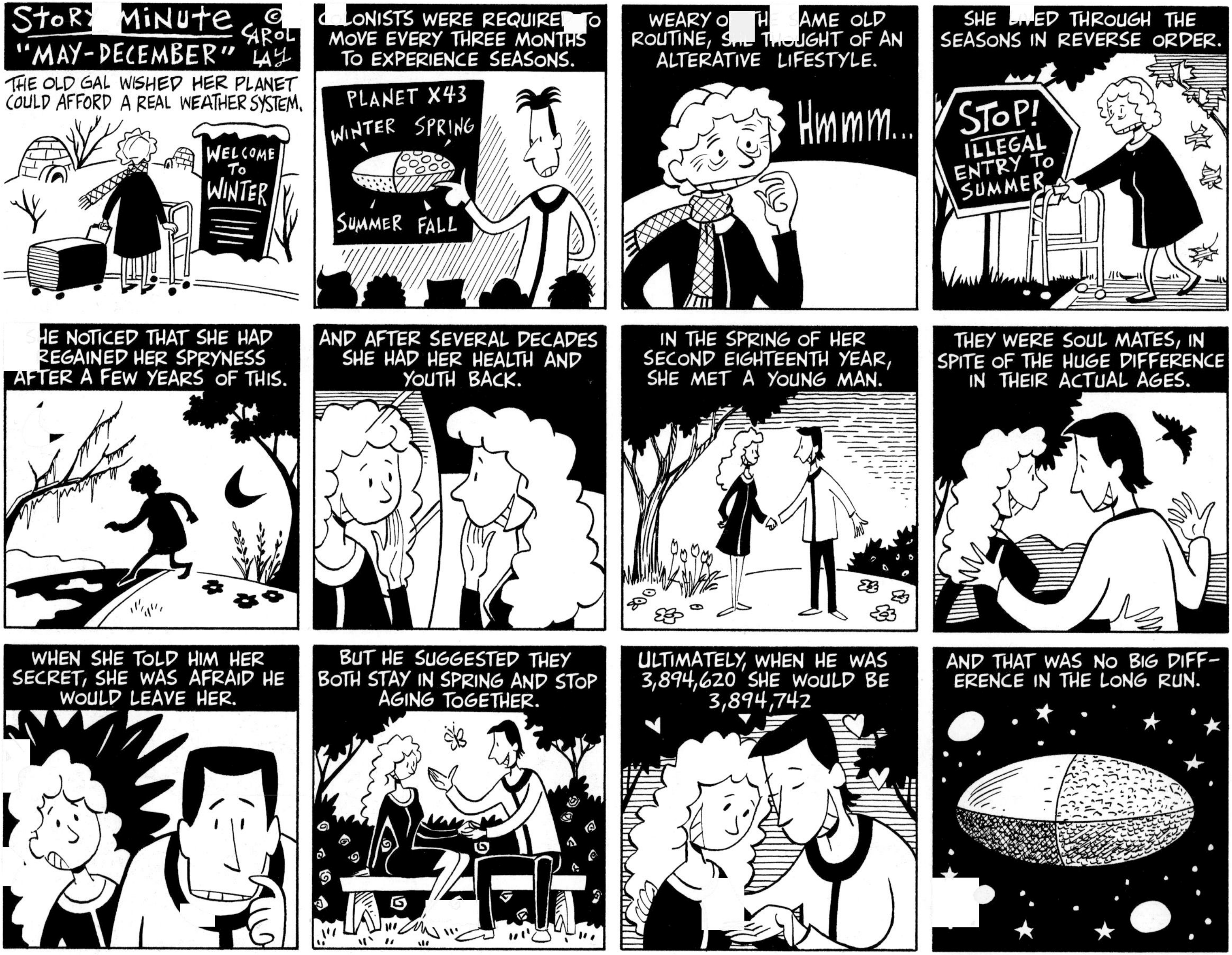
STORY MINUTE
"MAY-DECEMBER"
© CAROL LAY
THE OLD GAL WISHED HER PLANET COULD AFFORD A REAL WEATHER SYSTEM.
WELCOME TO WINTER
COLONISTS WERE REQUIRED TO MOVE EVERY THREE MONTHS TO EXPERIENCE SEASONS.
PLANET X43
WINTER
SPRING
SUMMER
FALL
WEARY OF THE SAME OLD ROUTINE, SHE THOUGHT OF AN ALTERATIVE LIFESTYLE.
HMMM...
SHE LIVED THROUGH THE SEASONS IN REVERSE ORDER.
STOP! ILLEGAL ENTRY TO SUMMER
SHE NOTICED THAT SHE HAD REGAINED HER SPRYNESS AFTER A FEW YEARS OF THIS.
AND AFTER SEVERAL DECADES SHE HAD HER HEALTH AND YOUTH BACK.
IN THE SPRING OF HER SECOND EIGHTEENTH YEAR, SHE MET A YOUNG MAN.
THEY WERE SOUL MATES, IN SPITE OF THE HUGE DIFFERENCE IN THEIR ACTUAL AGES.
WHEN SHE TOLD HIM HER SECRET, SHE WAS AFRAID HE WOULD LEAVE HER.
BUT HE SUGGESTED THEY BOTH STAY IN SPRING AND STOP AGING TOGETHER.
ULTIMATELY, WHEN HE WAS 3,894,620 SHE WOULD BE 3,894,742
AND THAT WAS NO BIG DIFF-ERENCE IN THE LONG RUN.

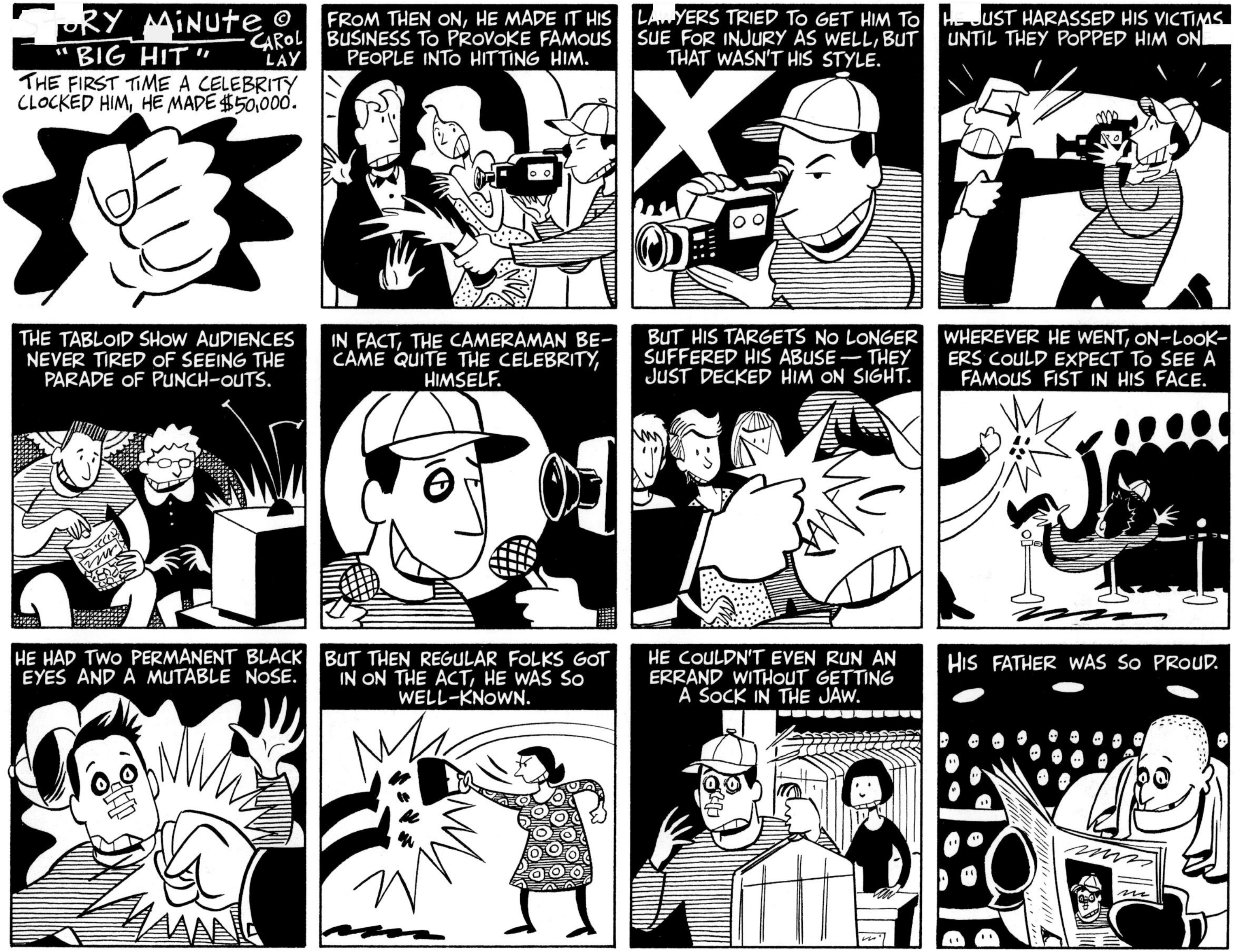
STORY MINUTE © CAROL LAY
"BIG HIT"
THE FIRST TIME A CELEBRITY CLOCKED HIM, HE MADE $50,000.
FROM THEN ON, HE MADE IT HIS BUSINESS TO PROVOKE FAMOUS PEOPLE INTO HITTING HIM.
LAWYERS TRIED TO GET HIM TO SUE FOR INJURY AS WELL, BUT THAT WASN'T HIS STYLE.
HE JUST HARASSED HIS VICTIMS UNTIL THEY POPPED HIM ON
THE TABLOID SHOW AUDIENCES NEVER TIRED OF SEEING THE PARADE OF PUNCH-OUTS.
IN FACT, THE CAMERAMAN BECAME QUITE THE CELEBRITY, HIMSELF.
BUT HIS TARGETS NO LONGER SUFFERED HIS ABUSE — THEY JUST DECKED HIM ON SIGHT.
WHEREVER HE WENT, ON-LOOKERS COULD EXPECT TO SEE A FAMOUS FIST IN HIS FACE.
HE HAD TWO PERMANENT BLACK EYES AND A MUTABLE NOSE.
BUT THEN REGULAR FOLKS GOT IN ON THE ACT, HE WAS SO WELL-KNOWN.
HE COULDN'T EVEN RUN AN ERRAND WITHOUT GETTING A SOCK IN THE JAW.
HIS FATHER WAS SO PROUD.

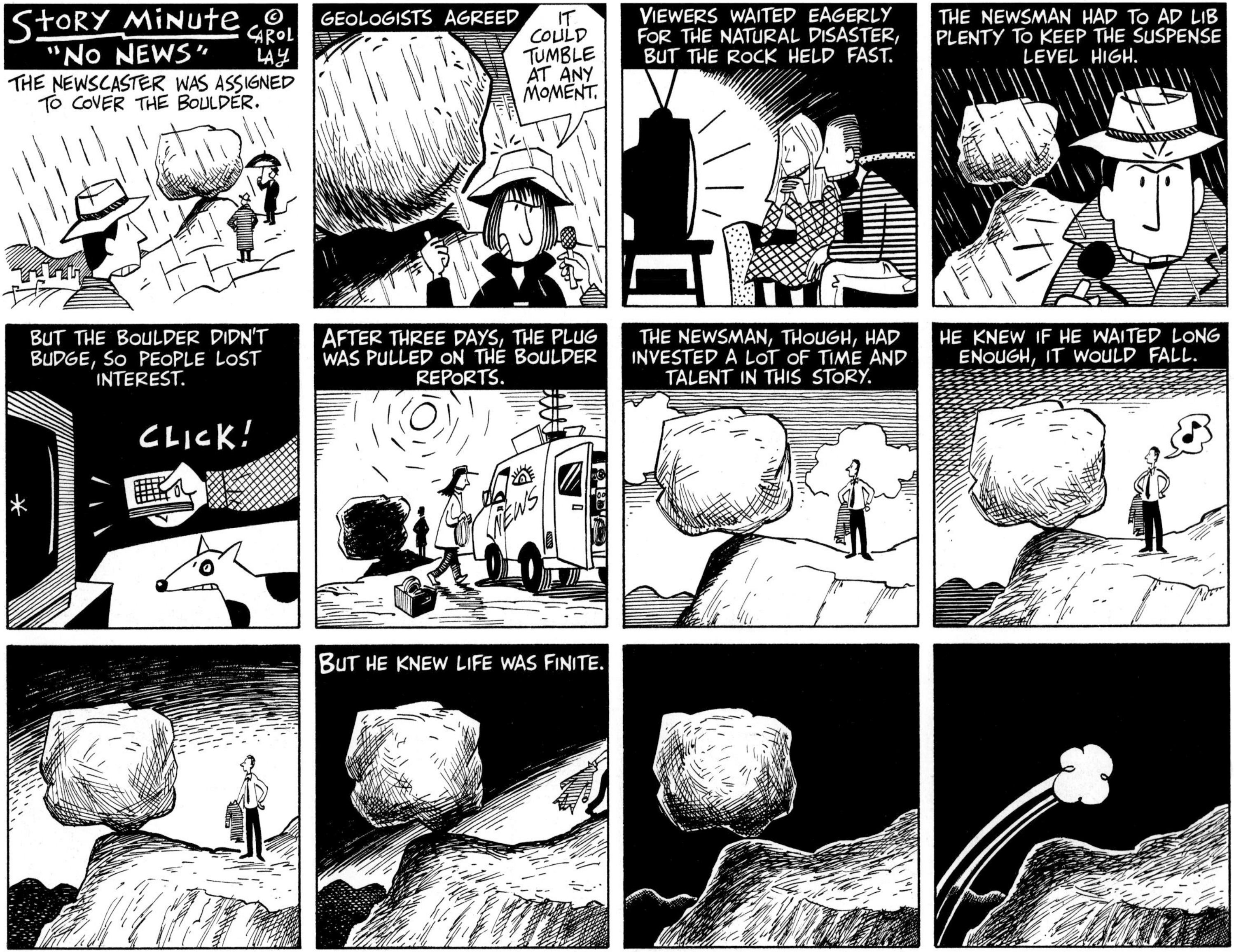
STORY MINUTE
"NO NEWS"
© CAROL LAY
THE NEWSCASTER WAS ASSIGNED TO COVER THE BOULDER.
GEOLOGISTS AGREED
IT COULD TUMBLE AT ANY MOMENT.
VIEWERS WAITED EAGERLY FOR THE NATURAL DISASTER, BUT THE ROCK HELD FAST.
THE NEWSMAN HAD TO AD LIB PLENTY TO KEEP THE SUSPENSE LEVEL HIGH.
BUT THE BOULDER DIDN'T BUDGE, SO PEOPLE LOST INTEREST.
CLICK!
AFTER THREE DAYS, THE PLUG WAS PULLED ON THE BOULDER REPORTS.
NEWS
THE NEWSMAN, THOUGH, HAD INVESTED A LOT OF TIME AND TALENT IN THIS STORY.
HE KNEW IF HE WAITED LONG ENOUGH, IT WOULD FALL.
BUT HE KNEW LIFE WAS FINITE.

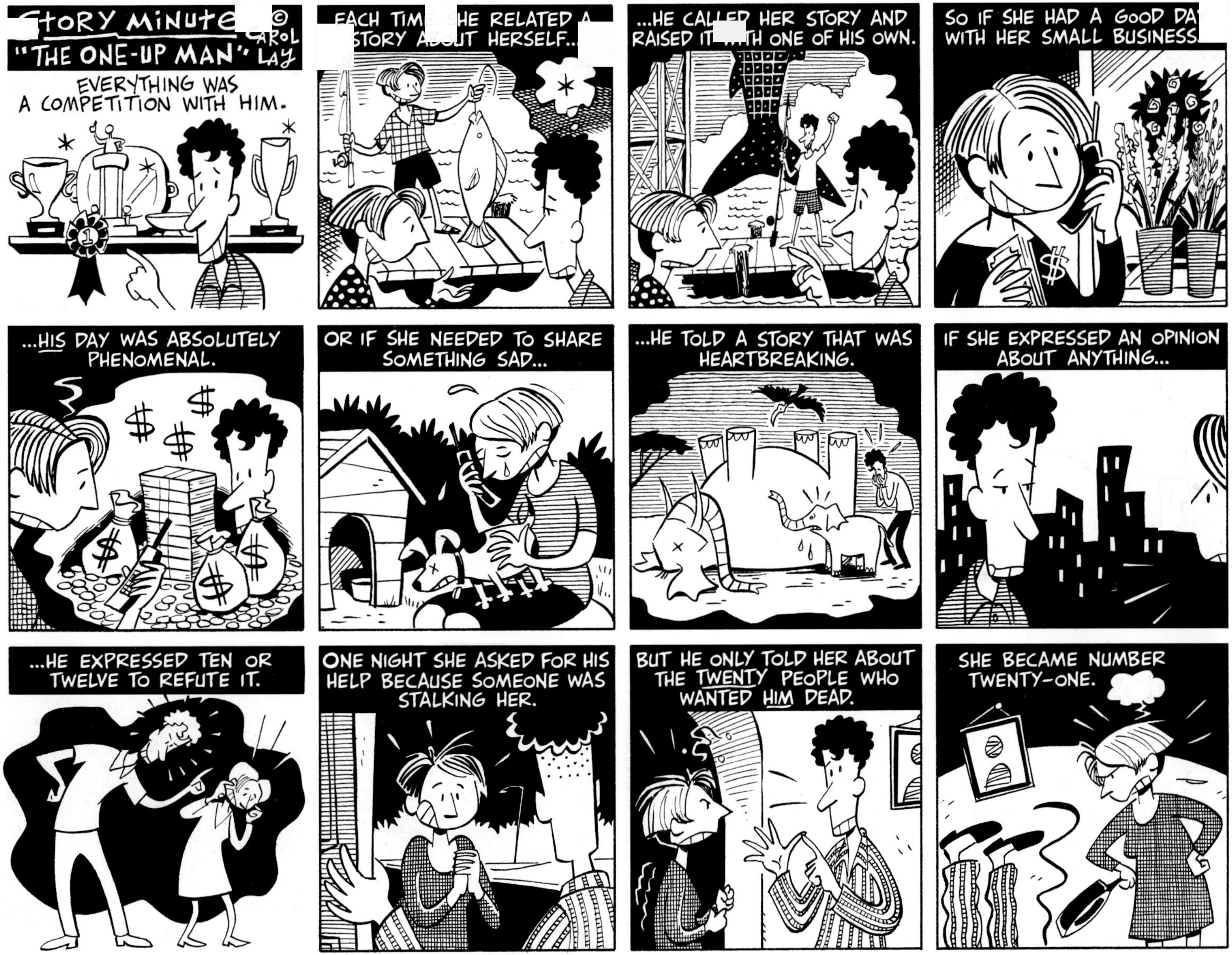
STORY MINUTE © CAROL LAY
"THE ONE-UP MAN"
EVERYTHING WAS A COMPETITION WITH HIM.
EACH TIME SHE RELATED A STORY ABOUT HERSELF...
...HE CALLED HER STORY AND RAISED IT WITH ONE OF HIS OWN.
SO IF SHE HAD A GOOD DAY WITH HER SMALL BUSINESS...
...HIS DAY WAS ABSOLUTELY PHENOMENAL.
OR IF SHE NEEDED TO SHARE SOMETHING SAD...
...HE TOLD A STORY THAT WAS HEARTBREAKING.
IF SHE EXPRESSED AN OPINION ABOUT ANYTHING...
...HE EXPRESSED TEN OR TWELVE TO REFUTE IT.
ONE NIGHT SHE ASKED FOR HIS HELP BECAUSE SOMEONE WAS STALKING HER.
BUT HE ONLY TOLD HER ABOUT THE TWENTY PEOPLE WHO WANTED HIM DEAD.
SHE BECAME NUMBER TWENTY-ONE.

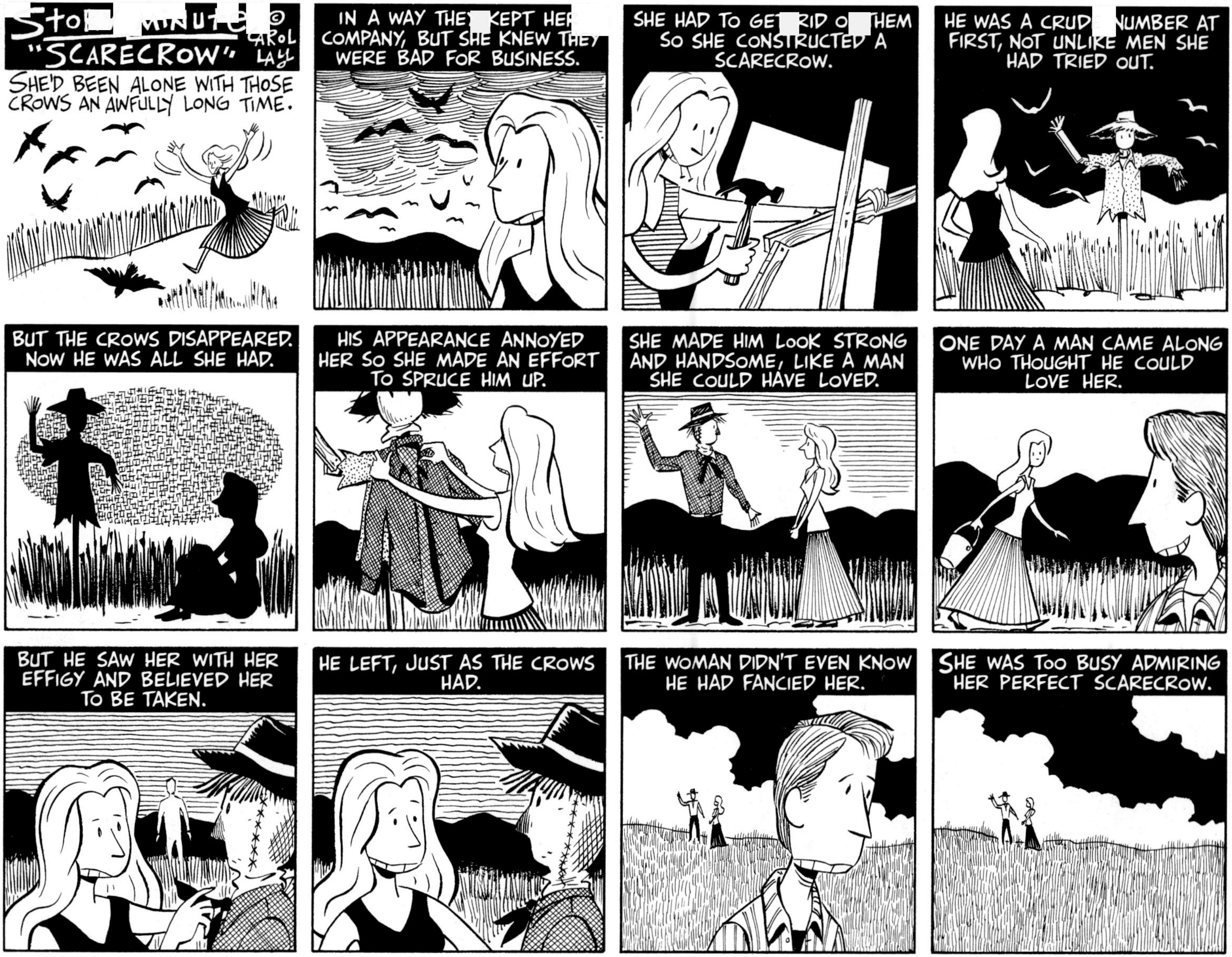
STO MINUTE © CAROL LAY
"SCARECROW"
SHE'D BEEN ALONE WITH THOSE CROWS AN AWFULLY LONG TIME.
IN A WAY THE KEPT HE COMPANY, BUT SHE KNEW THEY WERE BAD FOR BUSINESS.
SHE HAD TO GET RID O THEM SO SHE CONSTRUCTED A SCARECROW.
HE WAS A CRUD NUMBER AT FIRST, NOT UNLIKE MEN SHE HAD TRIED OUT.
BUT THE CROWS DISAPPEARED. NOW HE WAS ALL SHE HAD.
HIS APPEARANCE ANNOYED HER SO SHE MADE AN EFFORT TO SPRUCE HIM UP.
SHE MADE HIM LOOK STRONG AND HANDSOME, LIKE A MAN SHE COULD HAVE LOVED.
ONE DAY A MAN CAME ALONG WHO THOUGHT HE COULD LOVE HER.
BUT HE SAW HER WITH HER EFFIGY AND BELIEVED HER TO BE TAKEN.
HE LEFT, JUST AS THE CROWS HAD.
THE WOMAN DIDN'T EVEN KNOW HE HAD FANCIED HER.
SHE WAS TOO BUSY ADMIRING HER PERFECT SCARECROW.

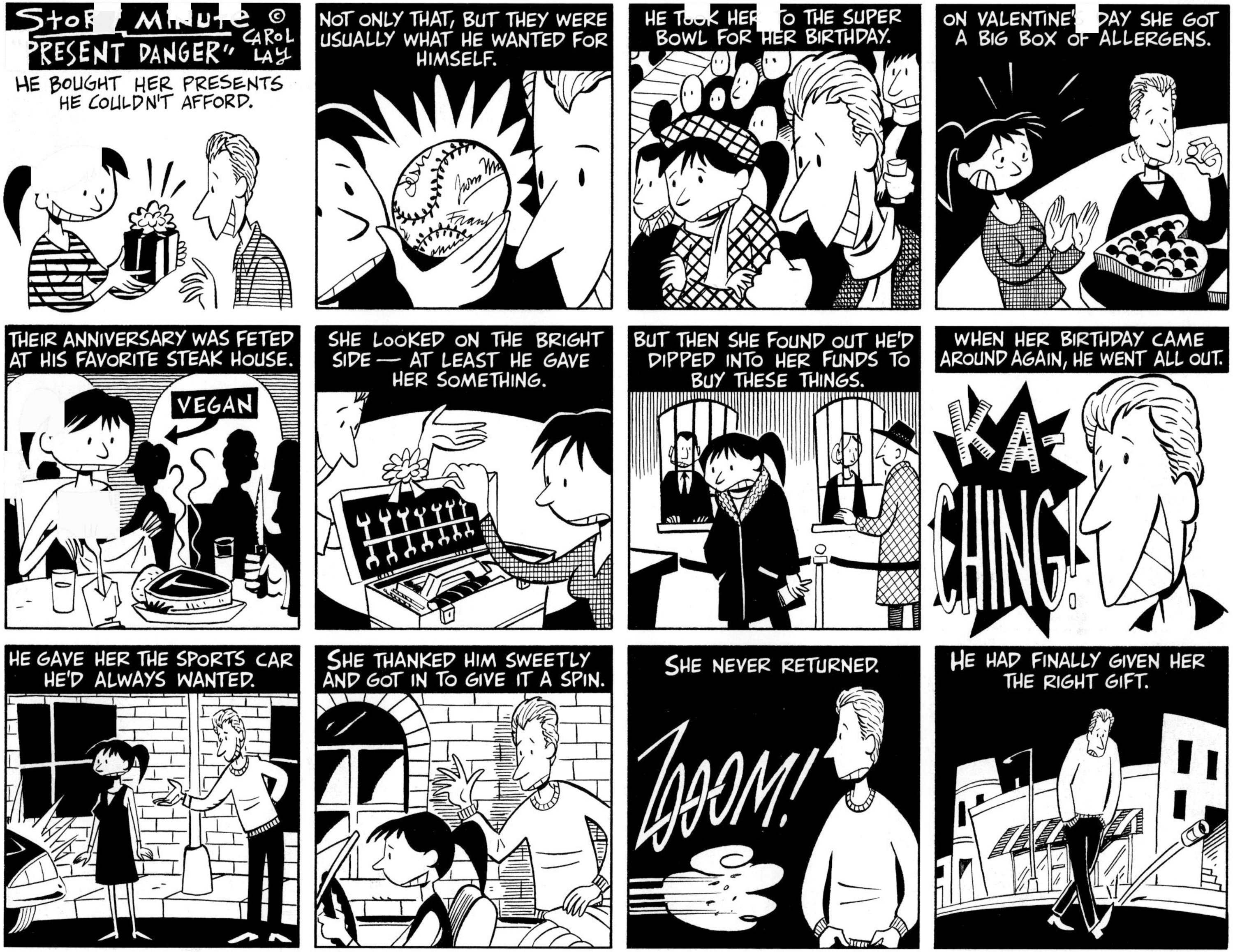
"PRESENT DANGER" © CAROL LAY
HE BOUGHT HER PRESENTS HE COULDN'T AFFORD.
NOT ONLY THAT, BUT THEY WERE USUALLY WHAT HE WANTED FOR HIMSELF.
HE TOOK HER TO THE SUPER BOWL FOR HER BIRTHDAY.
ON VALENTINE'S DAY SHE GOT A BIG BOX OF ALLERGENS.
THEIR ANNIVERSARY WAS FETED AT HIS FAVORITE STEAK HOUSE.
VEGAN
SHE LOOKED ON THE BRIGHT SIDE — AT LEAST HE GAVE HER SOMETHING.
BUT THEN SHE FOUND OUT HE'D DIPPED INTO HER FUNDS TO BUY THESE THINGS.
WHEN HER BIRTHDAY CAME AROUND AGAIN, HE WENT ALL OUT.
KA-CHING!
HE GAVE HER THE SPORTS CAR HE'D ALWAYS WANTED.
SHE THANKED HIM SWEETLY AND GOT IN TO GIVE IT A SPIN.
SHE NEVER RETURNED.
ZOOOM!
HE HAD FINALLY GIVEN HER THE RIGHT GIFT.

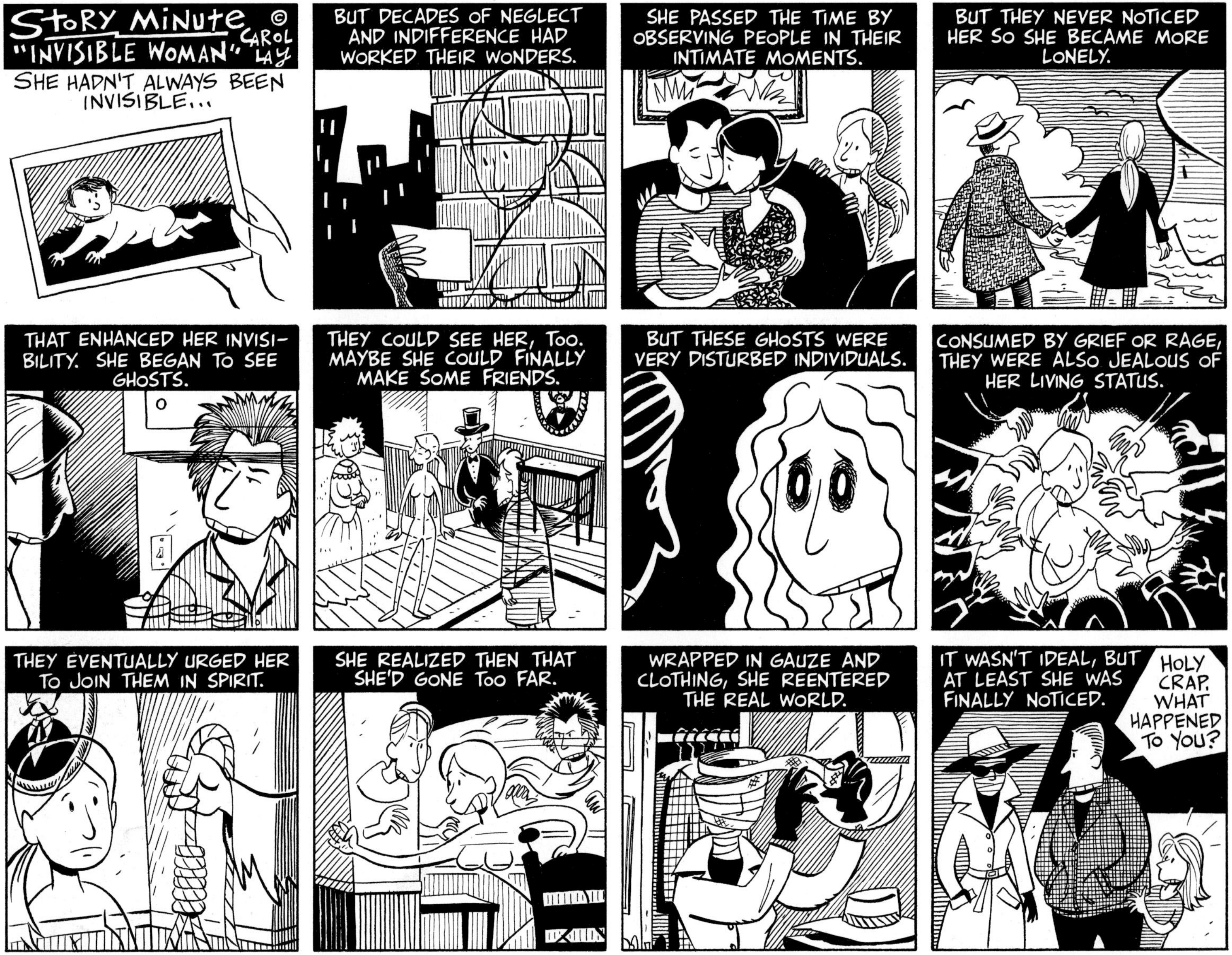
STORY MINUTE ©
CAROL LAY
"INVISIBLE WOMAN"
SHE HADN'T ALWAYS BEEN INVISIBLE...
BUT DECADES OF NEGLECT AND INDIFFERENCE HAD WORKED THEIR WONDERS.
SHE PASSED THE TIME BY OBSERVING PEOPLE IN THEIR INTIMATE MOMENTS.
BUT THEY NEVER NOTICED HER SO SHE BECAME MORE LONELY.
THAT ENHANCED HER INVISIBILITY. SHE BEGAN TO SEE GHOSTS.
THEY COULD SEE HER, TOO. MAYBE SHE COULD FINALLY MAKE SOME FRIENDS.
BUT THESE GHOSTS WERE VERY DISTURBED INDIVIDUALS.
CONSUMED BY GRIEF OR RAGE, THEY WERE ALSO JEALOUS OF HER LIVING STATUS.
THEY EVENTUALLY URGED HER TO JOIN THEM IN SPIRIT.
SHE REALIZED THEN THAT SHE'D GONE TOO FAR.
WRAPPED IN GAUZE AND CLOTHING, SHE REENTERED THE REAL WORLD.
IT WASN'T IDEAL, BUT AT LEAST SHE WAS FINALLY NOTICED.
HOLY CRAP. WHAT HAPPENED TO YOU?

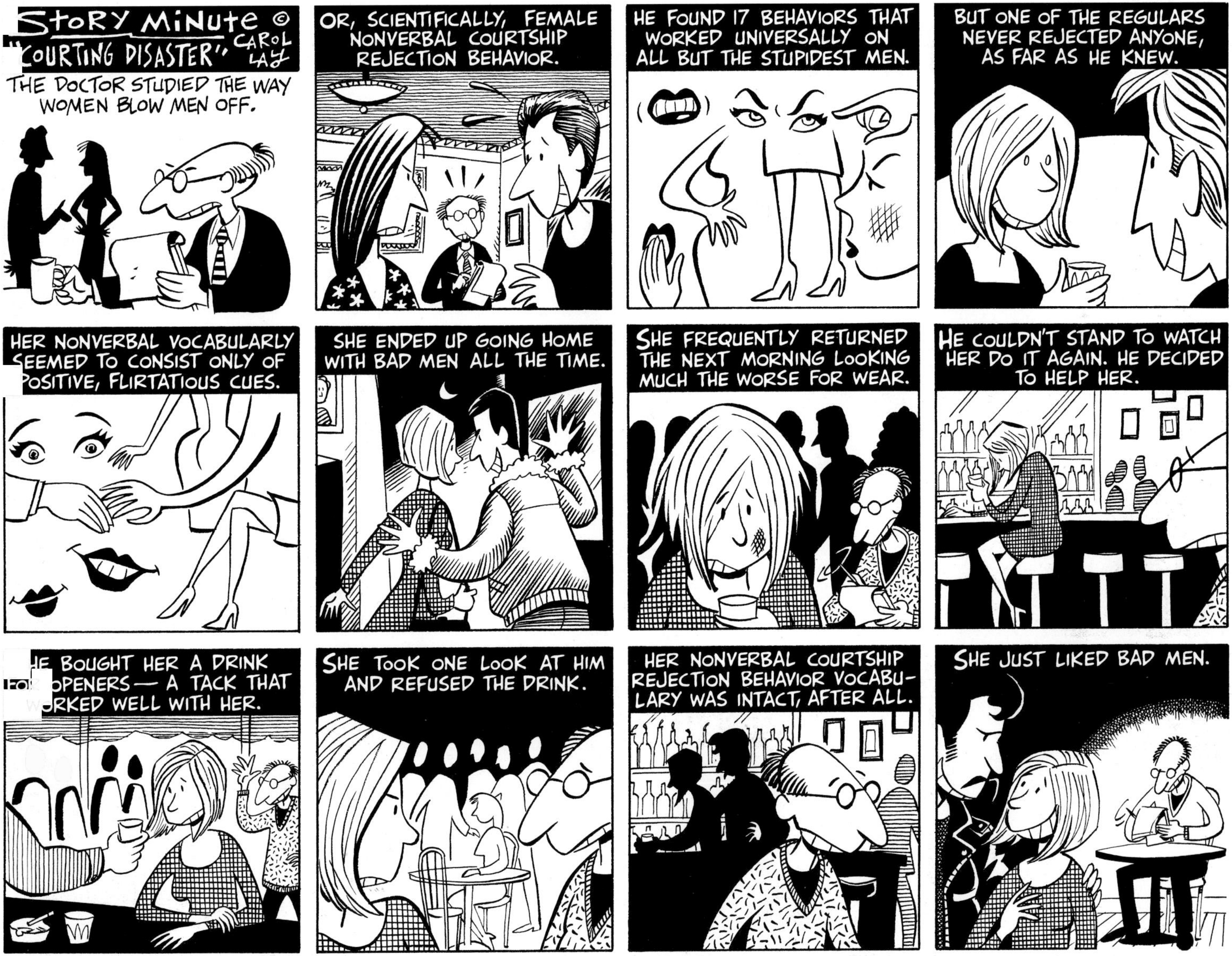
STORY MINUTE ©
"COURTING DISASTER"
CAROL LAY
THE DOCTOR STUDIED THE WAY WOMEN BLOW MEN OFF.
OR, SCIENTIFICALLY, FEMALE NONVERBAL COURTSHIP REJECTION BEHAVIOR.
HE FOUND 17 BEHAVIORS THAT WORKED UNIVERSALLY ON ALL BUT THE STUPIDEST MEN.
BUT ONE OF THE REGULARS NEVER REJECTED ANYONE, AS FAR AS HE KNEW.
HER NONVERBAL VOCABULARLY SEEMED TO CONSIST ONLY OF POSITIVE, FLIRTATIOUS CUES.
SHE ENDED UP GOING HOME WITH BAD MEN ALL THE TIME.
SHE FREQUENTLY RETURNED THE NEXT MORNING LOOKING MUCH THE WORSE FOR WEAR.
HE COULDN'T STAND TO WATCH HER DO IT AGAIN. HE DECIDED TO HELP HER.
E BOUGHT HER A DRINK
OPENERS— A TACK THAT
ORKED WELL WITH HER.
SHE TOOK ONE LOOK AT HIM AND REFUSED THE DRINK.
HER NONVERBAL COURTSHIP REJECTION BEHAVIOR VOCABU-LARY WAS INTACT, AFTER ALL.
SHE JUST LIKED BAD MEN.

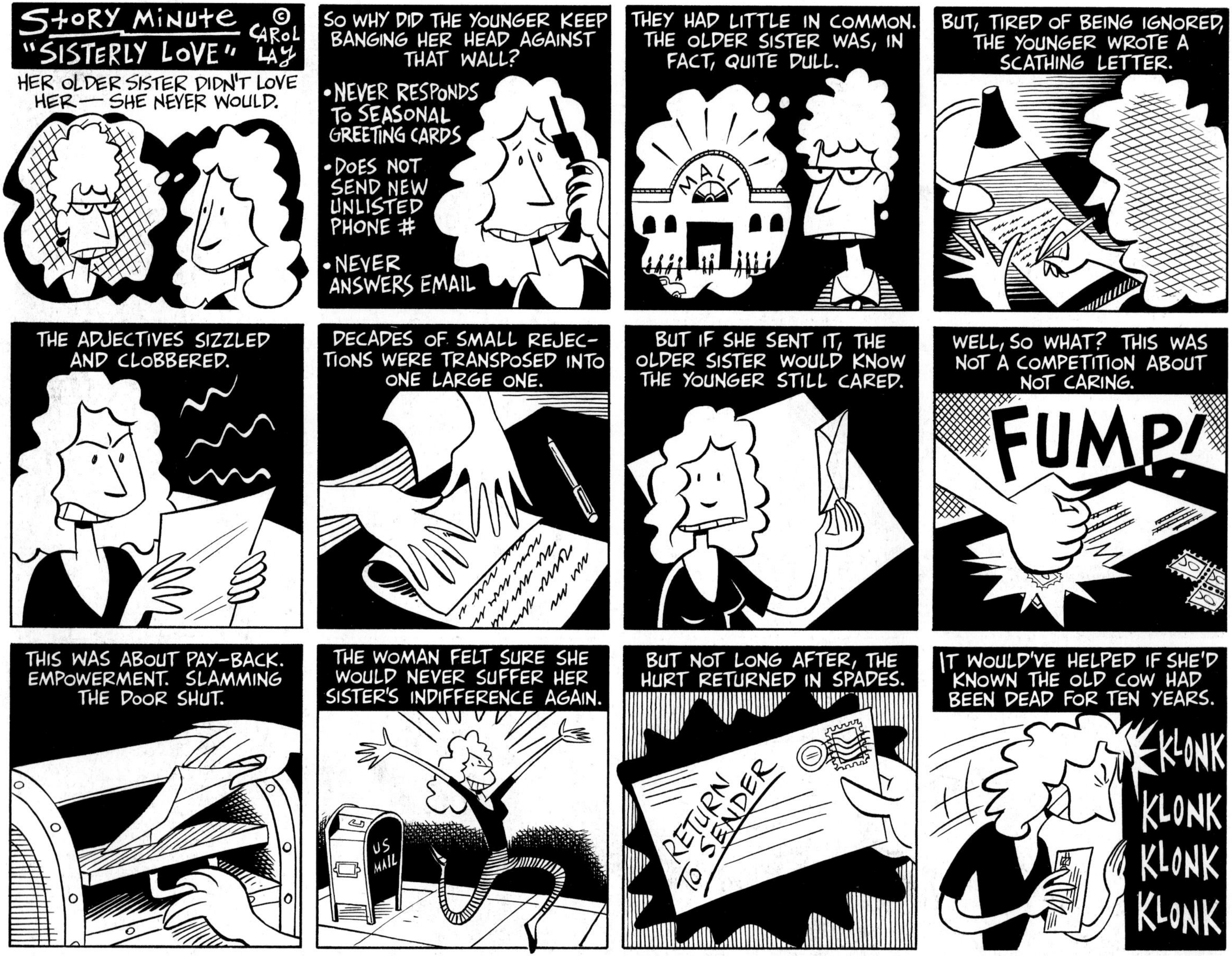
STORY MINUTE
"SISTERLY LOVE"
© CAROL LAY
HER OLDER SISTER DIDN'T LOVE HER — SHE NEVER WOULD.
SO WHY DID THE YOUNGER KEEP BANGING HER HEAD AGAINST THAT WALL?
• NEVER RESPONDS TO SEASONAL GREETING CARDS
• DOES NOT SEND NEW UNLISTED PHONE #
• NEVER ANSWERS EMAIL
THEY HAD LITTLE IN COMMON. THE OLDER SISTER WAS, IN FACT, QUITE DULL.
MALL
BUT, TIRED OF BEING IGNORED, THE YOUNGER WROTE A SCATHING LETTER.
THE ADJECTIVES SIZZLED AND CLOBBERED.
DECADES OF SMALL REJECTIONS WERE TRANSPOSED INTO ONE LARGE ONE.
BUT IF SHE SENT IT, THE OLDER SISTER WOULD KNOW THE YOUNGER STILL CARED.
WELL, SO WHAT? THIS WAS NOT A COMPETITION ABOUT NOT CARING.
FUMP!
THIS WAS ABOUT PAY-BACK. EMPOWERMENT. SLAMMING THE DOOR SHUT.
THE WOMAN FELT SURE SHE WOULD NEVER SUFFER HER SISTER'S INDIFFERENCE AGAIN.
US MAIL
BUT NOT LONG AFTER, THE HURT RETURNED IN SPADES.
RETURN TO SENDER
IT WOULD'VE HELPED IF SHE'D KNOWN THE OLD COW HAD BEEN DEAD FOR TEN YEARS.
KLONK
KLONK
KLONK
KLONK

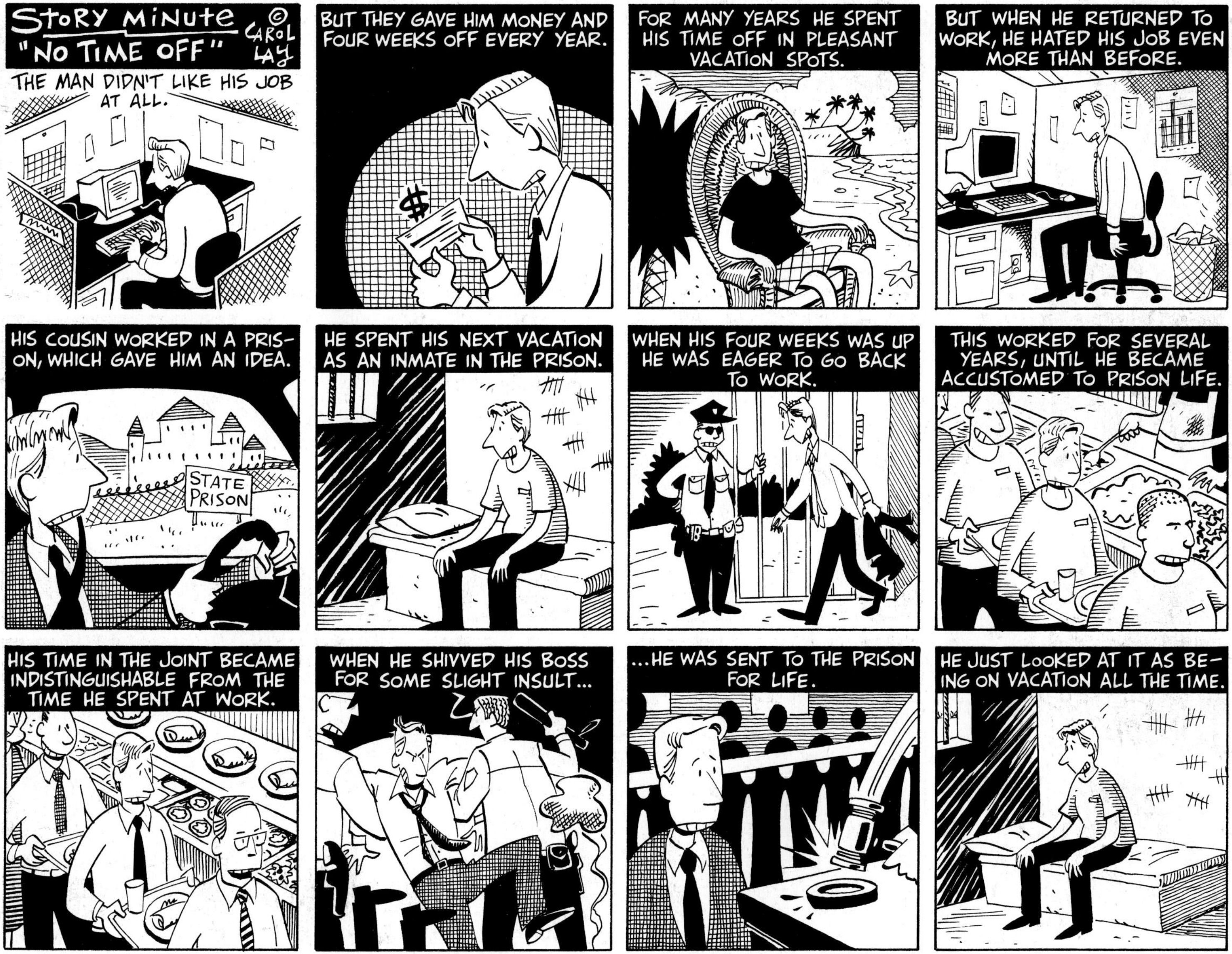
STORY MINUTE
"NO TIME OFF"
© CAROL LAY
THE MAN DIDN'T LIKE HIS JOB AT ALL.
BUT THEY GAVE HIM MONEY AND FOUR WEEKS OFF EVERY YEAR.
$
FOR MANY YEARS HE SPENT HIS TIME OFF IN PLEASANT VACATION SPOTS.
BUT WHEN HE RETURNED TO WORK, HE HATED HIS JOB EVEN MORE THAN BEFORE.
HIS COUSIN WORKED IN A PRISON, WHICH GAVE HIM AN IDEA.
STATE PRISON
HE SPENT HIS NEXT VACATION AS AN INMATE IN THE PRISON.
WHEN HIS FOUR WEEKS WAS UP HE WAS EAGER TO GO BACK TO WORK.
THIS WORKED FOR SEVERAL YEARS, UNTIL HE BECAME ACCUSTOMED TO PRISON LIFE.
HIS TIME IN THE JOINT BECAME INDISTINGUISHABLE FROM THE TIME HE SPENT AT WORK.
WHEN HE SHIVVED HIS BOSS FOR SOME SLIGHT INSULT...
...HE WAS SENT TO THE PRISON FOR LIFE.
HE JUST LOOKED AT IT AS BEING ON VACATION ALL THE TIME.

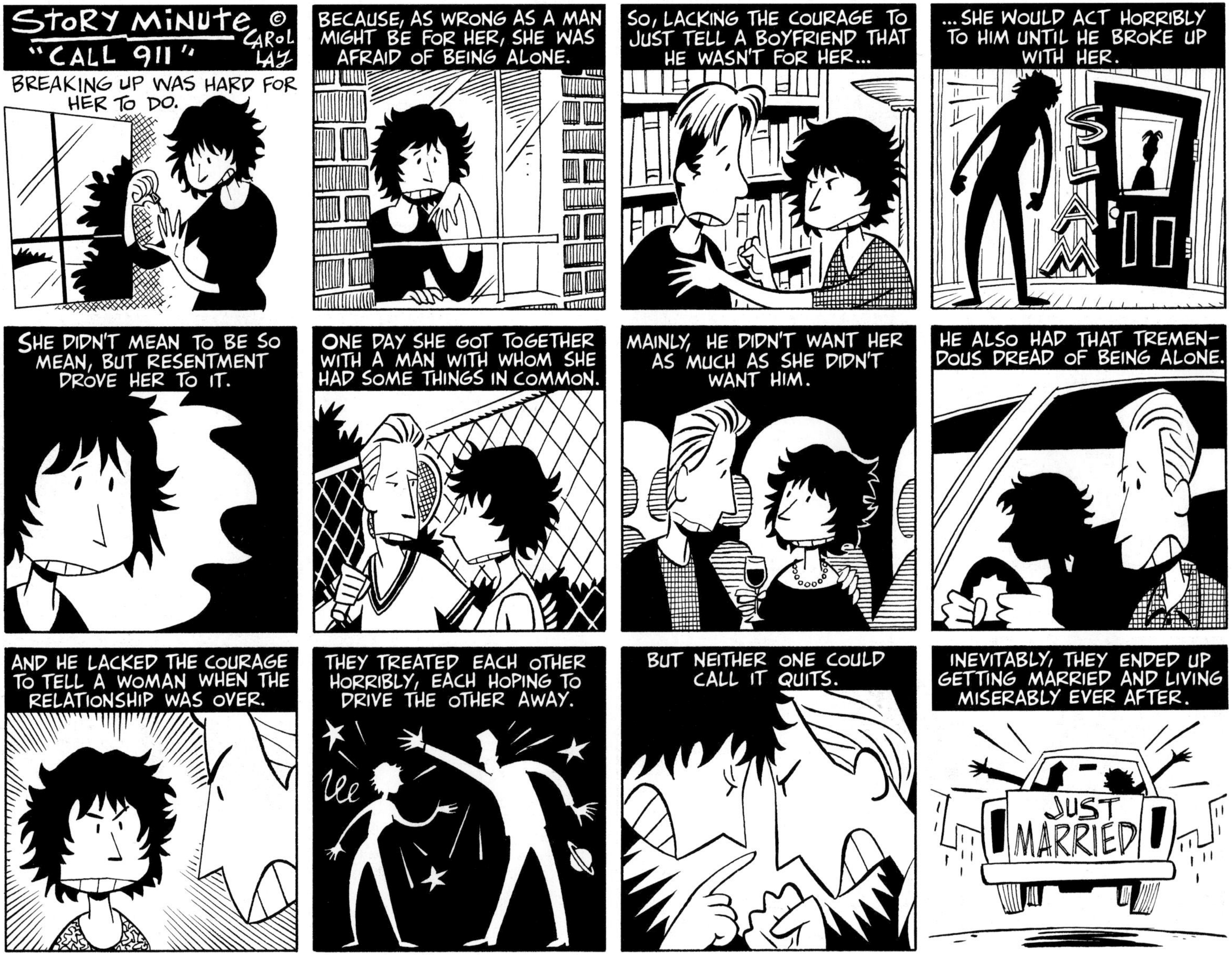
STORY MINUTE ©
"CALL 911"
CAROL LAY
BREAKING UP WAS HARD FOR HER TO DO.
BECAUSE, AS WRONG AS A MAN MIGHT BE FOR HER, SHE WAS AFRAID OF BEING ALONE.
SO, LACKING THE COURAGE TO JUST TELL A BOYFRIEND THAT HE WASN'T FOR HER...
...SHE WOULD ACT HORRIBLY TO HIM UNTIL HE BROKE UP WITH HER.
SLAM
SHE DIDN'T MEAN TO BE SO MEAN, BUT RESENTMENT DROVE HER TO IT.
ONE DAY SHE GOT TOGETHER WITH A MAN WITH WHOM SHE HAD SOME THINGS IN COMMON.
MAINLY, HE DIDN'T WANT HER AS MUCH AS SHE DIDN'T WANT HIM.
HE ALSO HAD THAT TREMENDOUS DREAD OF BEING ALONE.
AND HE LACKED THE COURAGE TO TELL A WOMAN WHEN THE RELATIONSHIP WAS OVER.
THEY TREATED EACH OTHER HORRIBLY, EACH HOPING TO DRIVE THE OTHER AWAY.
BUT NEITHER ONE COULD CALL IT QUITS.
INEVITABLY, THEY ENDED UP GETTING MARRIED AND LIVING MISERABLY EVER AFTER.
JUST MARRIED

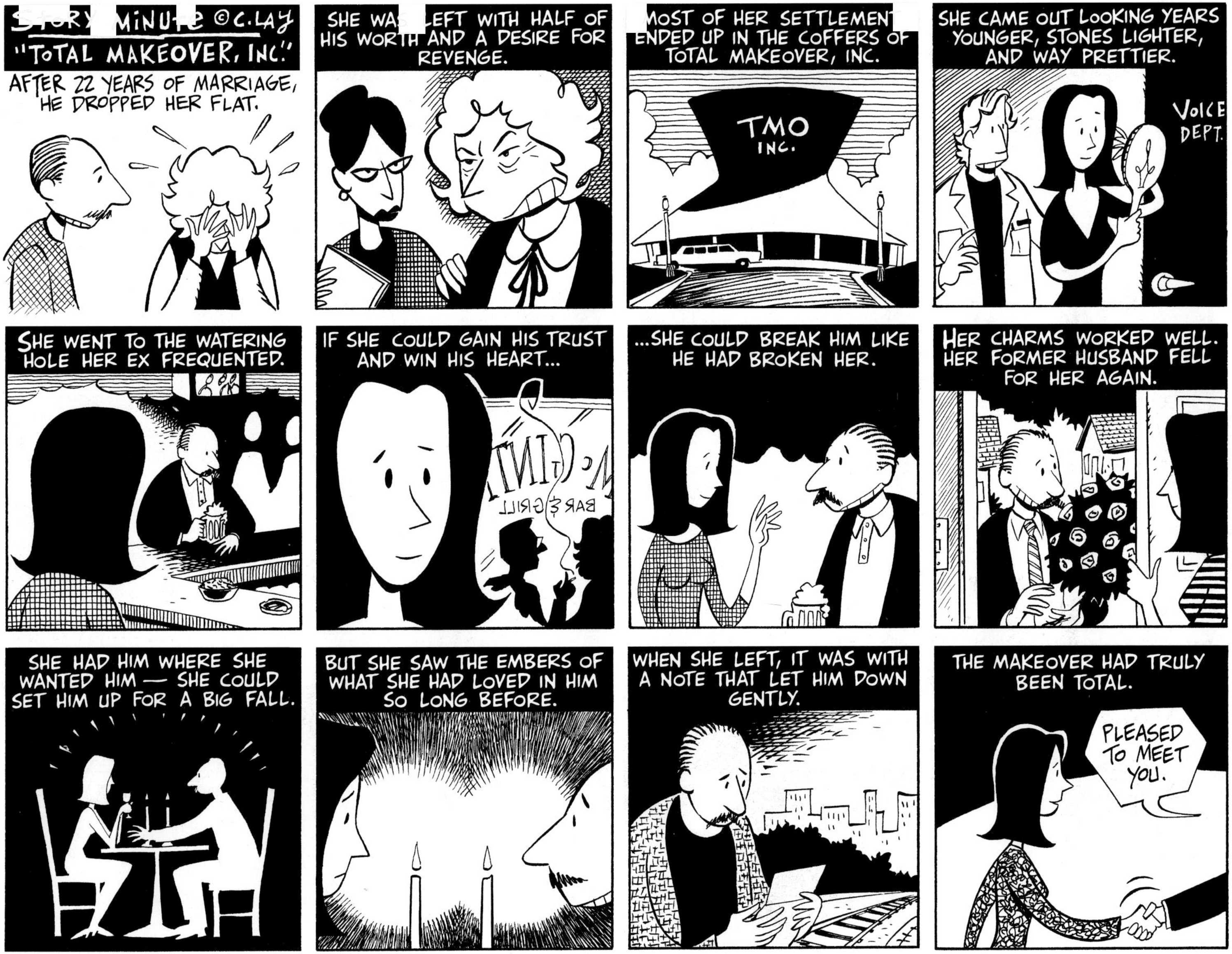

©C.LAY
"TOTAL MAKEOVER, INC."
AFTER 22 YEARS OF MARRIAGE, HE DROPPED HER FLAT.
SHE WAS LEFT WITH HALF OF HIS WORTH AND A DESIRE FOR REVENGE.
MOST OF HER SETTLEMENT ENDED UP IN THE COFFERS OF TOTAL MAKEOVER, INC.
TMO INC.
SHE CAME OUT LOOKING YEARS YOUNGER, STONES LIGHTER, AND WAY PRETTIER.
VOICE DEPT.
SHE WENT TO THE WATERING HOLE HER EX FREQUENTED.
IF SHE COULD GAIN HIS TRUST AND WIN HIS HEART...
BAR & GRILL
...SHE COULD BREAK HIM LIKE HE HAD BROKEN HER.
HER CHARMS WORKED WELL. HER FORMER HUSBAND FELL FOR HER AGAIN.
SHE HAD HIM WHERE SHE WANTED HIM — SHE COULD SET HIM UP FOR A BIG FALL.
BUT SHE SAW THE EMBERS OF WHAT SHE HAD LOVED IN HIM SO LONG BEFORE.
WHEN SHE LEFT, IT WAS WITH A NOTE THAT LET HIM DOWN GENTLY.
THE MAKEOVER HAD TRULY BEEN TOTAL.
PLEASED TO MEET YOU.

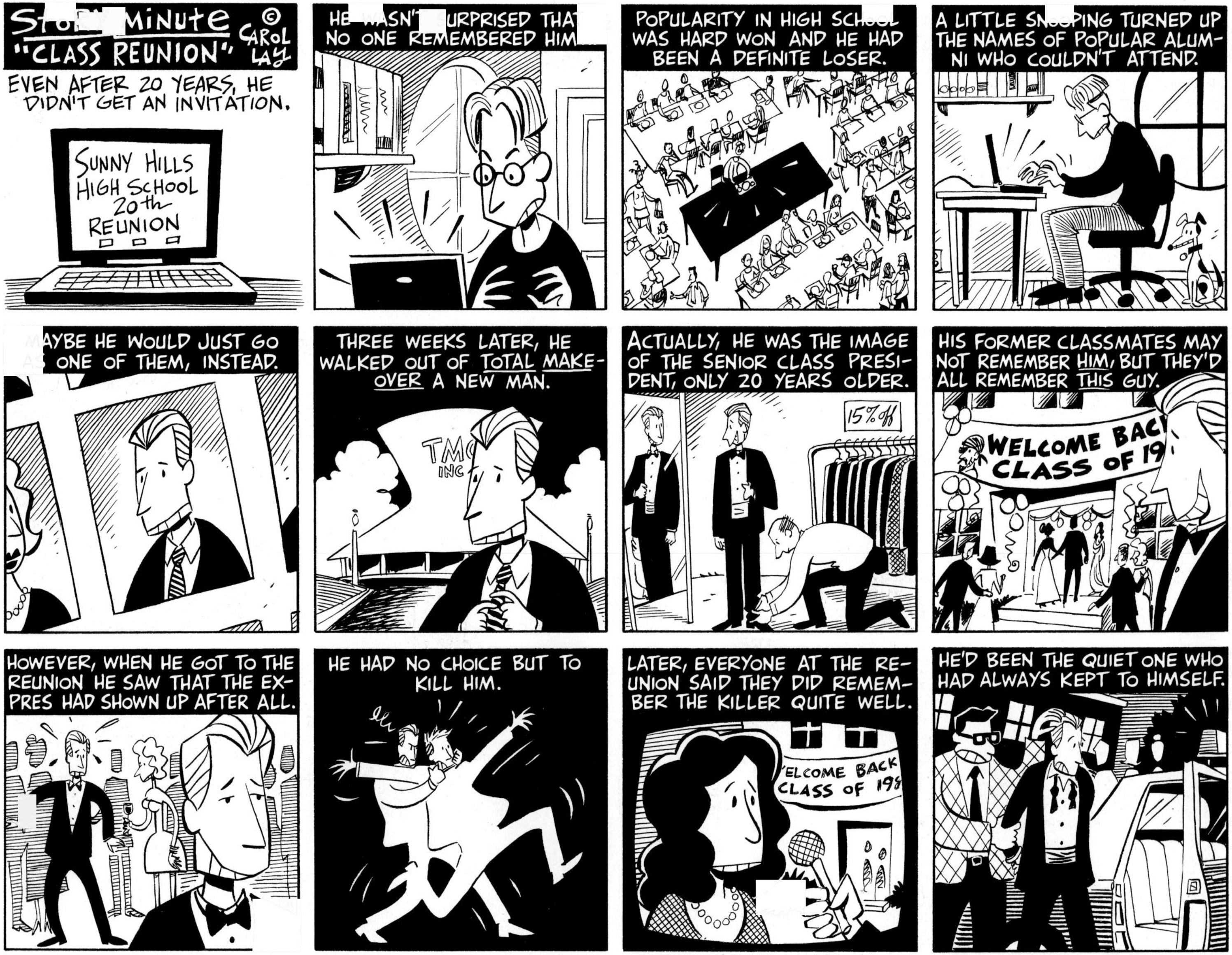

Minute
"CLASS REUNION"
© CAROL LAY
EVEN AFTER 20 YEARS, HE DIDN'T GET AN INVITATION.
SUNNY HILLS HIGH SCHOOL 20th REUNION
HE WASN'T URPRISED THAT NO ONE REMEMBERED HIM
POPULARITY IN HIGH SCHOOL WAS HARD WON AND HE HAD BEEN A DEFINITE LOSER.
A LITTLE SN PING TURNED UP THE NAMES OF POPULAR ALUMNI WHO COULDN'T ATTEND.
AYBE HE WOULD JUST GO ONE OF THEM, INSTEAD.
THREE WEEKS LATER, HE WALKED OUT OF TOTAL MAKEOVER A NEW MAN.
TMC INC
ACTUALLY, HE WAS THE IMAGE OF THE SENIOR CLASS PRESIDENT, ONLY 20 YEARS OLDER.
15% off
HIS FORMER CLASSMATES MAY NOT REMEMBER HIM, BUT THEY'D ALL REMEMBER THIS GUY.
WELCOME BAC CLASS OF 19
HOWEVER, WHEN HE GOT TO THE REUNION HE SAW THAT THE EX-PRES HAD SHOWN UP AFTER ALL.
HE HAD NO CHOICE BUT TO KILL HIM.
LATER, EVERYONE AT THE REUNION SAID THEY DID REMEMBER THE KILLER QUITE WELL.
ELCOME BACK CLASS OF 19
HE'D BEEN THE QUIET ONE WHO HAD ALWAYS KEPT TO HIMSELF.

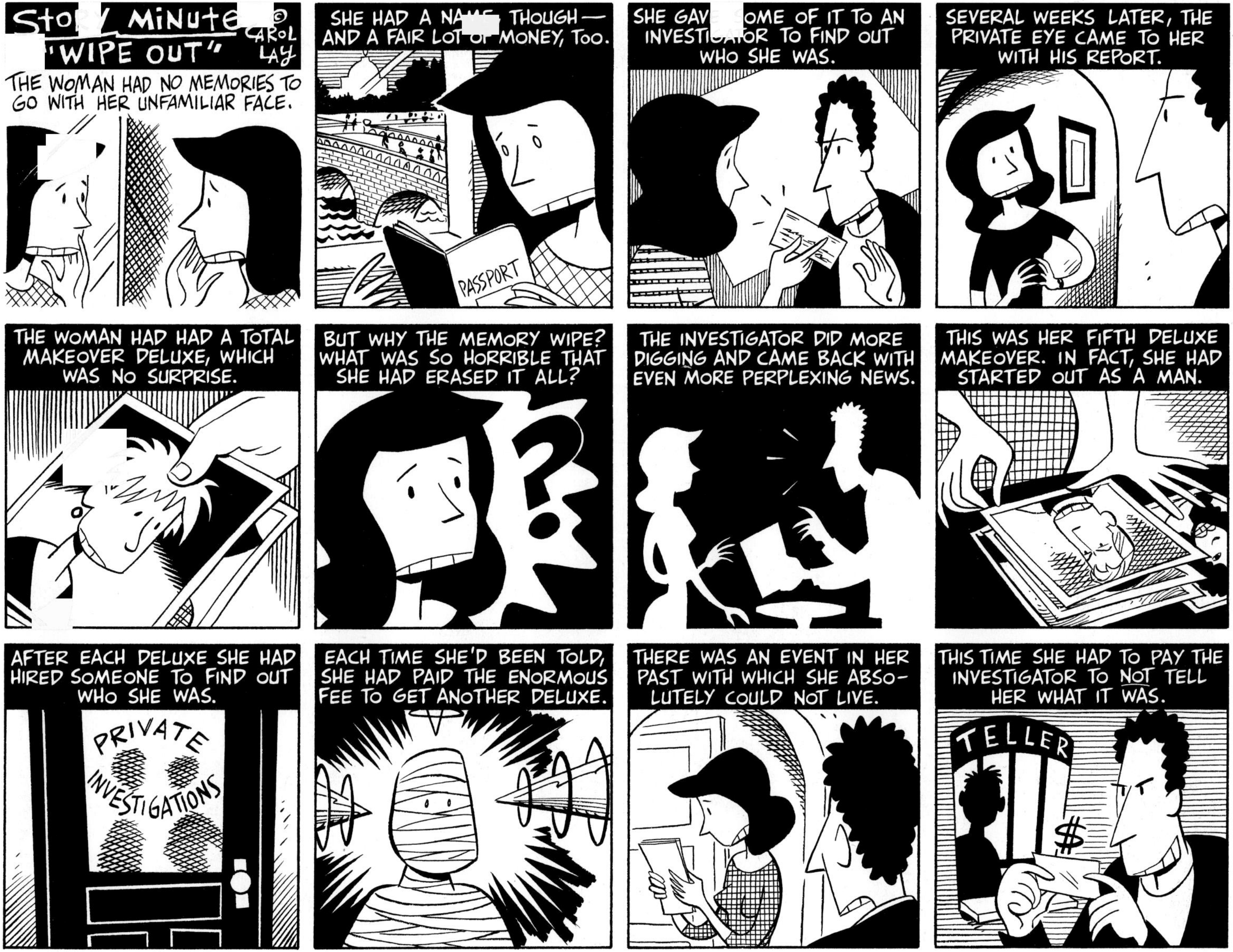

STO MINUTE
"WIPE OUT"
© CAROL LAY
THE WOMAN HAD NO MEMORIES TO GO WITH HER UNFAMILIAR FACE.
SHE HAD A NA THOUGH— AND A FAIR LOT O MONEY, TOO.
PASSPORT
SHE GAV OME OF IT TO AN INVESTI TOR TO FIND OUT WHO SHE WAS.
SEVERAL WEEKS LATER, THE PRIVATE EYE CAME TO HER WITH HIS REPORT.
THE WOMAN HAD HAD A TOTAL MAKEOVER DELUXE, WHICH WAS NO SURPRISE.
BUT WHY THE MEMORY WIPE? WHAT WAS SO HORRIBLE THAT SHE HAD ERASED IT ALL?
?
THE INVESTIGATOR DID MORE DIGGING AND CAME BACK WITH EVEN MORE PERPLEXING NEWS.
THIS WAS HER FIFTH DELUXE MAKEOVER. IN FACT, SHE HAD STARTED OUT AS A MAN.
AFTER EACH DELUXE SHE HAD HIRED SOMEONE TO FIND OUT WHO SHE WAS.
PRIVATE INVESTIGATIONS
EACH TIME SHE'D BEEN TOLD, SHE HAD PAID THE ENORMOUS FEE TO GET ANOTHER DELUXE.
THERE WAS AN EVENT IN HER PAST WITH WHICH SHE ABSO-LUTELY COULD NOT LIVE.
THIS TIME SHE HAD TO PAY THE INVESTIGATOR TO NOT TELL HER WHAT IT WAS.
TELLER
$

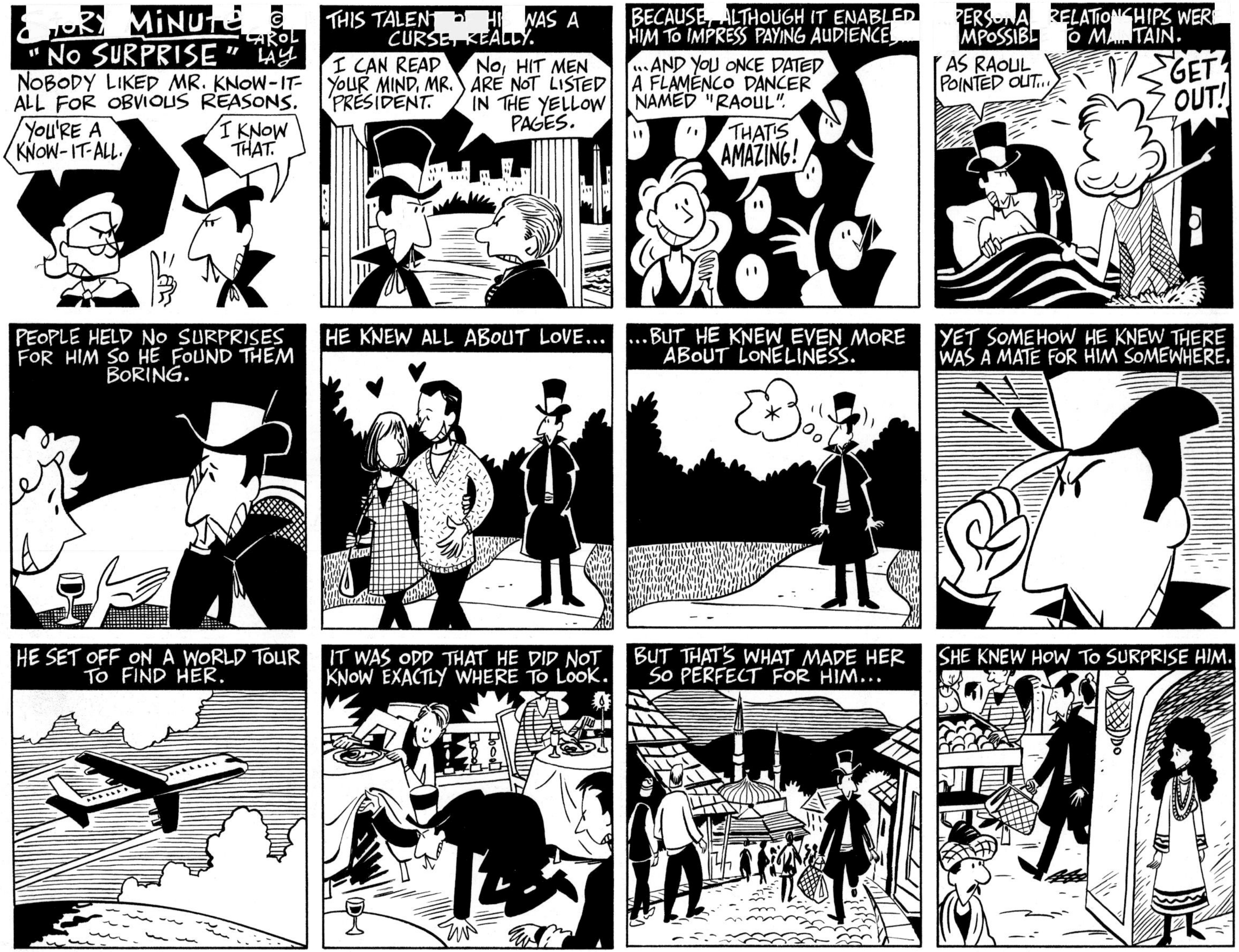
MINUT
"NO SURPRISE" © CAROL LAY
NOBODY LIKED MR. KNOW-IT-ALL FOR OBVIOUS REASONS.
YOU'RE A KNOW-IT-ALL.
I KNOW THAT.
THIS TALENT ... WAS A CURSE, REALLY.
I CAN READ YOUR MIND, MR. PRESIDENT.
NO, HIT MEN ARE NOT LISTED IN THE YELLOW PAGES.
BECAUSE, ALTHOUGH IT ENABLED HIM TO IMPRESS PAYING AUDIENCE...
...AND YOU ONCE DATED A FLAMENCO DANCER NAMED "RAOUL".
THAT'S AMAZING!
...PERSONAL RELATIONSHIPS WERE IMPOSSIBLE TO MAINTAIN.
AS RAOUL POINTED OUT...
GET OUT!
PEOPLE HELD NO SURPRISES FOR HIM SO HE FOUND THEM BORING.
HE KNEW ALL ABOUT LOVE...
...BUT HE KNEW EVEN MORE ABOUT LONELINESS.
YET SOMEHOW HE KNEW THERE WAS A MATE FOR HIM SOMEWHERE.
HE SET OFF ON A WORLD TOUR TO FIND HER.
IT WAS ODD THAT HE DID NOT KNOW EXACTLY WHERE TO LOOK.
BUT THAT'S WHAT MADE HER SO PERFECT FOR HIM...
SHE KNEW HOW TO SURPRISE HIM.

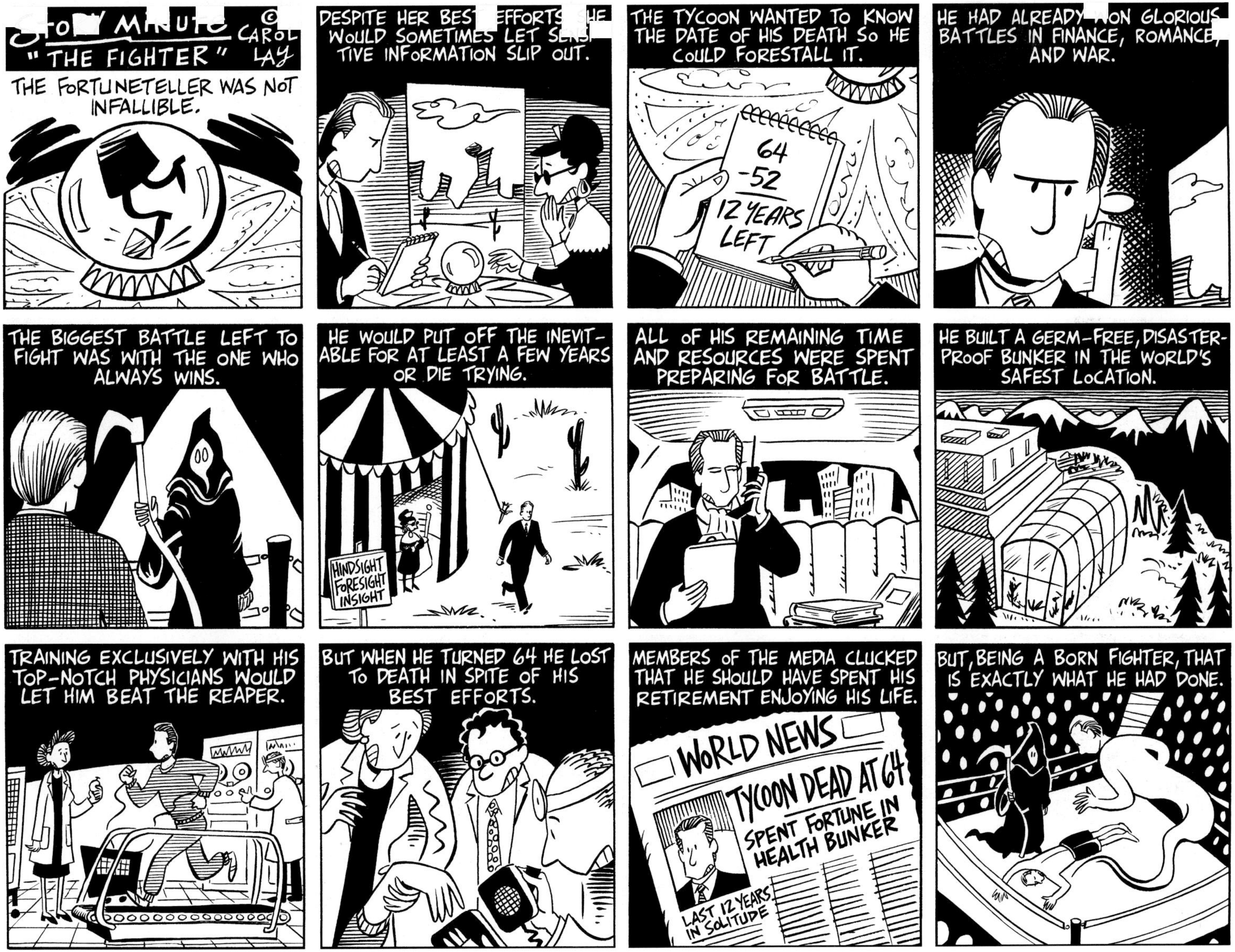

"THE FIGHTER"
© CAROL LAY
THE FORTUNETELLER WAS NOT INFALLIBLE.
DESPITE HER BEST EFFORTS SHE WOULD SOMETIMES LET SENSITIVE INFORMATION SLIP OUT.
THE TYCOON WANTED TO KNOW THE DATE OF HIS DEATH SO HE COULD FORESTALL IT.
64
-52
12 YEARS LEFT
HE HAD ALREADY WON GLORIOUS BATTLES IN FINANCE, ROMANCE, AND WAR.
THE BIGGEST BATTLE LEFT TO FIGHT WAS WITH THE ONE WHO ALWAYS WINS.
HE WOULD PUT OFF THE INEVITABLE FOR AT LEAST A FEW YEARS OR DIE TRYING.
HINDSIGHT
FORESIGHT
INSIGHT
ALL OF HIS REMAINING TIME AND RESOURCES WERE SPENT PREPARING FOR BATTLE.
HE BUILT A GERM-FREE, DISASTER-PROOF BUNKER IN THE WORLD'S SAFEST LOCATION.
TRAINING EXCLUSIVELY WITH HIS TOP-NOTCH PHYSICIANS WOULD LET HIM BEAT THE REAPER.
BUT WHEN HE TURNED 64 HE LOST TO DEATH IN SPITE OF HIS BEST EFFORTS.
MEMBERS OF THE MEDIA CLUCKED THAT HE SHOULD HAVE SPENT HIS RETIREMENT ENJOYING HIS LIFE.
WORLD NEWS
TYCOON DEAD AT 64
SPENT FORTUNE IN HEALTH BUNKER
LAST 12 YEARS IN SOLITUDE
BUT, BEING A BORN FIGHTER, THAT IS EXACTLY WHAT HE HAD DONE.

Carol Lay's weekly strip, "Story Minute," ran for almost twenty years in papers here and abroad, including the *LA Weekly* and *NY Press*, *Salon.com* and *Buzzle*, Tokyo and Hong Kong, Sweden and Norway, and a tiny daily paper on Gibraltar of all places.

Lay's strips and illustrations have appeared in *Newsweek*, *MAD Magazine*, The *Wall Street Journal*, and *The New Yorker*. She also writes and draws stories for *Simpsons* comic books (Bongo Comics Group).

Lay lives in L.A., mostly for the alliteration.

www.carollay.com

Other Titles by Carol Lay

Now, Endsville

Joy Ride

Strip Joint

Wonder Woman: Mythos (Justice League of America)

Goodnight, Irene: The Collected Stories of Irene Van De Kamp

The Big Skinny: How I Changed My Fattitude